CIMA PUBLISHING

The Complete November 2004 CIMA Examinations Question Papers with Examiner's Answers

Intermediate Level

ELSEVIER

AMSTERDAM BOSTON HEIDELBERG LONDON NEW YORK OXFORD
PARIS SAN DIEGO SAN FRANCISCO SINGAPORE SYDNEY TOKYO

CIMA Publishing
An imprint of Elsevier
Linacre House, Jordan Hill, Oxford OX2 8DP
30 Corporate Drive, Burlington, MA 01803

First Published 2005.

British Library Cataloguing in Publication Data
A catalogue record for this book is available from the British Library

ISBN 0 750667443

Printed and bound by Antony Rowe Ltd, Eastbourne

NOVEMBER 2004 INTERMEDIATE LEVEL

This book contains the **complete November 2004** CIMA Examination **Question Papers** with the **Examiner's Answers** for the **Intermediate level**, direct from CIMA and brought to you by CIMA Publishing, an imprint of Elsevier:

Paper 4	Finance
Paper 5	Business Taxation
Paper 6a	Financial Accounting (UK) Standards
Paper 6b	Financial Accounting (International) Standards
Paper 7a	Financial Reporting (UK) Standards
Paper 7b	Financial Reporting (International) Standards
Paper 8	Management Accounting Performance Management
Paper 9	Management Accounting Decision Making
Paper 10	Systems and Project Management
Paper 11	Organisational Management

Also available:

A companion book containing the complete November 2004 Question papers with Examiner's Answers for the Final Level. ISBN: 0750667451
Available from: www.cimapublishing.com

For all your future CIMA Qualification study needs: official CIMA Study Systems, Revision Cards, Exam Practice Kits, and CIMA interactive CD ROMS for the new syllabus visit:

www.cimapublishing.com or complete the order form at the back of this book

CIMA

November 2004 Examinations

Intermediate Level

Finance

(IFIN – Paper 4)

Question Paper 1

Examiner's Brief Guide to the Paper 16

Examiner's Answers 17

The answers published here have been written by the Examiner and should provide a helpful guide for both lecturers and students.

Published separately on the CIMA website (www.cimaglobal.com/students) from the end of February 2005 is a Post Examination Guide for this paper, which provides much valuable and complementary material including indicative mark information.

CIMA

Intermediate Level

Finance

4

IFIN

23 November 2004

Tuesday morning

INSTRUCTIONS TO CANDIDATES

Read this page before you look at the questions

You are allowed three hours to answer this question paper.
Answer the ONE question in Section A (this has 10 sub-questions). Answer the ONE question in Section B. Answer TWO questions ONLY from Section C.
Maths Tables and Formulae are provided.

SECTION A – 20 MARKS

ANSWER *ALL* TEN SUB-QUESTIONS – 2 MARKS EACH

Each of the sub-questions numbered from **1.1** to **1.10** inclusive, given below, has only ONE correct answer.

Required:

On the SPECIAL ANSWER SHEET opposite, place a circle "O" around the letter that gives the correct answer to each sub-question.
If you wish to change your mind about an answer, block out your first answer completely and then circle another letter. You will not receive marks if more than one letter is circled.
Please note that you will not receive marks for any workings to these sub-questions.

You must detach the special answer sheet from the question paper and attach it to the inside front cover of your answer book before you hand it to the invigilators at the end of the examination.

Question One

1.1 A fast-growing global business has a sales budget for next year based on a growth rate of 20% per month. The projected sales for the first month are $150 million. 25% of the sales are paid for by the buyers in the month of purchase and 70% in the following month, the remaining 5% turning into bad debts.

The expected cash receipts from sales in the THIRD month of next year would be

A $150 million.

B $171 million.

C $180 million.

D $216 million.

1.2 Examine the validity of the following statements:

Statement 1
When a yield curve is inverted, long-term interest rates are lower than short-term interest rates.

Statement 2
The most likely cause of an inverted yield curve is government or central bank action in increasing short-term rates.

	Statement 1	*Statement 2*
A	True	True
B	False	True
C	True	False
D	False	False

1.3 BACS (Bankers Automated Clearing Services) is an example of an electronic funds transfer system. Which of the following statements best describes this system?

A It is a facility used mainly to process payrolls and transactions involving standing orders and direct debits.

B It provides same day settlements for large amounts between banks who are members of the clearing system.

C It is a facility used by companies for international transactions.

D It is a network between participating banks for rapid transmission of foreign currencies.

1.4 A company has a current ratio of 2 : 1. It decides to use surplus cash to settle 30% of its total current liabilities.

The current ratio will

A decrease by more than 30%.

B decrease by less than 30%.

C increase by more than 30%.

D increase by less than 30%.

1.5 According to the traditional theory of capital structure, an increase in the use of debt relative to equity will have the following impact on the cost of capital:

A Weighted average cost of capital will always increase.

B Weighted average cost of capital will remain unchanged.

C Weighted average cost of capital will always decrease.

D Weighted average cost of capital may either increase or decrease.

1.6 In which ONE of the following circumstances is the Baumol cash management model likely to suggest an increase in a firm's cash balance?

A When there is an upward movement in interest rates.

B When the transaction cost of buying and selling securities goes up.

C When investors expect the rate of inflation to increase.

D When the firm discontinues a product line, leading to shrinking of its turnover.

1.7 Which ONE of the following is NOT a cause of float?

A Delay in billing.

B Delay in clearance.

C Delay in lodgement.

D Delay in transmission.

1.8 Examine the validity of the following statements:

Statement 1
If share prices move randomly, then technical analysis (that is chartism) will normally predict future share price movements.

Statement 2
If a stock market is semi-strong form efficient, then share prices will respond to new, publicly available information.

	Statement 1	*Statement 2*
A	True	True
B	False	True
C	True	False
D	False	False

1.9 Your company can make short-term investments in an account that pays interest at 5% per annum compounded semi-annually. Sufficient funds need to be invested in the account to be assured of receiving a sum of £500,000 after 6 months, to meet a potential liability.

Rounded to the nearest pound, the sum that needs to be invested is

A £487,500

B £487,656

C £487,805

D £487,950

1.10 To speed up the collection of receivables, a company is considering offering a 3% discount to customers who settle within 12 days, instead of the usual period of 85 days.

Taking into account the effect of compound interest, and based on a 365-day year, the effective annual cost of offering this cash discount would be approximately

A 3·00%.

B 3·09%.

C 15·46%.

D 16·45%.

(Total = 20 marks)

End of Section A

SECTION B – 30 MARKS

ANSWER THIS QUESTION

Question Two

Q Ltd, a family-owned dealer in fertiliser products, has been seeking to introduce greater professionalism in its managerial approach. To this end, the company appointed a full-time managing director two years ago who completely overhauled the marketing and working capital policies followed by the company, resulting in a sharp growth in turnover. Since the growth is expected to continue, the managing director has approached the company's bank for an increase in its overdraft facility.

In support of the application, he has submitted the company's summarised financial statements for the last two years, which are reproduced below:

Income statements	*2002*	*2003*
	£000	*£000*
Sales	39,600	70,800
Opening stock	1,000	1,780
Plus: Purchases	33,380	61,820
Less: Closing stock	(1,780)	(3,400)
Cost of sales	32,600	60,200
Gross profit	7,000	10,600
Selling, general and administrative expenses	(5,200)	(8,300)
Net profit	1,800	2,300
Dividend	1,620	1,620
Retained profit	180	680

Balance sheets	*2002*	*2003*
	£000	*£000*
Assets		
Current assets		
Cash	36	2
Trade debtors	2,304	4,480
Stocks	1,780	3,400
Total current assets	4,120	7,882
Net fixed assets	5,760	7,178
Total assets	**9,880**	**15,060**
Liabilities		
Current liabilities		
Trade creditors	1,800	5,200
Bank overdraft	900	2,000
Total current liabilities	2,700	7,200
Shareholders' funds		
Ordinary share capital	1,800	1,800
Reserves & surplus	5,380	6,060
Total equity	7,180	7,860
Total liabilities	**9,880**	**15,060**

Reviewing the company's performance, the managing director emphasised the effectiveness of his policies by pointing to the impressive increases in sales and profits, and also the big improvement in the operating cycle. But, to the surprise of Q Ltd's managing director, the bank has turned down the request for an increase in the overdraft facility on the grounds that the company is overtrading.

Alan Dimmock, the chairman and major shareholder of the company, wishes to take up the matter with the bank's senior management and has asked you, as the company's management accountant, to write him a report explaining what the bank means, and advising him on the extent to which its contention is justified.

Required:

Write a report to the chairman which includes:

(a) (i) An explanation of the term "overtrading", including a description of its symptoms, and how these symptoms might be caused.

(8 marks)

(ii) A summary of the steps that a company might take to rectify such a situation;

(4 marks)

(b) A discussion of the managing director's statement to the bank that the improvements in Q Ltd's key financial indicators are evidence of the success of the new policies. The second part of your report should include calculation of, and discussion of, any financial ratios that you consider relevant, particularly those relating to the operating cycle and to the bank's view that the company is overtrading.

(18 marks)

(Total = 30 marks)

End of Section B

SECTION C – 50 MARKS

ANSWER TWO QUESTIONS ONLY

Question Three

S plc is a well-established company in the food retailing industry. The company has paid-up share capital of £17·5 million in issue, consisting of ordinary shares with a par value of 50 pence. The shares are currently trading at a market price of 685 pence, ex-dividend.

Full year dividends for the last few financial years have been as follows:

Year ended 31 March	*1999*	*2000*	*2001*	*2002*	*2003*	*2004*
Dividend per share (in pence)	34	31	34	37	42	47

The company also has paid-up preference share capital of £75 million in issue, consisting of irredeemable preference shares with a par value of 100 pence. The preference shares, which pay an annual dividend of 8¼%, are currently trading at a market price of 75 pence ex-dividend. S plc has in issue £100 million of 6% debentures, the current price of which is £94 (per £100 nominal) ex interest. The debentures pay annual coupon interest and are redeemable at par in exactly six years' time. The effective corporation tax rate of S plc is 30%.

As part of their strategy for development of the company, S plc's directors are considering a new project for diversifying into retail banking. Although the company's long-term objective is to maintain the current pattern of capital structure, it proposes to use a new issue of 7% bonds to finance the initial capital investment of £100 million required for the retail banking venture. The company's managing director therefore feels that the coupon interest rate of 7% per annum on the new issue of bonds would be the appropriate discount rate to use for evaluating the new investment proposal. However, S plc's financial controller takes the view that the company's weighted average cost of capital would be more appropriate.

Required:

(a) Comment on the managing director's suggestion that the coupon interest rate of 7% on the new issue of bonds would be the appropriate discount rate for evaluating the new project.

(7 marks)

(b) Calculate the existing after-tax weighted average cost of capital (WACC) for S plc.

(12 marks)

(c) Discuss whether you consider it appropriate to use the company's existing WACC for evaluating the new project.

(6 marks)

(Total = 25 marks)

Question Four

P plc, a company engaged in the telecommunications industry, has paid-up capital consisting of 40 million ordinary shares of 50 pence each. P plc's current annual after-tax earnings are £4·8 million, and the company's shares are trading at a price/earnings multiple of 6·25. The company has developed new technology applications, for the promotion and marketing of which it needs to invest a further sum of £12 million. After lengthy discussions on the best way to raise long-term finance for the new investment, the Board has decided to raise the additional capital through a rights issue at a discount of 20% below the current market price. The company proposes to maintain its current annual dividend payout of £2·4 million for the foreseeable future.

One of the company's directors has questioned the size of the discount being considered, stating that it had always been her belief that shareholder interests would be best served by fixing as high an issue price for new shares as the market would bear. The newly-appointed chairman has explained to her that the size of the discount would be irrelevant for the company's shareholders. Unconvinced by this line of argument, she has asked for an evaluation of the likely impact for herself if she were to either take up the rights issue, sell the rights, or do nothing. She currently holds 520,000 shares in the company. Assume there are no other events which might influence P plc's share price during the period.

Required:

(a) Calculate the theoretical ex-rights share price assuming that the rights issue proceeds on the terms indicated. What would be the value of the right?

(7 marks)

(b) Evaluate the theoretical impact of the three courses of action open to the director, and of other factors which she might need to consider when taking a decision on whether or not to exercise her rights.

(11 marks)

(c) Identify and explain the main advantages of a rights issue as compared to an offer for sale, from the viewpoint of a company.

(7 marks)

(Total = 25 marks)

Question Five

R Inc has a substantial cash surplus, a significant part of which it needs to keep in a portfolio of marketable securities as a precautionary cash balance. This portfolio may be required at short notice for possible payments resulting from legal action against the company.

The company's financial controller has suggested investing this precautionary cash balance in short-term instruments like treasury bills, certificates of deposit or commercial paper through financial intermediaries. However, the managing director wants to know why the funds should not instead be invested in ordinary term deposits with retail or merchant banks.

The balance of surplus cash is to be invested in longer-term securities issued by an associate company. Due to a prevailing reverse yield gap situation, this investment is proposed to be made in the associate company's loan capital rather than its equity capital.

Required:

(a) Explain the main economic functions of financial intermediaries in the economy. Distinguish between retail and merchant banks, describing the most important ways in which each of these types of institution fulfils the functions of a financial intermediary.

(10 marks)

(b) (i) Identify the significant similarities/differences between treasury bills, certificates of deposit and commercial paper. Comment on the relative default risk of these three forms of short-term investment.

(5 marks)

(ii) Describe the other kinds of risk that should be considered when investing surplus cash, and explain why the managing director's suggestion would be less suitable in the particular case of R Inc.

(5 marks)

(c) Explain the terms "yield gap" and "reverse yield gap". In what circumstances might the reverse yield gap situation arise?

(5 marks)

(Total = 25 marks)

Question Six

T Limited, a medium-size exporter of machine tools, keeps large stocks of all required materials. The bulk of the company's stock value consists of one particularly high-cost component, for which it has a steady monthly requirement of 560 units. The current supplier of this component charges a price of £1,400 per unit. Including storage and theft insurance, the holding cost for this component is 10% of its value per year. The company has been negotiating with alternative suppliers with the aim of moving towards a Just in Time (JIT) purchasing system for the high-value component in question.

The location, delivery terms and internal quality control mechanisms of one prospective supplier are such that T Limited would be able to reduce the cost of placing and collecting orders (that is, the ordering cost) from the present level of £150 per order to an estimated level of only £34 per order. Although not exactly a JIT purchasing system, the new arrangement would enable T Limited to have more frequent deliveries of the item with smaller order quantities. However, the prospective new supplier would charge a higher price of £1,402 for the item. The new supplier would agree to discount its price to match the current supplier's price of £1,400, but only if T Limited agreed to a minimum order quantity of 140 units per order.

[Note: In the following calculations, the number of orders placed per year should, if necessary, be rounded upwards].

Required:

(a) Calculate the economic order quantity (EOQ) if T Limited were to switch to the new supplier at the full quoted price of £1,402. If this order size were used, calculate:

(i) the number of orders placed in a year;

(ii) the total annual variable cost (order cost plus stock carrying cost);

(iii) the total annual cost (purchase cost plus variable cost).

(6 marks)

(b) Evaluate whether it would be more cost-effective to purchase the EOQ at the full quoted price, or the larger quantity of 140 units per order at the discounted price of £1,400. Recommend an appropriate course of action for T Limited.

(5 marks)

(c) Discuss the problems that most firms might have in attempting to determine the EOQ.

(5 marks)

(d) Explain the term "JIT purchasing system" and how it might be achieved. Comment on the likely benefits from the introduction of such a system.

(9 marks)

(Total = 25 marks)

End of paper

Maths Tables and Formulae follow

MATHS TABLES AND FORMULAE

TABLES

Present value table

Present value of $1, that is $(1+r)^{-n}$ where r = interest rate; n = number of periods until payment or receipt.

Periods	Interest rates (*r*)									
(*n*)	1%	2%	3%	4%	5%	6%	7%	8%	9%	10%
1	0.990	0.980	0.971	0.962	0.952	0.943	0.935	0.926	0.917	0.909
2	0.980	0.961	0.943	0.925	0.907	0.890	0.873	0.857	0.842	0.826
3	0.971	0.942	0.915	0.889	0.864	0.840	0.816	0.794	0.772	0.751
4	0.961	0.924	0.888	0.855	0.823	0.792	0.763	0.735	0.708	0.683
5	0.951	0.906	0.863	0.822	0.784	0.747	0.713	0.681	0.650	0.621
6	0.942	0.888	0.837	0.790	0.746	0705	0.666	0.630	0.596	0.564
7	0.933	0.871	0.813	0.760	0.711	0.665	0.623	0.583	0.547	0.513
8	0.923	0.853	0.789	0.731	0.677	0.627	0.582	0.540	0.502	0.467
9	0.914	0.837	0.766	0.703	0.645	0.592	0.544	0.500	0.460	0.424
10	0.905	0.820	0.744	0.676	0.614	0.558	0.508	0.463	0.422	0.386
11	0.896	0.804	0.722	0.650	0.585	0.527	0.475	0.429	0.388	0.350
12	0.887	0.788	0.701	0.625	0.557	0.497	0.444	0.397	0.356	0.319
13	0.879	0.773	0.681	0.601	0.530	0.469	0.415	0.368	0.326	0.290
14	0.870	0.758	0.661	0.577	0.505	0.442	0.388	0.340	0.299	0.263
15	0.861	0.743	0.642	0.555	0.481	0.417	0.362	0.315	0.275	0.239
16	0.853	0.728	0.623	0.534	0.458	0.394	0.339	0.292	0.252	0.218
17	0.844	0.714	0.605	0.513	0.436	0.371	0.317	0.270	0.231	0.198
18	0.836	0.700	0.587	0.494	0.416	0.350	0.296	0.250	0.212	0.180
19	0.828	0.686	0.570	0.475	0.396	0.331	0.277	0.232	0.194	0.164
20	0.820	0.673	0.554	0.456	0.377	0.312	0.258	0.215	0.178	0.149

Periods	Interest rates (*r*)									
(*n*)	11%	12%	13%	14%	15%	16%	17%	18%	19%	20%
1	0.901	0.893	0.885	0.877	0.870	0.862	0.855	0.847	0.840	0.833
2	0.812	0.797	0.783	0.769	0.756	0.743	0.731	0.718	0.706	0.694
3	0.731	0.712	0.693	0.675	0.658	0.641	0.624	0.609	0.593	0.579
4	0.659	0.636	0.613	0.592	0.572	0.552	0.534	0.516	0.499	0.482
5	0.593	0.567	0.543	0.519	0.497	0.476	0.456	0.437	0.419	0.402
6	0.535	0.507	0.480	0.456	0.432	0.410	0.390	0.370	0.352	0.335
7	0.482	0.452	0.425	0.400	0.376	0.354	0.333	0.314	0.296	0.279
8	0.434	0.404	0.376	0.351	0.327	0.305	0.285	0.266	0.249	0.233
9	0.391	0.361	0.333	0.308	0.284	0.263	0.243	0.225	0.209	0.194
10	0.352	0.322	0.295	0.270	0.247	0.227	0.208	0.191	0.176	0.162
11	0.317	0.287	0.261	0.237	0.215	0.195	0.178	0.162	0.148	0.135
12	0.286	0.257	0.231	0.208	0.187	0.168	0.152	0.137	0.124	0.112
13	0.258	0.229	0.204	0.182	0.163	0.145	0.130	0.116	0.104	0.093
14	0.232	0.205	0.181	0.160	0.141	0.125	0.111	0.099	0.088	0.078
15	0.209	0.183	0.160	0.140	0.123	0.108	0.095	0.084	0.079	0.065
16	0.188	0.163	0.141	0.123	0.107	0.093	0.081	0.071	0.062	0.054
17	0.170	0.146	0.125	0.108	0.093	0.080	0.069	0.060	0.052	0.045
18	0.153	0.130	0.111	0.095	0.081	0.069	0.059	0.051	0.044	0.038
19	0.138	0.116	0.098	0.083	0.070	0.060	0.051	0.043	0.037	0.031
20	0.124	0.104	0.087	0.073	0.061	0.051	0.043	0.037	0.031	0.026

Cumulative present value of $1 per annum, Receivable or Payable at the end of each year for *n* years $\frac{1-(1+r)^{-n}}{r}$

Periods	Interest rates (*r*)									
(*n*)	1%	2%	3%	4%	5%	6%	7%	8%	9%	10%
1	0.990	0.980	0.971	0.962	0.952	0.943	0.935	0.926	0.917	0.909
2	1.970	1.942	1.913	1.886	1.859	1.833	1.808	1.783	1.759	1.736
3	2.941	2.884	2.829	2.775	2.723	2.673	2.624	2.577	2.531	2.487
4	3.092	3.808	3.717	3.630	3.546	3.465	3.387	3.312	3.240	3.170
5	4.853	4.713	4.580	4.452	4.329	4.212	4.100	3.993	3.890	3.791
6	5.795	5.601	5.417	5.242	5.076	4.917	4.767	4.623	4.486	4.355
7	6.728	6.472	6.230	6.002	5.786	5.582	5.389	5.206	5.033	4.868
8	7.652	7.325	7.020	6.733	6.463	6.210	5.971	5.747	5.535	5.335
9	8.566	8.162	7.786	7.435	7.108	6.802	6.515	6.247	5.995	5.759
10	9.471	8.983	8.530	8.111	7.722	7.360	7.024	6.710	6.418	6.145
11	10.368	9.787	9.253	8.760	8.306	7.887	7.499	7.139	6.805	6.495
12	11.255	10.575	9.954	9.385	8.863	8.384	7.943	7.536	7.161	6.814
13	12.134	11.348	10.635	9.986	9.394	8.853	8.358	7.904	7.487	7.103
14	13.004	12.106	11.296	10.563	9.899	9.295	8.745	8.244	7.786	7.367
15	13.865	12.849	11.938	11.118	10.380	9.712	9.108	8.559	8.061	7.606
16	14.718	13.578	12.561	11.652	10.838	10.106	9.447	8.851	8.313	7.824
17	15.562	14.292	13.166	12.166	11.274	10.477	9.763	9.122	8.544	8.022
18	16.398	14.992	13.754	12.659	11.690	10.828	10.059	9.372	8.756	8.201
19	17.226	15.679	14.324	13.134	12.085	11.158	10.336	9.604	8.950	8.365
20	18.046	16.351	14.878	13.590	12.462	11.470	10.594	9.818	9.129	8.514

Periods	Interest rates (*r*)									
(*n*)	11%	12%	13%	14%	15%	16%	17%	18%	19%	20%
1	0.901	0.893	0.885	0.877	0.870	0.862	0.855	0.847	0.840	0.833
2	1.713	1.690	1.668	1.647	1.626	1.605	1.585	1.566	1.547	1.528
3	2.444	2.402	2.301	2.322	2.283	2.246	2.210	2.174	2.140	2.106
4	3.102	3.037	2.974	2.914	2.855	2.798	2.743	2.690	2.639	2.589
5	3.696	3.605	3.517	3.433	3.352	3.274	3.199	3.127	3.058	2.991
6	4.231	4.111	3.998	3.889	3.784	3.685	3.589	3.498	3.410	3.326
7	4.712	4.564	4.423	4.288	4.160	4.039	3.922	3.812	3.706	3.605
8	5.146	4.968	4.799	4.639	4.487	4.344	4.207	4.078	3.954	3.837
9	5.537	5.328	5.132	4.946	4.772	4.607	4.451	4.303	4.163	4.031
10	5.889	5.650	5.426	5.216	5.019	4.833	4.659	4.494	4.339	4.192
11	6.207	5.938	5.687	5.453	5.234	5.029	4.836	4.656	4.486	4.327
12	6.492	6.194	5.918	5.660	5.421	5.197	4.988	7.793	4.611	4.439
13	6.750	6.424	6.122	5.842	5.583	5.342	5.118	4.910	4.715	4.533
14	6.982	6.628	6.302	6.002	5.724	5.468	5.229	5.008	4.802	4.611
15	7.191	6.811	6.462	6.142	5.847	5.575	5.324	5.092	4.876	4.675
16	7.379	6.974	6.604	6.265	5.954	5.668	5.405	5.162	4.938	4.730
17	7.549	7.120	6.729	6.373	6.047	5.749	5.475	5.222	4.990	4.775
18	7.702	7.250	6.840	6.467	6.128	5.818	5.534	5.273	5.033	4.812
19	7.839	7.366	6.938	6.550	6.198	5.877	5.584	5.316	5.070	4.843
20	7.963	7.469	7.025	6.623	6.259	5.929	5.628	5.353	5.101	4.870

FORMULAE

Valuation models

(i) Irredeemable preference share, paying a constant annual dividend, d, in perpetuity, where P_0 is the ex-div value:

$$P_0 = \frac{d}{k_{\text{pref}}}$$

(ii) Ordinary (equity) share, paying a constant annual dividend, d, in perpetuity, where P_0 is the ex-div value:

$$P_0 = \frac{d}{k_e}$$

(iii) Ordinary (equity) share, paying an annual dividend, d, growing in perpetuity at a constant rate, g, where P_0 is the ex-div value:

$$P_0 = \frac{d_1}{k_e - g} \quad \text{or} \quad P_0 = \frac{d_0[1+g]}{k_e - g}$$

(iv) Irredeemable (undated) debt, paying annual after tax interest, $i[1 - t]$, in perpetuity, where P_0 is the ex-interest value:

$$P_0 = \frac{i[1-t]}{k_{d\,\text{net}}}$$

or, without tax:

$$P_0 = \frac{i}{k_d}$$

(v) Future value of S, of a sum X, invested for n periods, compounded at r% interest: $S = X[1 + r]^n$

(vi) Present value of \$1 payable or receivable in n years, discounted at r% per annum:

$$PV = \frac{1}{[1+r]^n}$$

(vii) Present value of an annuity of \$1 per annum, receivable or payable for n years, commencing in one year, discounted at r% per annum:

$$PV = \frac{1}{r}\left[1 - \frac{1}{[1+r]^n}\right]$$

(viii) Present value of \$1 per annum, payable or receivable in perpetuity, commencing in one year, discounted at r% per annum:

$$PV = \frac{1}{r}$$

(ix) Present value of \$1 per annum, receivable or payable, commencing in one year, growing in perpetuity at a constant rate of g% per annum, discounted at r% per annum:

$$PV = \frac{1}{r-g}$$

Cost of Capital

(i) Cost of irredeemable preference capital, paying an annual dividend, d, in perpetuity, and having a current ex-div price P_0:

$$k_{pref} = \frac{d}{P_0}$$

(ii) Cost of irredeemable debt capital, paying annual net interest, $i[1 - t]$, and having a current ex-interest price P_0:

$$k_{d\,\text{net}} = \frac{i[1-t]}{P_0}$$

(iii) Cost of ordinary (equity) share capital, paying an annual dividend, d, in perpetuity, and having a current ex-div price P_0:

$$k_e = \frac{d}{P_0}$$

(iv) Cost of ordinary (equity) share capital, having a current ex-div price, P_0, having just paid a dividend, d_0, with the dividend growing in perpetuity by a constant g% per annum:

$$k_e = \frac{d_1}{P_0} + g \quad \text{or} \quad k_e = \frac{d_0[1+g]}{P_0} + g$$

(v) Cost of ordinary (equity) share capital, using the CAPM:

$$k_e = R_f + [R_m - R_f]\beta$$

(vi) Weighted average cost of capital, k_0:

$$k_0 = k_e\left[\frac{V_E}{V_E + V_D}\right] + k_d\left[\frac{V_D}{V_E + V_D}\right]$$

Stock management

(i) Economic Order Quantity

$$\text{EOQ} = \sqrt{\frac{2C_oD}{C_h}}$$

where:
C_o = cost of placing an order
C_h = cost of holding one unit in stock for one year
D = annual demand

Cash management

(i) Optimal sale of securities, Baumol model:

$$\text{Optimal sale} = \sqrt{\frac{2 \times \text{Annual cash disbursements} \times \text{Cost per sale of securities}}{\text{interest rate}}}$$

(ii) Spread between upper and lower cash balance limits, Miller-Orr model:

$$\text{Spread} = 3\left[\frac{\frac{3}{4} \times \text{transaction cost} \times \text{variance of cash flows}}{\text{interest rate}}\right]^{\frac{1}{3}}$$

Other

(i) Theoretical ex-rights price

$$\text{TERP} = \frac{1}{N+1}\left[(N \times \text{cum rights price}) + \text{issue price}\right]$$

where N = number of shares required to buy one new share

The Examiner for IFIN offers to future candidates and to lecturers using this booklet for study purposes, the following background and guidance on the questions included in this examination paper.

Section A – compulsory

Question One presents 10 objective test sub-questions designed to test knowledge, understanding and techniques across a wide range of syllabus topics. They are of varying lengths and test a mix of computational and qualitative skills.

Section B – compulsory

Question Two tests candidates' conceptual understanding of how liquidity problems manifest themselves in an organisation, and how the problems can be managed. To properly demonstrate this understanding, candidates are also required to show analytical and evaluative skills by calculating and commenting on the significance of various appropriate financial ratios. Candidates are required to do this in the form of a report which also, incidentally, tests their knowledge and understanding of corporate objectives and the role of financial management.

Section C – choice of questions

Question Three part (a) tests candidates' conceptual understanding of the rationale for the use of the weighted average cost of capital (WACC), rather than the coupon on debentures, as the appropriate opportunity cost for the evaluation of investment decisions. Part (b) requires candidates to show analytical skill in calculating the costs of different sources of long-term capital, and the WACC. Part (c) tests candidates' understanding of the limitations of the WACC in the evaluation of investment decisions.

Question Four part (a) requires candidates to show analytical skill in calculating a theoretical ex-rights price and the value of a right. Part (b) requires candidates' to evaluate three different courses open to a shareholder who has been allocated rights shares. Part (c) requires identification and explanation of the relative merits of a rights issue as compared to the raising of finance through an offer for sale.

Question Five part (a) tests candidates' knowledge and understanding of the role of financial intermediation in the economy, and the differing roles of two types of institution. Part (b) tests candidates' understanding of the differences between three different avenues of short-term investment and their relative merits. Part (c) tests candidates' understanding of two terms and the circumstances in which one of them might arise.

Question Six part (a) requires analysis of a company's existing EOQ and annual inventory cost in respect of an item of stock. Part (b) requires evaluation of the cost impact of proposed changes in inventory management policy. Part (c) requires candidates to discuss the problems that companies might face in doing such an analysis and evaluation using the EOQ model. Part (d) tests candidates' knowledge and understanding of the JIT purchasing system.

CIMA

The Examiner's Answers for Finance

SECTION A

Answers to Question One

1.1	A	B	**(C)**	D
1.2	A	B	**(C)**	D
1.3	**(A)**	B	C	D
1.4	A	B	C	**(D)**
1.5	A	B	C	**(D)**
1.6	A	**(B)**	C	D
1.7	**(A)**	B	C	D
1.8	A	**(B)**	C	D
1.9	A	B	**(C)**	D
1.10	A	B	C	**(D)**

Explanations follow for answers to objective test questions involving calculations

1.1

Month	*1*	*2*	*3*
Sales	150	180	216
25%	37·5	45	54
70%		105	126
Total	37·5	150	180

Therefore the answer is C

1.4

Original current ratio = $^{2}/_{1}$ = 2

Settlement = 0·3

New current ratio = $^{1.7}/_{0.7}$ = 2·42

Increase = $^{2.42}/_{2}$

Thus the increase is = 21%

Therefore the answer is D

1.6

Note inflation would increase interest rates, increasing the denominator of the model; shrinkage of turnover would reduce the annual demand for cash, reducing the numerator.

Therefore the answer is B

1.9

[500,000 ÷ $1{\cdot}025^1$ = 487,805]

Therefore the answer is C

1.10

365 ÷ 73 = 5 compounding periods
$[1 + (3/97)]^5 - 1$ = 16·45% approx.

Therefore the answer is D

SECTION B

Answer to Question Two

Requirement (a)

REPORT

To:	The Chairman, Q Limited
From:	Management Accountant
Date:	25 November 2004

This is with reference to your query on the bank's response to our request for an increase in our overdraft facility. Overtrading refers to a situation where turnover is increased without a matching increase in equity or other long-term sources of funds. The main cause is the failure to make adequate financing provision for rapidly increasing turnover, particularly in high growth enterprises. There can also be other causes such as escalation of project costs, making it necessary to use short-term sources of funds to finance long-term investments.

Symptoms and their possible causes:

- Sales increase very quickly in relation to capital employed, resulting in sharp increases in the ratio of sales to fixed assets.
- The increase in sales would result in a higher level of debtors and other current assets.
- The increased investment in current assets needed to support the increased sales are financed mainly from short-term sources like creditors and bank overdrafts, resulting in a declining current ratio and quick ratio.
- The cash position will become tight, to alleviate which bank overdrafts and other borrowings are likely to increase, resulting in higher gearing.
- Delay in paying creditors would be reflected in higher average payment periods.
- Increased short-term borrowings and trade credit would cause the net working capital to decline, and it may even become negative. Negative net working capital implies a current ratio less than unity (current assets less than current liabilities), and a business in such a position is likely to face considerable difficulty in meeting its current liabilities. Even where the current ratio is satisfactory, any erosion of net working capital would worsen the liquidity of the business and make it more vulnerable to cyclical risk (the pressures that surface in a recession – fall in turnover and margins, delay in realising receivables, drying up of credit – all put an immediate squeeze on liquidity).
- Tangible and intangible costs such as increased cost of borrowing, disruption in supplies due to delay in settling bills, stiffening of credit terms by suppliers, loss of management time in firefighting, liquidity crises and so on, would cause downward pressure on profitability.

Other causes of overtrading symptoms

A situation similar to that resulting from overtrading can be caused due to other reasons such as:

- Repayment of a loan without raising sufficient long-term funds for the repayment (either in the form of profit accruals or a fresh loan) can drain cash from the firm, creating the symptoms.

- Excessive dividend payout not backed by sufficient profit accruals can result in depressing the equity and creating similar symptoms.

- Using short-term sources of funds to finance long-term investments will depress net working capital, resulting in overtrading symptoms.

Solutions to overtrading

- The short-term solutions would be to either

  - restrict the growth in turnover to manageable proportions;

  - or improve working capital management so that the investment in current assets in relation to the level of sales is reduced (that is better inventory control, credit policy and debt collection).

- The long-term solution is to provide more long-term funds for working capital purposes – that is improve the net working capital position of the firm.

Requirement (b)

The Managing Director is correct in highlighting that the sales have increased dramatically. However, calculation of key working capital ratios indicate a worsening liquidity position:

Some relevant ratios:

	2002	*2003*
Gross profit margin	17·68%	14·97%
Net profit margin	4·54%	3·25%
Sales to fixed assets	6·87	9·86
Current ratio	1·53	1·09
Quick ratio	0·87	0·62
Net working capital	£1,420,000	£682,000
Debt/equity ratio	12·53%	25·44%
Stock turnover period	15·56 days	15·70 days
Debtors collection period	21·24 days	23·10 days
Creditors payment period	19·68 days	30·70 days
Operating cycle	17·12 days	8·10 days

The Managing Director is correct in highlighting that the sales and profits have increased dramatically. However, although profits have increased in absolute terms, net profit margin has declined, probably due to increased selling expenses (including discounts).

A low operating cycle can be either an indication of efficient working capital management or a sign of a very tight working capital situation caused by overtrading. The latter seems to be the case here, because the reduction is not due to better current asset management, but rather due to delay in payment of creditors.

Similarly, the higher fixed asset turnover ratio could be either an indication of more efficient utilisation of assets or a sign of overtrading. Financial ratio analysis should be done with care, looking at the overall picture. Ideally, ratios of other similar companies, or industry average ratios should be scrutinised for comparison.

The declining liquidity ratios are classic indicators of overtrading, indicating that the current assets may soon be insufficient to cover the company's maturing obligations.

The big increase in creditor days is a cause for concern, as loss of supplier goodwill could result in delays or difficulties in obtaining timely supplies.

Given the financial situation of the company, the bank is unlikely to increase its exposure unless more long-term funds are brought in to shore up the net working capital, which has fallen to dangerous levels.

Management Accountant

SECTION C

Answer to Question Three

Requirement (a)

The following points should be brought out:

- The interest rate charged by the bank reflects the risk of the bank's debt, which is affected by factors like seniority of the debt, security available and so on, hence, it is likely to be lower than the business risk of the company's projects. It would be inappropriate to use this as a hurdle rate for projects whose risk is borne by the equity investors.

- Moreover, borrowing for this project will result in increasing the company's financial risk, and consequently, the rate of return required by the equity shareholders, that is it will increase the company's overall cost of capital.

- Different sources of finance are used to achieve a company's target capital structure, and this "pool of funds" is used to invest in projects. Companies often find it economical to minimise issue costs by raising one source of finance at a time. They may therefore move towards their target capital structure unevenly, by raising marginal amounts of debt and equity by turn. The marginal cost of capital will fluctuate from low levels when debt is the marginal choice, to high levels when equity is used. It is therefore more appropriate to use the average cost of the pool of funds as the discount rate for all projects.

- In any case, it is the after-tax yield on the bonds (and not the coupon rate of interest) that would represent the appropriate cost of debt.

Requirement (c)

The ex-dividend share price is 705 – 20 = 685p

Let dividend growth rate = g

$34p \times (1 + g)^5 = 47p \qquad (1 + g)^5 = 47 \div 34 = 1{\cdot}3824$

$1 + g = 5\sqrt{1 \cdot 3824} = 1{\cdot}0669 \qquad g = 6{\cdot}69\%$ approx

$D_1 = D_0 \times (1 + g) = 47 \times (1 + 0{\cdot}0669) = 50{\cdot}14p$

$$k_e = \frac{D_1}{P_o} + g = \frac{50 \cdot 14}{685} + 0 \cdot 0669 = 14\% \text{ approx}$$

Cost of preference share capital:

The dividend payable on each preference share is 8·25% on the face value of 100 pence = 8·25p.

Using the rearranged formula for valuing a perpetuity:

$$K_p = \frac{D}{P_o} = \frac{8 \cdot 25}{75} = 11\%$$

The cost of borrowing through fixed rate debentures can be found by calculating the after-tax yield on the company's existing debt.

After-tax coupon on 6% debentures = 6 x (1 - 0·30) = £4·2

$(4{\cdot}2 \times AF_{k\%,6}) + 100/(1 + k)^6 = 94$

To find the yield (k) calculate the IRR through interpolation:

Try 5%: $(4{\cdot}2 \times 5{\cdot}076) + 100/1{\cdot}05^6 - 94 = 21{\cdot}32 + 74{\cdot}62 - 94 = 1{\cdot}94$
Try 6%: $(4{\cdot}2 \times 4{\cdot}917) + 100/1{\cdot}06^6 - 94 = 20{\cdot}65 + 70{\cdot}5 - 94 = -2{\cdot}85$

$$\text{Yield} = 5 + \left[\frac{\quad \times 1}{1\cdot 94 - (-2\cdot 85)}\right] = 5\cdot 4\%$$

				£m
MV of equity	=	35m x £6·85	=	239·75
MV of preference share capital	=	75m x £0·75	=	56·25
MV of debentures	=	1m x £94	=	94·00
Capital employed				390·00

WACC = (14 x 239·75/390) + (11 x 56·25/390) + (5·4 x 94/390)

Requirement (c)

(i) The project being financed should have the same systematic risk as the company's existing operations. The new venture is in a different line of activity to S plc's existing business.

(ii) The project should be marginal. This one is not – the investment of £100 million is just over 25% of the market value of capital employed.

(iii) The company's existing capital structure should remain unchanged. This project is to be financed by a new issue of debentures, which will alter the capital structure, the cost of capital would be affected in the short-term – It is not clear for how long.

Answer to Question Four

Requirement (a)

(i) Current earnings per share: 4·8 ÷ 40 = 12 pence

∴ current market price of share = 12 x 6·25 = 75 pence

Subscription price = 75 x (1 - 0·36) = 48 pence

Value of rights issue = £12 million

Number of rights issue = 12 million ÷ 0·48 = 25 million shares

Total number of shares after rights issue = 40 million + 25 million = 65 million shares

Rights terms 25 million for 40 million shares = 5 for 8

$$TERP = \left[75 \times \frac{40}{65}\right] + \left[48 \times \frac{25}{65}\right] = 64 \cdot 62 \text{ pence}$$

(ii) Current earnings yield = $^{12}/_{75}$ = 16%

Earnings yield on new funds = $^{2\cdot4}/_{12}$ = 20%

$$TERP = \left[75 \times \frac{40}{65}\right] + \left[48 \times \frac{20}{16} \times \frac{25}{65}\right] = 69 \cdot 23 \text{ pence}$$

Alternatively:

		£m
Market capitalisation (pre-issue) 40m x 0·75	=	30
Yield-adjusted value of proposed rights issue = 12 x (20/16)	=	15
Total value of company following the rights issue	=	45

Ex-rights price of share = £45 ÷ 65 = 69·23 pence

(iii) The yield-adjusted value of the right = 69·23 - 48 = 21·23 pence

The rights issue is 25 : 40 = 1 : 1·6 ∴ the owner of 520,000 shares will be eligible to get 325,000 rights shares, making up a total of 845,000 shares

Value of the shareholding before the rights issue = 520,000 x £0·75 = 390,000

Evaluation of the alternatives:

Take up the rights		£
Value of the holding, ex-rights	= 845,000 x 0·6923 =	584,994
Less: Cost of taking up rights	= 325,000 x 0·48 =	(156,000)
Net value		428,994

Sell the rights		£
Value of the holding, ex-rights	= 520,000 x 0·6923 =	359,996
Sale proceeds of rights	= 325,000 x 0·2123 =	68,998
Net value		428,994

Thus, there would theoretically be no loss of value for the shareholder if the rights are either taken up or sold. Sale of the rights would, however, incur some transaction costs.

[Note: Similar calculations using the TERP would be acceptable]

If the director did nothing she would be left with her original 520,000 shares, which at the ex-rights price, would have a value of only £359,996, representing a loss of value of £68,998. However, to limit the loss of value that might arise from doing nothing, the underwriters to a rights issue are required to sell the shares allotted to such shareholders, and pass on to them any surplus realised over the issue price. Since the surplus ought to be at least equal to the amount that would have been realised by sale of the rights, there should again be no value loss for the shareholder – although transaction costs would again be incurred.

However, shareholders who sell their rights (or whose rights are sold on their behalf) do suffer dilution of ownership and earnings. Particularly if the shareholder is dependent on dividend earnings, the reduction in the company's dividend per share paid from 6·5 pence (2·6m/40m) to 4 pence (2·6m/65m) would have an adverse impact on the shareholder's cash flow.

Thus, if the shareholder does not take up her rights she may be seriously inconvenienced by having a proportion of her capital in the company forcibly realised. Although this money can be immediately reinvested in the same company or in other companies by buying in the market, this will involve transactions costs.

Requirement (b)

Main advantages of a rights issue compared to an offer for sale:

- Relatively cheap (that is lower issue costs);
- Pricing not a critical factor;
- High success rate – deep discounts common (deeper the discount, lower the chance of the issue failing due to a dip in the market place);
- Underwriting not essential (although it is rarely dispensed with);
- Dilution restricted to those shareholders who choose not to take up rights.

Answer to Question Five

Requirement (a)

The main economic roles played by financial intermediaries are:

Volume transformation ("Parcelling"): Breaking down large loans to companies into smaller loans from individuals (like in wholesale/retail markets).

Maturity transformation: Companies usually long-term funds for investment in assets over a period of time, whereas investors generally prefer their investments to be liquid and easily realisable in the short-term. Financial markets and institutions reconcile these two conflicting needs by:

- Borrowing short and lending long;
- Providing liquidity in the secondary markets.

Risk transformation: Risky loans to the users of funds are converted into relatively safe investments by the lenders of funds, by spreading the risk through diversification. Financial institutions also make use of economies of scale to offer specialised risk management expertise at lower cost.

Reduction of *transaction costs* through economies of scale, thereby contributing towards the efficient pricing of securities.

Offering *financial expertise* and *advice* to both lenders and borrowers, through *specialisation*.

Retail banks mainly fulfil the parcelling, maturity transformation and risk transformation roles by collecting small and short-maturity savings for larger and longer-maturity lending. Their cash distribution and money transmission activities reduce transaction costs in the transfer of funds.

Since merchant banks deal in large amounts, and have a high proportion of term deposits, their role in parcelling and maturity transformation is secondary. Their primary roles lie in:

- Risk transformation through acceptance and discount facilities, development of risk management products, arranging large foreign exchange deals, and so on.
- Offering financial expertise and advice to fund managers in investment activity and to the corporate sector in activities like mergers and acquisitions, new security issues and so on.

- Reduction of brokerage costs by acting as intermediaries in arranging large-scale loans.

Requirement (b)

- *Maturity:* T-Bills and CP are short-term investments (CP: 7 to 270 days; T-Bills: 6 to 180 days); CDs can be for both short and long term maturities (7 days to 5 years).

- *Trading:* All three negotiable. But, like T-Bills, CP is usually a non-interest-bearing instrument that trades at a discount to face value. CDs, on the other hand, trade at the discounted maturity value (including interest on the principal)

- *Default risk:* T-Bills are backed by government guarantee. CDs are issued by banks, and CPs by any public corporation – credit rating is important.

Apart from default risk, other important types of risk when investing surplus cash are price risk (the risk that the value of the investment will vary with changes in interest rates – the longer the maturity of the instrument, the more sensitive it will be to interest rate changes), and liquidity risk (the risk that it would be difficult or costly to exit the investment at short notice).

Liquidity of the short-term investment would be an important consideration in S plc's situation. Since bank term deposits are not as liquid as negotiable instruments that can be freely traded in the market, they would be less suitable as an investment in this particular case.

Requirement (c)

The yield gap arises from the dividend yield on shares being higher than the interest yield on debt, due to the higher risk borne by equity investors. Reverse yield gap refers to the situation where the dividend yield on shares is *lower* than the interest yield on debt. This could be due to a share being highly priced in spite of its paying a low dividend, due to investors' expectations with regard to its future growth potential (compared to shares, the growth potential of debt instruments is highly limited).

Answer to Question Six

Requirement (a)

Monthly demand = 560 units;
Annual demand = 6,720 units.
Price per unit = £1,400

EOQ = $\sqrt{(2 \times 6{,}720 \times 150) \div (0 \cdot 10 \times 1{,}400)}$ = **120 units**

The number of orders that should be placed in a year = 6,720 ÷ 120 = **56**

Annual ordering cost = 56 x £150 = £8,400

Annual holding cost = (120 x £1,400 x 0·10) ÷ 2 = £8,400

Total variable cost = 8,400 + 8,400 = £16,800

Annual purchase cost = 6,720 x £1,400 = £9,408,000

Total annual cost = **£9,424,800**

Requirement (b)

New EOQ = $\sqrt{(2 \times 6{,}720 \times 34) \div (0{\cdot}10 \times 1{,}402)}$ = **57 units**

The number of orders that should be placed in a year = 6,720 ÷ 57 = 118 (approx)
Annual ordering cost = 118 x £34 = £4,012
Annual holding cost = (57 x £1,402 x 0·10) ÷ 2 = £3,995·70
Total variable cost = 4,012 + 3,995·70 = £8,007·70
Annual purchase cost = 6,720 x £1,402 = £9,421,440
Total annual cost = **£9,429,447·70**

If the higher order quantity of 140 units is agreed at the discounted price of £1,400:

The number of orders that should be placed in a year = 6,720 ÷ 140 = **48**
Annual ordering cost = 48 x £34 = £1,632
Annual holding cost = (140 x £1,400 x 0·10) ÷ 2 = £9,800
Total variable cost = 1,632 + 9,800 = £11,432
Annual purchase cost = 6,720 x £1,400 = £9,408,000
Total annual cost = **£9,419,432**

It would be preferable to take the large quantity discount from the new supplier. Otherwise, the higher price of £1,402 would outweigh the benefit gained from the lower order cost of £34.

Requirement (c)

Problems faced by companies in determining the EOQ:

- It is practically difficult to make accurate estimates of annual usage, ordering costs and holding (carrying) cost; even the purchase price may be subject to variation between periods and between different suppliers.

- The EOQ formula is based on an assumption that stock is consumed at a constant rate – that is the average level of stock is equal to the quantity ordered divided by two; but, in practice, stock may not be used at a constant rate.

Requirement (d)

JIT purchasing techniques seek to keep stock at a minimum by buying stocks in such a way that the delivery coincides with their use. This can only be achieved by maintaining very close liaison and rapport with suppliers in order to eliminate the two main reasons for high stock levels – viz long lead times and uncertainty regarding supply. This can be achieved by giving more business to a smaller number of suppliers by entering into long-term supply contracts – this can lead to better quality and greater reliability.

The main benefits from JIT purchasing would stem from smaller, more frequent supplies, resulting in lower stock levels and reduced inventory holding costs. There would be less pressure on storage space. The supplier would have greater responsibility for quality control. leading to further benefits from reduced inspection costs and fewer quality problems.

CIMA

November 2004 Examinations

Intermediate Level

Business Taxation

(IBTX – Paper 5)

Question Paper	1
Examiner's Brief Guide to the Paper	13
Examiner's Answers	14

The answers published here have been written by the Examiner and should provide a helpful guide for both lecturers and students.

Published separately on the CIMA website (www.cimaglobal.com/students) from end of February 2005 is a Post Examination Guide for this paper, which provides much valuable and complementary material including indicative mark information.

CIMA

Intermediate Level

Business Taxation

5

IBTX

23 November 2004

Tuesday afternoon

INSTRUCTIONS TO CANDIDATES

Read this page before you look at the questions

You are allowed three hours to answer this question paper.
Answer the ONE question in Section A (this has 10 sub-questions). Answer the ONE question in Section B. Answer TWO questions ONLY from Section C.
A Taxation Table is provided.

SECTION A – 20 MARKS

ANSWER *ALL* TEN SUB-QUESTIONS – 2 MARKS EACH

Question One

1.1 On 1 September 2003, K Ltd places an order with L Ltd for a machine costing £12,000 exclusive of VAT for delivery before 30 September 2003. L Ltd completes the machine on 28 September, but does not deliver it to K Ltd until 2 October 2003. K Ltd pays the full amount due (including VAT) into L Ltd's bank account by direct transfer on 7 October 2003 and L Ltd issues a VAT invoice three days later.

The VAT tax point is

A 1 September 2003.

B 2 October 2003.

C 7 October 2003.

D 10 October 2003.

1.2 A company has been making up its accounts annually at 31 May for many years. For the year ended 31 May 2003 it did not submit its Annual Return (CT600) until 31 October 2004.

What is the latest date by which the Inland Revenue can commence an investigation into the company's return?

A 31 October 2005

B 31 January 2006

C 31 May 2005

D 31 December 2005

1.3 Class 1A National Insurance Contributions in respect of 2003/2004 must be paid by

A 19 May 2004.

B 5 July 2004.

C 19 July 2004.

D 31 July 2004.

1.4 X Ltd had been making up accounts annually to 31 May for several years. Early in 2003, the directors decided to make up accounts to 31 August 2003 (instead of 31 May 2003) and annually thereafter at 31 August.

The **two** chargeable accounting periods for CT purposes will be

A	1 June 2002 – 31 March 2003	and	1 April 2003 – 31 August 2003.
B	1 June 2002 – 31 May 2003	and	1 June 2003 – 31 August 2003.
C	1 June 2002 – 31 December 2002	and	1 January 2003 – 31 August 2003.
D	1 June 2002 – 31 August 2002	and	1 September 2002 – 31 August 2003.

1.5 H Ltd, a UK resident company with no associated companies, made up accounts for the **nine**-month period to 30 September 2003. The total taxable profits for this period were £40,000, including £5,000 of FII.

The CT liability for the period will be

A £6,650.

B £6,235.

C £10,500.

D £10,085.

1.6 J Ltd, a large company for CT quarterly payment purposes, made up accounts for the **eight**-month period to 31 August 2003.

The **final** payment under the quarterly system (ignoring any balance payable on the usual due date) will be payable by

A 14 July 2003.

B 14 October 2003.

C 14 December 2003.

D 14 January 2004.

1.7 During its accounting year ended 31 March 2004, K Ltd sold a painting that had been hanging in the boardroom for several years. The selling price was £7,200 and the cost plus indexation allowance amounted to £4,800.

The chargeable gain will be

A £2,400

B £1,200

C £400

D £2,000

1.8 K Ltd incurred legal fees during its twelve-month accounting period ended 31 December 2003 on the following:

Directors' service contracts	£12,000
On a loan to be used to purchase new business premises	£9,000
Defending an action for faulty workmanship	£6,000
Bringing a Tax appeal to the High Court	£16,000
Obtaining planning permission to extend a factory	£8,000

In arriving at the company's Schedule DI profit, the amount to be added back will be

A £16,000.

B £22,000.

C £27,000.

D £37,000.

1.9 An employee paying higher rate tax is provided with a motor car throughout 2003/04 and the assessable benefit is agreed at £3,300. The employee has underpaid tax for the year 2002/03 of £80, which is to be collected via his PAYE code number for 2003/04.

The correct code number for 2003/04 is

A 461L

B 131L

C 95L

D 111L

1.10 S Ltd is a company which is partially exempt for VAT purposes. For its quarter ended 30 June 2003, its unattributable input VAT, which cannot be linked directly to its chargeable supplies or exempt supplies, is £8,000.

Its sales for the quarter comprised:

Zero rated –	£20,000
Standard rated	£7,000 (excluding VAT)
Exempt	£9,000

The amount of the **unattributable** input VAT of £8,000 it may recover for the quarter is

A £2,000.

B £2,483.

C £5,517.

D £6,000.

(Total = 20 marks)

End of Section A

SECTION B – 40 MARKS

ANSWER THIS QUESTION

Question Two

For the purpose of this scenario you are the chief accountant of H Ltd, a UK resident company with a number of interests in UK and overseas companies.

Your assistant has prepared the following diagram of the structure of the group together with some explanatory notes. The figures represent the percentages of the voting shares held in each case. Apart from H Ltd's acquisition of 80% of P Inc on 1 January 2004, all of the holdings were acquired several years ago.

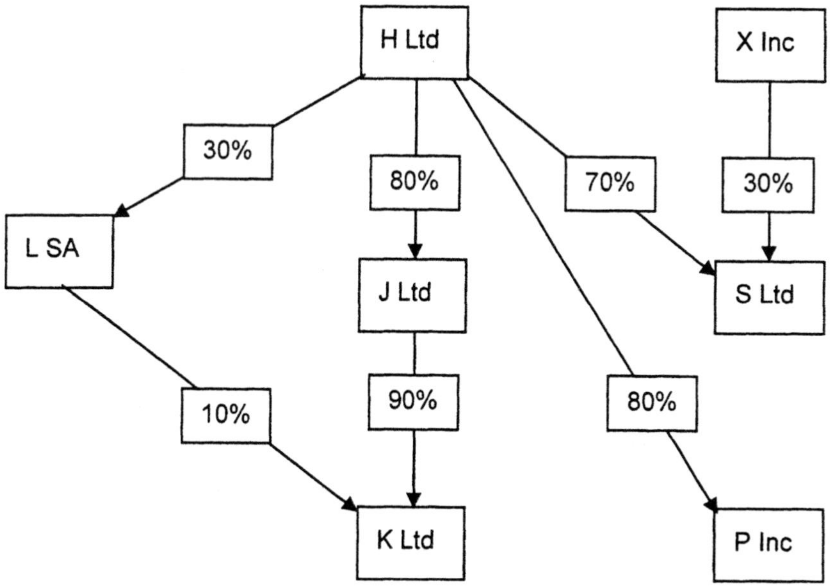

Notes:

1 Apart from L SA and X Inc and P Inc, all of the companies were incorporated in and trade in, the UK.

2 P Inc is centrally managed and controlled from the UK. It operates in a country where the only rate of CT is 10%.

3 L SA is incorporated abroad and is wholly managed abroad in a country where the rate of CT is 12%. 30% of its shares are owned by UK resident individuals.

During discussions with your managing director he raised the following points:

(i) He indicated that H Ltd is considering operating a number of new profitable businesses in overseas countries. He wishes to know about the taxation implications of running them as branches of H Ltd or as separate subsidiaries, incorporated and managed overseas.

(ii) He advised you that the board of H Ltd is considering transferring the management of P Inc to its country of operation and he wishes to know the tax consequences of this decision. It is anticipated that P Inc will sustain trading losses for at least the next accounting year, but will thereafter become profitable.

Shortly after 31 March 2004, the date to which all of the companies make up accounts for twelve months, your assistants collate the results which are shown in the following table:

	H Ltd	*S Ltd*	*P Inc*	*J Ltd*	*K Ltd*	*L SA*
	£000	*£000*	*£000*	*£000*	*£000*	*£000*
Schedule DI profit	320				110	120
Schedule DI Loss		(240)	(280)	(200)		
Schedule A	100		20		30	
Capital gain		80		60		
Capital loss					(90)	

Notes:

1 The capital gain arising in J Ltd was on an asset sold on 30 April 2003 and the capital loss in K Ltd arose from a sale in September 2003. S Ltd's gain arose on an asset sold in November 2003. All these sales were to third parties.

2 The profit in L SA has been computed in accordance with UK tax law.

3 None of the companies paid any dividends.

4 For the year ended 31 March 2003, H Ltd had chargeable profits of £400,000 and K Ltd and L SA both had profits of less than £200,000.

Required:

(a) Draft a report to the board of directors showing the final corporation tax liabilities for the profit making companies in the group in respect of the year ended 31 March 2004, indicating in each case when the liabilities have been or will be paid. Your report should explain:

- The application of the associated companies rules in the case of the group.
- The nature of the reliefs which have been claimed, indicating why you chose to claim the reliefs in the manner in which you did.
- The nature of any elections which were required to be made to minimise the liabilities of group companies.
- The effect of the presence of L SA on the CT liability of H Ltd.

Your calculations of the liabilities of the various group companies should be included in an appendix to your report and references to the figures in the appendix should be shown in the body of your report.

The report (including *3 marks* for presentation)	*(20 marks)*
Your appendix	*(12 marks)*

(Total for requirement (a) = 32 marks)

(b)

Draft a separate report to the managing director on the two points raised by him in his discussion with you.

Point (i)	*(5 marks)*
Point (ii)	*(2 marks)*
Presentation	*(1 mark)*

(Total for requirement (b) = 8 marks)

(Total marks for question = 40 marks)

End of Section B

SECTION C – 40 MARKS

ANSWER TWO QUESTIONS ONLY

Question Three

All of the ordinary share capital of A Ltd, a UK resident company, had, until 30 September 2003 been owned by M Ltd, also a UK resident company which had two other wholly owned UK resident subsidiaries – N Ltd and O Ltd. On that date, M Ltd sold 30% of the shares of A Ltd to a company resident in Germany.

You establish that, in August 1999, M Ltd had transferred a building to A Ltd under group arrangements on a no gain/no loss basis. At the date of transfer the building had a market value of £240,000. It had cost M Ltd £100,000 in August 1987 and an extension was added in June 1994 at a cost of £40,000.

During the year to 31 March 2004, N Ltd had incurred a capital loss of £40,000 and O Ltd a capital loss of £20,000.

A Ltd had the following disposals during its accounting year to 31 March 2004:

1 **June 2003**
Sold rights to shares for £25,000. This arose from a holding of 30,000 ordinary shares in C Ltd which A Ltd had purchased in October 1994 for £160,000. When C Ltd made a rights issue in June 2003, A Ltd did not wish to exercise its rights and these were sold for £25,000. The market value of the 30,000 shares still held by A Ltd on the day following the rights issue was £280,000.

2 **September 2003**
An office building held by A Ltd as an investment and not used for its trade was sold for £250,000. This building had originally been purchased in June 1972 for £30,000 and since then the following capital expenditure had been incurred on the building:

December 1977	£25,000
October 1981	£30,000
June 1991	£20,000
August 2000	£10,000

A global election was in place and the agreed market value of the building at 31 March 1982 was £75,000.

Required:

(a) Compute the chargeable gains on A Ltd for the year ended 31 March 2004, arising from **each** of the above transactions assuming all relevant claims are made.

(16 marks)

(b) Assuming A Ltd had other chargeable income for the year amounting to £13,500, compute the **total** CT payable by A Ltd and state when this will be payable.

(4 marks)

(Total = 20 marks)

Relevant Indexation Factors are:

March 1982 – September 2003	1·297	August 1987 – August 1999	0·622
June 1994 – August 1999	0·144	October 1994 – June 2003	0·249
August 2000 – September 2003	0·070	June 1991 – September 2003	0·361

Question Four

(a) For the quarter ended 30 June 2003, T Ltd, a company registered for VAT, had turnover comprising £210,000 of supplies which were standard rated, £20,000 which were zero rated and £50,000 which were exempt.

The input VAT on expenditure during the quarter was allocated as follows:

	£
Attributable to standard rated sales	24,000
Attributable to exempt sales	10,000
Attributable to Zero rated sales	1,000
Unattributable	15,000

Required:

Compute the amount of input VAT that T Ltd may recover in respect of the quarter ended 30 June 2003, explaining clearly how you arrived at your answer. There is no special method being applied.

State what adjustment may be required at the end of the company's normal accounting year.

(8 marks)

(b) You are the chief accountant of R Ltd, a rapidly growing successful company engaged in software engineering. The company employs a number of highly skilled workers who have all been provided with motors cars by the company, with unrestricted private use. The managing director has read that the company and the employees could be better off, from a tax point of view, if the employees were to provide their own cars for business use and claim mileage rates.

Required:

Prepare a report for the managing director explaining the operation of the car benefits arrangements, including fuel benefits, which will apply in 2003/04. Your answer should deal with both

(i) employees who have to do over 20,000 business miles per year and with a very small amount of private mileage.

(ii) employees who do less than 4,000 business miles per year with a large amount of private mileage.

(12 marks)

(Total = 20 marks)

Question Five

TG Ltd, a UK manufacturing company making up accounts at 31 March each year, had the following Industrial Buildings in use at 1 April 2003:

Building A
This building had been purchased new on 1 April 1978 at a total cost of £80,000, excluding the cost of land.

Building B
This building had been purchased new on 1 April 1987 at a cost of £140,000 including £33,000 for the cost of the land and £36,000 in respect of administration offices.

Building C
This building had been purchased second hand from Q Ltd on 1 April 1991 for £180,000, excluding the cost of land. It had originally cost Q Ltd £115,000 new on 1 April 1983.

All of the above buildings had been brought into use immediately on purchase and had been used at all times for qualifying purposes for Industrial Buildings allowance.

Building D
This building, situated in an Enterprise Zone, had been purchased by TG Ltd on 1 April 2001 for £140,000 excluding the cost of land, and the company had claimed Initial Allowance of 55% in the year ended 31 March 2002 and thereafter had claimed the maximum allowances available.

During the year ended 31 March 2003, the directors of TG Ltd were planning the purchase, on 1 April 2003, of one additional secondhand qualifying building on which they were prepared to spend £160,000. They had narrowed the choice down to the following three buildings, each of which would be suitable for the business and each of which would cost £160,000, excluding the cost of land.

(i) Originally purchased by the previous owner for £110,000 on 1 April 1976.

(ii) Originally purchased by the previous owner for £140,000 on 1 April 1979.

(iii) Originally purchased by the previous owner for £170,000 on 1 April 2001.

All of the above prices are exclusive of the cost of the land.

All of the above buildings were brought into use by the original owners on the date of purchase and have always been used for industrial purposes.

Required:

Compute the maximum Industrial Buildings Allowances that may be claimed by TG Ltd for the year ended 31 March 2004, assuming the most tax efficient choice was made concerning the building which was purchased on 1 April 2003.

(20 marks)

Question Six

(a) X Ltd, a UK resident company, controls 80% of the ordinary shares of Y Ltd, also UK resident.

Both companies make up accounts to 31 March 2004.

In May 2003, W Ltd, a major supplier of raw materials to both X Ltd and Y Ltd, was experiencing serious cash flow problems. Had this company ceased to trade it would have created serious problems for X Ltd. After careful consideration and after having a valuation report on W Ltd prepared by a firm of accountants at a cost of £6,000, X Ltd made a loan to W Ltd of £70,000.

In December 2003, W Ltd paid X Ltd interest on the loan of £5,000 which was credited to X Ltd's profit and loss account. In February 2004, one of W Ltd's major customers became insolvent. As a result, W Ltd was unable to pay back any of the loan from X Ltd who wrote it off in its profit and loss account.

The results for the year ended 31 March 2004 were:

X Ltd	Profit of £60,000 – after writing off the above loan and related costs and crediting the interest received from W Ltd.
Y Ltd	Profit of £280,000.

Required:

Demonstrate how the above transactions would be dealt with by X Ltd for taxation purposes and indicate how the group of X Ltd and Y Ltd can gain maximum relief under the loan relationship rules. You should show how much CT has been saved by your treatment.

(10 marks)

(b) You are the Financial Controller of D Ltd, a small UK resident manufacturing company engaged in the software industry. The recent taxable profits have been between £250,000 to £280,000 per year.

Your chairman calls you to a meeting at which he informs you that 90% of the company's share capital, which is currently owned by the four directors in equal amounts, is about to be acquired by an American resident company. This company already has thirty five European subsidiaries, including four resident in the UK.

Required:

Draft a brief report to the chairman, setting out the UK tax implications for D Ltd as a result of the takeover. You should also discuss the effect on the CT liability of D Ltd.

(10 marks)

(Total = 20 marks)

End of paper

The Taxation Table follows

The Chartered Institute of Management Accountants

Intermediate Level | November 2004 examination

Business Taxation

In answering the questions in this paper, the following tax rates and reliefs should be used.

CORPORATION TAX:	*Financial year 2002 (year ended 31 03 2003)* ***and*** *Financial year 2003 (year ended 31 03 2004)*
Large companies – total profits over	£1·5 million
Rate of tax for large companies	30%
Small companies – total profits up to	£300,000
Rate of tax for small companies	19%
Threshold for new small company rate – total profits up to	£10,000
Rate of tax for a new small company	0%
Starting point for small company rate of 19%	£50,000 (total profits)
Taper relief fractions:	
£10,000 – £50,000	$^{19}/_{400}$
£300,000 – £1·5 million	$^{11}/_{400}$
Taper relief formula – all years	(M - P) x I/P x appropriate fraction above
Rate for grossing up dividends – all years	$^{10}/_{9}$

INCOME TAX:	*2002/2003* ***and*** *2003/2004*
Rate of income tax on interest received and paid	20% (to and from individuals)
Rate of income tax on charges paid/received	22% (to and from individuals)

Note: Interest and charges paid to and received from UK companies from 1 April 2001 are gross.

CAPITAL GAINS TAX:
The relevant indexation factors are given in **Question Three**.

VALUE ADDED TAX:
The 2003/04 registration threshold is £56,000.

PERSONAL TAXATION:

Personal Allowance 2003/04	£4,615
NIC CLASS 1A and 1B - 2003/04	12·8%

The Examiner for IBTX offers the following background and guidance on the questions included in this examination paper.

Section A – compulsory

Question One provides 10 objective test sub-questions which cover most of the knowledge based topics within the syllabus, including, on this occasion, one on the capital gains tax treatment of chattels. A few of the questions require only basic calculations.

Section B – compulsory

Question Two is a wide-ranging question covering most core areas of the syllabus, but in a fairly basic fashion. Had these items been examined separately, they would have been regarded as easy. However, when they are presented in a narrative style, it appears candidates are unable to summarise the main points in the question.

Given that there are **four marks** available for presentation, it will be important that great care is taken in organising the answer and producing it exactly in the manner required by the question. None of the tasks require a great level of technical knowledge.

The requirement makes it quite clear that any detailed calculations are to be shown in appendices and **not** in the body of the reports.

The important aspect of this type of question is the ability to assimilate and organise the information given and to produce a clear report providing the information being sought by the directors of the company.

Finally, candidates can be re-assured that if an early mistake is made in a calculation of say one of the capital gains, then no further marks will be lost if the "wrong" figure is correctly used in the remainder of the answer.

Section C – two questions from four

This section is where candidates are expected to demonstrate some in-depth technical knowledge of topics from any part of the syllabus and where detailed calculations will be required. The four questions are equally balanced in terms of degree of difficulty.

Question Three is the guaranteed CGT question and because it is always examined, candidates should prepare thoroughly for it. There is evidence that this is the case and high marks will be scored here.

Question Four part (a) requires sound knowledge of the operation of the partial exemption rules in VAT. In past questions, candidates have shown weaknesses in this important topic. Part (b) covers a recurring basic choice for many employees (and their employers) – take the car or the cash?

Question Five is on Industrial Buildings Allowances, a topic examined on many occasions in this syllabus and its predecessors. It has the standard choice situation – which building to buy?

Question Six part (a) is on Loan Relationships, another topic examined on many occasions in this syllabus. Part (b) is again a well-examined topic – what are the tax implications when a UK company is acquired by a non-UK resident parent?

CIMA

The Examiner's Answers for Business Taxation

SECTION A

Answers to Question One

> **Examiner's Note:**
> On the examination paper, candidates were asked to circle the letter of the answer they thought was correct. However, the answers below are presented in special answer sheet format for ease of reference.

1.1	A	B	C	(D)
1.2	A	(B)	C	D
1.3	A	B	(C)	D
1.4	A	(B)	C	D
1.5	(A)	B	C	D
1.6	A	B	(C)	D
1.7	A	B	C	(D)
1.8	(A)	B	C	D
1.9	A	B	C	(D)
1.10	A	B	C	(D)

Explanations follow for deriving the answers to the objective test questions		
1.1	Response D	Because the invoice was issued on 10 October 2003, within 14 days of the actual tax point (2 October 2003 – delivery date), the invoice date becomes the actual tax point. Had the receipt of cash been before 2 October that date would be the actual tax point.
1.2	Response B	The anniversary of the actual return date is 31 October 2005 and the enquiry can be opened up until the next quarter date – 31 January 2006.
1.3	Response C	Payment of Class 1A NIC is due by 19 July 2004.
1.4	Response B	A long period of accounts must be split into **two** CAPs – the first is the 12 months from the start of the long period and the second is the remaining period. This long period started on 1 June 2002.
1.5	Response A	With profits of £40,000 for a **nine** month period (£53,333 for 12 month period) H Ltd is a small company and pays CT @ 19% on £35,000 = £6,650.
1.6	Response C	The final quarterly payment must be made $3^1/_2$ months after the end of the CAP to 31 August 2003 – 14 December 2003.
1.7	Response D	The actual gain is £7,200 - £4,800 = £2,400 but the gain cannot exceed $^5/_3$ x (7,200 - 6,000) = £2,000.
1.8	Response A	The **only disallowable** item is the Tax Appeal.
1.9	Response D	The Code Number comprises: PA £4,615 *Less*: Car BIK £3,300 Unpaid tax £80 x 100/40 200 — 3,500 £1,115 Code Number 111L
1.10	Response D	Unattributable VAT reclaimable = Zero rated + standard rate sales/total sales = 27,000/36,000 = 75% x £8,000 = £6,000

SECTION B

Answer to Question Two

Requirement (a)

TO BOARD OF DIRECTORS OF H LTD

REPORT ON TAXATION LIABILITIES OF GROUP MEMBERS

Date: May 2004

1 INTRODUCTION

As you will see from the attached appendix, I have now calculated the final CT liabilities of each of the profit making members of the group, after making appropriate claims and elections to minimise the liabilities. These claims are explained later in this report.

The final liabilities were as follows:

H Ltd	£22,200 – Payable by 1 January 2005
K Ltd	£30,395 – Payable by 1 January 2005

The liability of H Ltd includes £10,800 in respect of our interest of 30% in L SA, which is a Controlled Foreign Company (CFC).

2 RELIEFS AVAILABLE AND CLAIMS MADE

2.1 ASSOCIATED COMPANY RULES
It would be helpful to start by explaining that, as there are **four** other companies under our control, this means that there are **five** associated companies for CT purposes. The effect of this is that the thresholds at which each company starts to be treated as a large company is reduced from £1·5 million to £300,000. The lower limit is similarly scaled down to £60,000 so that any company with profits lying between these thresholds is paying CT at 32·75%. I have claimed the reliefs described below so as to eliminate as much of this high marginal rate of CT as possible.

2.2 RELIEFS AVAILABLE AND CLAIMS MADE
In preparing the computation shown in the appendix, I have taken advantage of two main forms of relief.

The first is **Consortium Relief**. Because we own 70% of S Ltd and X Inc owns 30%, S Ltd is a consortium company and we are able to claim relief for 70% of S Ltd's remaining trading losses of £160,000 amounting to £112,000. This claim is possible as a result of provisions introduced in the Finance Act 2000, which allows a consortium to include non-resident companies such as X Inc.

The most important relief is **Group Relief**, the application of which has reduced the group liability considerably. Companies are in a group relationship where at least 75% of voting power is held directly or indirectly by another UK company. Shares held by a UK company via a non-UK resident (L SA) company are taken into account.

On this basis our tax group comprises H Ltd, J Ltd, K Ltd, and P Inc. S Ltd is **not** in the group. All of the losses of P Inc (from 1 January 2004), which is deemed to be UK resident for tax purposes because it is managed in the UK, are available against the chargeable profits of other group members from 1 January 2004 (the date of acquisition).

This means that total group relief group relief of £70,000 is available ($^{3}/_{12}$ x £280,000) and this has been applied wholly against H Ltd as part of the strategy of eliminating all of the income on which H Ltd is paying at 32·75%.

J Ltd's loss of £200,000 has been relieved – £178,000 against H Ltd to reduce taxable profits to £60,000 and £22,000 against K Ltd. S Ltd is able to use the balance of its losses (£80,000) against its own gain of £80,000.

The final claim made was in connection with the **capital gains and losses** which arose in group companies. All of the companies qualifying for group relief as above are also in a group for capital gains purpose. While it is not possible to surrender capital losses from one group member to another, it is possible, as a result of changes introduced in the Finance Act 2000, for J Ltd and K Ltd to jointly elect to deem that the asset sold by J Ltd in April 2003, was transferred to K Ltd on a no gain/no loss basis. This allows K Ltd use its capital loss to eliminate the gain on J Ltd's asset. K Ltd will have £30,000 of unused capital losses carried forward.

3 THE HOLDING IN L SA

Our 30% holding in this company has two kinds of effects – some positive and some negative.

The positive aspects are twofold. As indicated above, the presence of L SA allowed K Ltd to be part of H Ltd's group for group relief purposes, allowing K Ltd to benefit from J Ltd's trading losses

The main negative aspect is that because of a number of factors, L SA is regarded as a CFC and H Ltd has to pay tax on its share of the profits of that company. This rule only affects UK companies owning more than 25% of a CFC and if our interest in L SA was reduced below that level we would not have to pay CFC tax.

I hope this report has made matters clear regarding our final taxation position.

Chief Accountant

Requirement (b)

REPORT TO MANAGING DIRECTOR RE ISSUES RAISED **June 2004**

You raised two main issues in our recent discussion and I can now provide you with the following information:

(i) Method of operating overseas activities

If the activity is run as a branch of our company then its profits will simply be merged with our UK activities and charged to UK CT. Relief will be given for any foreign tax suffered, but limited to our rate of UK CT. If the branch made a trading loss then this loss would be set against the UK profits, but only if such losses cannot be relieved against overseas profits.

If it is run as a separate subsidiary, we would possibly be taxed in the UK on any dividends remitted to the UK. We would not be able to utilise any losses of the overseas subsidiary. Almost certainly such a subsidiary could fall within the definition of a CFC with the consequences outlined in the main report.

(ii) Change of P Inc's Management

Such an action would result in P Inc ceasing to be UK resident and we would be unable to claim group relief for its losses next year. In addition, when it does make profits we could be taxed on these under CFC rules.

Chief Accountant

APPENDIX

Group comprises H Ltd, J Ltd, K Ltd, and, (from 1 January 2004), P Inc

COMPUTATION OF THE CT LIABILITIES OF THE VARIOUS GROUP COMPANIES

(Note that S Ltd has been excluded as it is not a member of the group)

	H Ltd	**K Ltd**	**P Inc**
	£	£	£
Schedule D I	320,000	110,000	–
Other Income	100,000	30,000	20,000
	420,000	140,000	20,000
Gains – J Ltd £60 - K Ltd (£90)			
Eliminated by election			
Less: P Inc's loss – S 393 (1a)			(20,000)
P Inc's loss to H Ltd – s402			
$^{3}/_{12}$ x £280,000	(70,000)		
J Ltd's Loss of £200,000 to H Ltd/K Ltd	(178,000)	(22,000) Balance	
Maximum relief to reduce to Small company threshold			
Consortium Relief to H Ltd			
70% of S Ltd's loss £160,000	(112,000)		
Taxable profits	60,000	118,000	
CT payable – @ 30%		35,400	
@ 19%	11,400		
Taper Relief (300 – 118) x $^{11}/_{400}$		(5,005)	
CFC Tax on share of L SA's income:			
30% x £120,000 @ 30%	10,800		
Tax payable	22,200	30,395	

Both H Ltd and K Ltd will pay these liabilities by **1 January 2005**.

S Ltd's gain of £80,000 is eliminated by its trading losses of £240,000 leaving £160,000.

Answer to Question Three

Requirement (a)

The following gains become chargeable for the year ended 31 March 2004:

As a result of A Ltd ceasing to be a member of a capital gains tax group, the gain on any asset transferred to A Ltd (under group arrangements) in the previous six years now becomes chargeable – as a "de-merged" gain on **A Ltd**.

	£	£
MV at date of Transfer – August 1999		240,000
Less: Original cost August 1987	100,000	
IA to August 1999 x 0·622	62,200	
Cost of Extension June 1994	40,000	
IA to August 1999 x 0·144	5,760	207,960
Chargeable gain		32,040

This de-merged gain on A Ltd can be eliminated by re-allocating this gain to **N Ltd**, which it can use against its capital losses of **£40,000**.

June 2003 – Sale of rights
Since the amount received from the rights exceeds 5% of the total value of rights plus the retained shares (£305,000) the small disposal exemption cannot apply.

	£	£	£
Proceeds from rights		25,000	
Deemed cost – October 1994:			
£160,000 x 25,000/(25,000 + 280,000)	13,115		
IA to June 2003 x 0·249	3,266	16,381	
Chargeable gain		8,619	8,619

September 2003 – Sale of building – Can use **only MV at 31/3/1982**

	£	£
Proceeds	250,000	
Less: Cost/MV up to March 1982	(75,000)	
June 1991	(20,000)	
August 2000	(10,000)	
Unindexed Gain	145,000	
B/fwd	145,000	
Less IA		
£75,000 x 1·297	(97,275)	
£20,000 x 0·361	(7,220)	
£10,000 x 0·070	(700)	
Chargeable gains	39,805	39,805
Total gains		48,424
Less: Balance of losses from N Ltd and O Ltd by election £60,000 - £32,040		27,960
Chargeable gains		20,464

Requirement (b)

CT computation for year ended 31 March 2004	£
Capital gains as above	20,464
Other income	13,500
	33,964

As there were **four** associated companies at one time during the year the thresholds are divided by four and become:

Starting rate	Lower limit	£2,500	Upper Limit	£12,500
Small Company	Lower Limit	£75,000	Upper Limit	£375,000

BG is a small company and the CT payable is £33,964 x 19%		£6,453·16
Due date	1 January 2005	

Answer to Question Four

Requirement (a)

Quarter ended 30 June 2003

The recoverable input VAT comprises:

Attributable to Standard rated sales – fully recoverable	£24,000
Attributable to exempt supplies – non-recoverable	
Attributable to zero rated sales	1,000
Unattributable directly – partially recoverable in	
Proportion to standard + zero rated sales – ***83%** x £15,000 =	12,450
*** 210+ 20/280 x 100 = 82.14% rounded up to 83%***	£37,450

Since the total input VAT attributable to exempt sales £10,000 + **17%** x £15,000 = £12,550 is > than £625 per month on average, the *de minimis* exempt input VAT rule does not apply Note that this already exceeds the annual *de minimis figure of £7,500.*

At the year end, the total recoverable input VAT for the whole year will be calculated using the **total sales and VAT figures for the whole year**. If this figure differs from the total allowed under the quarterly calculations then an **annual adjustment** will be made in the first quarter of the new year.

Requirement (b)

Report to Managing Director **November 2004**

General Description of the Car Benefit system where employer provides a car

The taxable benefit in kind (BIK) arising when an employee is provided with a motor car by the employer is quantified under two headings:

- A Car BIK and a Charge for use of fuel for private mileage;
- The car benefit is arrived at by applying a percentage factor to the list price of the car including any accessories costing over £100;
- This percentage is based on the level of CO_2 emissions made by the car – the higher the level of emissions, the higher the percentage;
- The lowest figure is 15% and the highest 35% – for diesel cars a further 3% is added;
- The mileage covered (business and private) has no effect on the car BIK;

- The Fuel BIK is arrived at by taking the same percentage arrived at above and applying it, for 2003/04 to a standard figure of £14,400;
- The employer can claim **full** capital allowances on cars provided;
- The company must pay class 1A NIC at 12·8% on all above BIK;

Where employees provide their own car (regardless of size) for Business use

- In this case, the employee can be paid by the employer, tax free, 40p per mile for each of the first 10,000 **business miles** covered by them and, also tax free, 25p per mile for each business mile above 10,000 in any tax year (known as the AMAP rates);
- The employee will generally pay for all petrol;
- Where the employer does **not** pay these rates, then the employee may make a claim for a deduction from his taxable income equivalent to the amount which **could** have been paid. Where the employer pays **less** than the above rates, the employee can make a claim for the difference;
- If employees are paid **more** than these rates the excess is taxable and liable to class 1 NIC;
- The employer can claim a Schedule DI deduction for such amounts and is not required to pay class 1A NIC on them.

Approach to be adopted

- Employees covering 20,000 business miles will almost certainly be better off providing their own car and claiming the above AMAP rates;
- With only small amounts of private mileage the employee would be also better off under AMAP arrangements since he would not have a charge of £14,400 x say 25% = £3,600;
- The employer would not have the cost of buying and servicing the car and would not have class 1A NIC;
- Employees with only 4,000 business miles are probably better off getting a car provided by the employer as he can have unlimited private mileage. The amount he could claim under the AMAP scheme would be very low.

Conclusion

Allowing the manager to purchase his own car will leave the company slightly better off – certainly no worse off, and the company will save in terms of cash flow and administration reductions (no P11D entries and calculations.)

Answer to Question Five

Industrial Building Computation Year ended 31 March 2004	*IBA*
Building A This building is 25 years old at 31 March 2003 and therefore no IBAs for year ended 31 March 2004	£nil
Building B The cost of land must be excluded and, since the cost of the Administration buildings exceeded 25% of qualifying cost*, this does not qualify for IBA. This leaves IBA on £71,000 @ 4% * £36,000/£107,000	£2,840
Building C TG Ltd is entitled to allowances each year equal to **lower** of original cost or price paid = £115,000, spread over remaining 17 years of buildings 25 year life = £115,000/17 =	6,765
Building D An Initial Allowance of 55% (£77,000) was claimed in the year ended 31 March 2002 and the maximum – 25% of £140,000 = £35,000 was claimed in the year ended 31 March 2003. This leaves a balance of £28,000 to be claimed for 31 March 2004	28,000

Additional Second Hand Building

The IBA 31/3/2004 for each of the proposed buildings is:

		IBA
(i)	Over 25 years old	£nil
(ii)	There is only **one year** of life left	140,000
(iii)	23 years remain IBA = £160,000/23 =	6,957
Total IBA for year ended 31 March 2004 =		£177,605

Answer to Question Six

Requirement (a)

Adjustment of X Ltd's profit:	£
Per accounts	60,000
Non-trade loan written off	70,000
Costs of loan written off	6,000
Non trade loan interest received	(5,000)
Adjusted Schedule DI	131,000

Non-trading deficit:	
Non-trading expenses loan + costs	(£76,000)
Non-trading income from loan	5,000
Non-trading deficit	(£71,000)

Set off:	*X Ltd*	*Y Ltd*
Profits	£131,000	£280,000

Thresholds – 2 associated companies
£300,000/2 = £150,000

X Ltd is paying CT at 19%		
Y Ltd is paying £130,000 @ 32·75%		
Surrender deficit to Y Ltd		(71,000)

CT saved by this approach – £71,000 @ (32·75% - 19%) = £9,762·50

Requirement (b)

The Report, addressed to the chairman, should make the following points:

- Assuming the American parent company "controls" all of the companies, there will now be 37 associated companies and the CT threshold will become:
  Large company £1·5m/37 = £40,540 and Small Company £300,000/37 = £8,108.
- Assuming D Ltd's profits are greater than this it will now pay CT at 30% instead of 19%.
- If D Ltd's profits consistently (for two successive years) exceed £40,540, then the company will be required to pay its CT on a quarterly basis.
- If any of the other UK companies are 75% subsidiaries of the American parent, then D Ltd could claim group relief or, if it makes a trading loss, it could surrender it to another UK 75% subsidiary for common accounting periods.
- In addition, assets could be transferred from one 75% UK subsidiary to another on a no gain/no loss basis. This could allow capital gains to be taxed at the lower rate or for losses to be set against gains. UK group companies can elect to deem that assets were transferred between group companies **before** being sold to third parties.
- Capital Losses brought forward **at the date of acquisition** may not be used to shelter gains in other group companies arising **after the date of acquisition**.
- The fellow UK subsidiaries could elect for a group VAT registration if this could result in savings in administration costs and/or improvements in cash flow.

CIMA

November 2004 Examinations

Intermediate Level

Financial Accounting – UK Standards

(IFNA – Paper 6a)

Question Paper	1
Examiner's Brief Guide to the Paper	17
Examiner's Answers	18

The answers published here have been written by the Examiner and should provide a helpful guide for both lecturers and students.

Published separately on the CIMA website (www.cimaglobal.com/students) from the end of March 2005 is a Post Examination Guide for this paper, which provides much valuable and complementary material including indicative mark information.

UK STANDARDS UK STANDARDS UK STANDARDS UK STANDARDS UK STANDARDS UK STANDARDS

CIMA

Intermediate Level

Financial Accounting – UK Accounting Standards

6a

IFNA

24 November 2004

Wednesday morning

INSTRUCTIONS TO CANDIDATES

Read this page before you look at the questions

You are allowed three hours to answer this question paper.
This question paper is based on UK ACCOUNTING STANDARDS. **If you require the paper based on International Accounting Standards, please speak immediately to the invigilator.**
Answer the ONE question in Section A (this has 10 sub-questions). Answer the ONE question in Section B. Answer TWO questions ONLY from Section C.

SECTION A – 20 MARKS

ANSWER *ALL* TEN SUB-QUESTIONS – 2 MARKS EACH

Question One

1.1 When an external auditor is unable to agree the accounting treatment of a material item with the directors of a company, but the financial statements are not seriously misleading, he will issue

A an unqualified audit report.

B an adverse opinion.

C a qualified audit report using "except for".

D an unqualified audit report using "except for".

1.2 According to SSAP 19 – *Accounting for investment properties*, an investment property has to meet some of the following criteria:

(i) Completely let to a third party
(ii) Completely let to a subsidiary
(iii) Partly occupied by the company and partly let to a third party
(iv) Let at a commercial rent
(v) Let at a discounted rent
(vi) Held for investment
(vii) Held for use in the business

An investment property is a property owned by the company that meets the following SSAP 19 criteria:

A (i), (v) and (vi)

B (ii), (v) and (vii)

C (iii), (iv) and (vi)

D (i), (iv) and (vi)

1.3 X plc, a quoted company, had the following results for the year ended 30 September 2004:

	£m
Profit before tax	2,400
Tax	700
Profit after tax	1,700

X plc also had the following balances at 30 September 2004:

Share capital of 680 million shares at a nominal value of £0·50 each

Closing stock market price per share at 30 September 2004 was £10

X plc's P/E ratio is:

A 0·25

B 2·0

C 2·9

D 4·0

1.4 In some circumstances, company directors set aside the detailed provisions contained in the Companies Act 1985 and Accounting Standards and use their own accounting methods.

This setting aside of detailed regulations could be:

(i) Creative accounting
(ii) Applying the "true and fair view override"
(iii) Illegal manipulation of accounting data

A (i) only

B (ii) only

C (iii) only

D (i) or (iii)

1.5 Z Ltd entered into a finance lease agreement on 1 November 2002. The lease was for five years, the fair value of the asset acquired was £45,000 and the interest rate implicit in the lease was 7%. The annual payment was £10,975 in arrears.

The total amount due to creditors (less than one year plus more than one year) under the lease at 31 October 2004 was

A £27,212.

B £28,802.

C £29,350.

D £40,108.

1.6 W Ltd owns two properties, property 1 and property 2. As economic circumstances have worsened recently, W Ltd has carried out an impairment review of its properties. The values calculated during the review are as follows:

All values are at 31 October 2004:

	Book value	*Net realisable value*	*Value in use*
	£000	*£000*	*£000*
Property 1	1,650	1,500	1,400
Property 2	2,500	2,300	2,600

According to FRS 11 – *Impairment of fixed assets and goodwill*, the values that W Ltd should use in its balance sheet at 31 October 2004 are

	Property 1	*Property 2*
	£000	*£000*
A	1,400	2,300
B	1,400	2,600
C	1,500	2,300
D	1,500	2,500

1.7 Using the requirements set out in SSAP 17 – *Accounting for Post Balance Sheet Events*, which of the following would be classified as an adjusting post balance sheet event in financial statements ended 31 March 2004 that were approved by the directors on 31 August 2004?

A A reorganisation of the company, proposed by a director on 31 January 2004 and agreed by the Board on 10 July 2004.

B A strike by the workforce which started on 1 May 2004 and stopped all production for 10 weeks before being settled.

C A claim on an insurance policy for damage caused by a fire in a warehouse on 1 January 2004. No provision had been made for the receipt of insurance money at 31 March 2004 as it was uncertain that any money would be paid. The insurance company settled with a payment of £1·5 million on 1 June 2004.

D The company had made large export sales to the USA during the year. The year end debtors included £2 million for amounts outstanding that were due to be paid in US dollars between 1 April 2004 and 1 July 2004. By the time these amounts were received, the exchange rate had moved in favour of the company and the equivalent of £2·5 million was actually received.

1.8 N Ltd started business on 1 September 2003. The following balances were extracted from the books of N Ltd on 31 August 2004:

	£000	*£000*
Sales		161
Cost of sales:		
Purchases	151	
Closing stock	26	
		125
Gross profit		36
Trade debtors		25
Trade creditors		16

Assume a 365 day trading year.

Using the information above, N Ltd's average working capital cycle for the year ended 31 August 2004 (to the nearest day) was

A 81 days.

B 94 days.

C 113 days.

D 171 days.

1.9 R plc redeemed its redeemable preference shares with a cash payment, paying a premium of 25%. The shares redeemed were as follows:

	£
Nominal value of preference shares redeemed	95,000
Cash paid on redemption	118,750

How much should be debited to distributable profits and how much should be credited to the capital redemption reserve?

	Distributable profits	*Capital redemption reserve*
	£	£
A	23,750	95,000
B	95,000	118,750
C	118,750	118,750
D	118,750	95,000

1.10 S Ltd revalues its properties to current value each year. One of S Ltd's warehouses, in its balance sheet at its September 2003 current value of £1,200,000, was sold on 29 September 2004 for £900,000 with an option to repurchase after four years at £1,093,956 (£900,000 plus compound interest for four years at 5% per annum).

The warehouse's current value at 29 September 2004 was £1,380,000.

How should S Ltd treat this transaction in its financial statements for the year ended 30 September 2004?

A As a sale of the warehouse recording a loss on disposal of £300,000.

B Revalue the warehouse to £1,380,000 and record £900,000 as a loan received.

C Revalue the warehouse to £1,380,000 and record a loss on disposal of £480,000.

D Leave the warehouse in its balance sheet at £1,200,000 and record £900,000 as a loan received.

(Total = 20 marks)

End of Section A

SECTION B – 30 MARKS

ANSWER THIS QUESTION

Question Two

ZZ Ltd produces two different ranges of products, range A and range B. The range A brand was developed in-house, but the range B brand name was purchased seven years ago.

The B product range has been losing popularity and sales have been in sharp decline for the last two years. By the end of the third quarter of 2002, the level of sales had declined to a point where the directors decided it was no longer viable to produce the B product range. A provision of £100,000 for closure costs was set up in the accounts for the year ended 30 September 2003. The closure was delayed until 1 January 2004 when the production lines ceased production and all the assets relating to the B product range were put up for sale.

ZZ Ltd's trial balance at 30 September 2004 is shown below:

	£000	*£000*
10% Debentures 2010		2,600
Administration expenses – A product range	96	
Administration expenses – B product range	34	
Bank & Cash	3,192	
Brand name – B product range	197	
Buildings at cost	2,500	
Cash received on disposal of factory		2,000
Cash received on disposal of machinery		50
Closure costs	125	
Corporation tax	20	
Cost of goods sold – A product range	513	
Cost of goods sold – B product range	127	
Creditors		90
Debenture interest paid – half year	130	
Debtors	140	
Distribution costs – A product range	92	
Distribution costs – B product range	12	
Land at valuation at 30 September 2003	1,500	
Machinery and equipment at cost	1,706	
Ordinary shares £1 each, fully paid		1,500
Profit & loss account at 30 September 2003		436
Provision for amortisation of brand name – B product range at 30 September 2003		138
Provision for closure costs at 30 September 2003		100
Provision for deferred tax at 30 September 2003		203
Provision for depreciation at 30 September 2003:		
Buildings		860
Machinery and equipment		415
Revaluation reserve		900
Sales – A product range		1,260
Sales – B product range		42
Stock at 30 September 2004 – A product range	210	
	10,594	10,594

Further information:

(i) The assets relating to the B product range were disposed of as follows:

- The land and the factory buildings were sold on 1 March 2004 for £2,000,000.
- The machinery was sold for £50,000 on the same date.
- All the cash received is included in the trial balance.
- The purchased brand name was deemed to have no value and should be written off. The book values of the assets sold were:

Asset type	*Cost*	*Valuation*	*Accumulated depreciation*
	£000	*£000*	*£000*
Land	300	750	0
Buildings	400		220
Machinery and equipment	462		195

(ii) Buildings are depreciated at 5% per annum on the straight-line basis. Machinery is depreciated at 25% per annum using the reducing balance method. Depreciation is treated as a cost of sales.

(iii) There were no purchases of tangible fixed assets during the year.

(iv) ZZ Ltd's accounting policy for amortisation and depreciation is to charge a full year in the year of acquisition and make no charge in the year of disposal.

(v) The directors decided to downsize the company and used the cash received to repay loans rather than invest in new production facilities. The debentures were redeemed on 30 September 2004. A payment equal to the nominal value outstanding, plus accrued interest to date, was made from the bank account on 30 September 2004. This transaction has not been recorded in the trial balance.

(vi) The directors estimate the corporation tax charge on the year's profits at £113,000. The balance on the corporation tax account is the amount remaining after settling the amount due for the year ended 30 September 2003.

(vii) The deferred tax provision needs to be reduced to £170,000.

(viii) The directors have proposed a final dividend of £200,000, no interim dividend was paid during the year.

Required:

(a) Prepare the tangible fixed assets note to the accounts for the year ended 30 September 2004.

(6 marks)

(b) Prepare the profit and loss account for ZZ Ltd for the year ended 30 September 2004 and its balance sheet at that date. These should be in a form suitable for publication and in accordance with all current regulations.

(24 marks)

> Notes to the financial statements are not required (except as specified in requirement (a)) but all workings must be clearly shown. DO NOT prepare a statement of accounting policies, a statement of total recognised gains and losses or a reconciliation of movements in shareholders funds.

(Total for Question Two = 30 marks)

End of Section B

SECTION C – 50 MARKS

ANSWER TWO QUESTIONS ONLY

Question Three

Requirement (a)

FRS 18 – *Accounting policies*, distinguishes between accounting policies and estimation techniques.

Required:

Explain the difference between accounting policies and estimation techniques; give an example of each.

(4 marks)

Requirement (b)

The directors of U plc have recently made four changes to their accounting treatment of certain items for the year ended 30 September 2004:

Change 1

U plc has been depreciating its factory machines on the straight-line basis over six years, assuming no residual value. U plc replaced all of its machines at the same time on 1 October 2000 at a cost of £1,300,000.

The directors of U plc have decided to change the method of machinery depreciation to the reducing balance method, as they think that it will more accurately reflect usage of the machines and will give a true and fair view. Effective from 1 October 2003, all machinery will be depreciated at 25% per annum using the reducing balance method.

(5 marks)

Change 2

U plc manufactures refrigerators and freezers and sells them with a one-year warranty. It applies the requirements of FRS 12 – *Provisions, contingent liabilities and contingent assets* to its financial accounts. U plc has made a provision for future warranty claims each year.

U plc did not keep accurate records of previous warranty claims, so when FRS 12 became effective, it estimated future warranty claims based on an estimated 10% of sales turnover. It also started keeping accurate records of warranty claims.

U plc has decided to change its method of calculating the provision for warranty claims to the weighted average of the last three years' actual claims paid.

A warranty claim provision of £900,000, calculated on the old basis, has already been entered in the accounts for the year ended 30 September 2004.

Year to 30 September	*2002*	*2003*	*2004*
	£000	*£000*	*£000*
Sales	7,500	8,000	9,000
Actual warranty claims paid	375	400	325

(6 marks)

Change 3
U plc did not previously capitalise interest incurred in connection with the construction of tangible fixed assets. All interest was charged to the profit and loss account each year. The directors have now decided that, in future, interest incurred on construction contracts will be added to the cost of construction. U plc's trial balance shows that construction costs of tangible fixed assets completed in the year ended 30 September 2004 were £1,400,000. Interest directly attributable to the construction was £56,000 during the year; this has been included in the trial balance under interest paid.

(5 marks)

Change 4
U plc owns an office building, which it purchased for £250,000 ten years ago (1 October 1993) for use by its employees. U plc has charged depreciation on the office building at 2% per annum on the straight line basis.

All of U plc's employees have now moved to other premises and U plc has let the office building to a third party on an operating lease. Effective from 1 October 2003, the directors have decided to reclassify the office building as an investment property and to carry it in its balance sheet at valuation without any depreciation, as required by SSAP 19 – *Accounting for investment properties*. The office building was valued at £450,000 on 1 October 2003.

(5 marks)

Required:

For each of the four changes above:

(i) Identify the accounting policy and estimation technique involved and explain whether U plc is making a change in accounting policy or a change in estimation technique or neither.

(ii) Prepare the accounting entries required in U plc's profit and loss account and balance sheet to implement changes 1 to 4 above for the year ended 30 September 2004 and explain the need for such entries.

(The breakdown of marks is shown against each change detailed above)

(Total for Requirement (b) = 21 marks)

(Total for Question Three = 25 marks)

Question Four

JK plc is considering entering a long-term business arrangement with another organisation to provide a full range of contract services for the construction industry.

The selected organisation must be in a strong financial position and be able to survive and prosper in both the immediate future and the medium term.

JK plc has two possible candidates for the business arrangement, CDE Ltd and VWX Ltd. Both candidates have a high reputation for the provision of their services. Neither company carries any significant stocks.

Summarised profit and loss account for the year ended 31 October 2004

	CDE Ltd	*VWX Ltd*
	£000	*£000*
Turnover	11,200	9,800
Operating profit	990	966
Interest payable	(202)	(70)
Profit before tax	788	896
Tax	(190)	(240)
Profit after tax	598	656
Dividends	(320)	(400)
Retained profit for the year	278	256
Retained profit b/fwd	22	739
Retained profit c/fwd	300	995

Balance sheets at 31 October 2004

	CDE Ltd		*VWX Ltd*	
	£000	*£000*	*£000*	*£000*
Tangible fixed assets		2,000		2,500
Current assets	1,950		1,995	
Creditors: amounts falling due within one year				
Bank loan 2005	(1,110)		0	
Creditors	(630)		(990)	
	(1,740)		(990)	
		210		1,005
		2,210		3,505
Creditors: amounts falling due after more than one year				
Loans 2010-2015		(1,410)		(1,010)
		800		2,495
Capital and reserves:				
Ordinary share capital		400		1,000
Share premium		100		500
Retained profits		300		995
		800		2,495

Requirement (a)

As the trainee management accountant you have been asked to prepare a draft report to the Finance Director, based on the information given above, analysing the financial strengths and weaknesses of each of the candidate organisations and their suitability for a long-term business arrangement with JK plc.

(*Note:* You should ignore the further information given in requirement (b) for this draft report.)

(19 marks)

Requirement (b)

VWX Ltd regularly revalues all its tangible fixed assets which are carried in its balance sheet at current value. CDE Ltd has not revalued any assets and carries all its assets at depreciated historical cost. If CDE Ltd were to revalue its assets at 31 October 2004, its tangible fixed assets would increase by £2,750,000.

All other accounting policies of the two organisations are substantially the same.

Required:

Explain, with supporting calculations, how the revaluation of CDE Ltd's fixed assets will affect its financial ratios and whether this would have any effect on your conclusions regarding CDE Ltd's suitability for a long-term business arrangement with JK plc.

(6 marks)

(Total for Question Four = 25 marks)

Question Five

Requirement (a)

A general manager in your organisation has recently enrolled on a management course at the local college. She is studying a module on finance and accounting and is having some difficulty understanding the theory. She has asked you, the trainee management accountant, if you could explain the consultative process used to produce a new Financial Reporting Standard (FRS).

(5 marks)

Requirement (b)

E Ltd, a food retailer, decided to start a home delivery service from 1 November 2002. As E Ltd had no vehicles suitable for use by the new service, it purchased three small delivery vehicles to enable them to provide the service.

The invoice for the vehicles included the following details:

	£
Cost price - per vehicle	12,000
Less: Trade discount	(2,400)
	9,600
Delivery charge	250
One vehicle	9,850
Three vehicles	29,550
1 year's insurance for the three vehicles	2,100
Total cost of three vehicles	31,650

By 31 October 2003, there had been a general price increase in all new delivery vehicles of 25%. The directors of E Ltd decided to revalue all three of their delivery vehicles to 125% of their net book value at 31 October 2003.

During the next year, it became apparent that the delivery service was so successful that the delivery vehicles were now too small. On 1 April 2004, E Ltd traded in the three delivery vehicles for three new larger vehicles. The new larger delivery vehicles cost £18,000 each and the vendor allowed a trade-in value of £9,000 for each of the old vehicles. E Ltd paid the balance of £9,000 per vehicle on 1 May 2004.

All vehicles are depreciated using the reducing balance method at 25% per annum, charged on a time basis.

E Ltd purchased new computer equipment, costing £5,000, to assist in running the delivery service. The software required to provide the service was also purchased at the same time. The initial cost of the delivery scheduling software was £950 plus the cost of adapting the software to E Ltd's detailed specifications £2,600. The computer equipment and the adapted software were delivered on 1 November 2002, and brought into use at once. During December 2002, the software developed reliability problems, often crashing for no apparent reason. E Ltd's in-house programmer spent time resolving these problems at an estimated cost of £2,000 in December 2002 and £1,000 in January 2003. E Ltd depreciates all computer equipment and software on a straight line basis over four years, assuming no residual value.

The Accounting Standards Board's (ASB) *Statement of Principles for Financial Reporting* (SoP) describes the asset recognition process as:

- Initial recognition
- Subsequent remeasurement
- Derecognition

Required:

(i) Apply the ASB's SoP asset recognition process to the above situations and explain the relevance of each stage of the process to each of the situations.

(6 marks)

(ii) Prepare profit and loss account and balance sheet extracts for the years ended 31 October 2003 and 31 October 2004 to show how the above transactions would be recorded. Explain your treatment with reference to appropriate Accounting Standards.

(14 marks)

(Total for Requirement (b) = 20 marks)

(Total for Question Five = 25 marks)

Question Six

Requirement (a)

M plc operates a copper mine in a remote part of a country which is designated a national park. To obtain the licence to operate the mine, M plc had to agree to a number of conditions. One condition is that at the end of the useful economic life of the mine, M plc will remove all above ground buildings and equipment and will reinstate the land on which they were situated. They also agreed to landscape all the waste tips and to plant them with trees normally found in the area. The estimated cost of all of this work is £3 million.

The initial costs of building the required premises, preparing the mine for operation and other set-up costs were £5 million and have been charged to tangible fixed assets – assets under construction.

M plc paid the government £10 million for a licence to operate the mine for 25 years. This has been debited to tangible fixed assets. The mine commenced operations on 1 October 2003.

Required:

Calculate the value of the amounts that M plc should show in its profit and loss account for the year ended 30 September 2004 and its balance sheet at that date. Justify your treatment of each item by reference to appropriate Accounting Standards.

(9 marks)

Requirement (b)

N plc manufactures a range of electrical products for home and portable personal entertainment. Demand for products can fall drastically at very short notice, often due to a product having been superseded by a new product.

At 30 September 2004, N plc's stock balance included the following:

	Total cost	*Total normal sales value*
	£000	*£000*
20,000 personal cassette tape players	18	27
5,000 basic CD players	45	90
Damaged DVD players	10	20

At 30 September 2004, the 20,000 personal cassette tape players had been in stock an average of 18 months. These cassette tape players are no longer manufactured. During November 2004, N plc found a buyer for its whole stock of cassette tape players; the total agreed price was £10,000.

The market for the basic CD players has contracted as higher specification models and DVD players have entered the market. N plc's sales director estimates that the basic CD players will only sell for £10 each.

A quantity of DVD players were found to be damaged and were unable to be sold in their current condition. The DVD players had a zero scrap value. These units could be repaired at a total cost of £5,000; they could then be sold for a total of £12,000.

Required:

Advise N plc how it should treat the above stock items in its profit and loss account for the year ended 30 September 2004 and how it should value the stock in its balance sheet at that date. Your answer should refer to appropriate Accounting Standards.

(7 marks)

Requirement (c)

D Ltd purchased all its tangible fixed assets new three years ago on 1 October 2001. The tangible fixed assets cost £720,000 and all qualified for capital allowances at 25% per annum on the reducing balance method. D Ltd's depreciation policy is to depreciate tangible fixed assets at 20% per annum using the straight-line method and assuming no residual value. D Ltd pays corporation tax at 30%.

Required:

(i) Calculate D Ltd's deferred tax balance at the end of each of the years ended 30 September 2002, 2003 and 2004.

(5 marks)

(ii) Using the Accounting Standards Board's (ASB) *Statement of Principles for Financial Reporting* (SoP) definitions of assets and liabilities, justify the deferred tax balances at 30 September 2002, 2003 and 2004.

(4 marks)

(Total for requirement (c) = 9 marks)

(Total for Question Six = 25 marks)

End of paper

The Examiner for IFNA offers to future candidates and to lecturers using this booklet for study purposes, the following background and guidance on the questions included in this examination paper.

Section A — compulsory

Question One consists of 10 objective test sub-questions, designed to cover a variety of syllabus topics not covered elsewhere in the paper and addressing a selection of learning outcomes in all sections of the syllabus.

Section B — compulsory

Section B is a single question for 30 marks. **Question Two** requires a specific note to the accounts, which is consistent with the information I presented at the last Lecturers' Conference. As previously stated, I intend using this compulsory question as a final account preparation question in each exam. I said at the Lecturers' Conference that this question will not always be a P&L account and balance sheet and could include any published final accounts statement.

The last exam in May 2004 had a cash flow statement, so this one is back to a profit and loss account and balance sheet. The question includes a range of the usual adjustments and a substantial element on closure of a segment and disposal of the assets concerned. FRS 3 formats for discontinued activities must be used.

Section C – two questions from four

Question Three is on FRS 18 and accounting policies. The accounting policy and estimation technique must be identified for a range of situations. Accounting entries then have to be prepared to record the changes.

Question Four part (a) requires the analysis of two companies to be considered for a long-term business arrangement venture. A range of accounting ratios need to be calculated and analysed. Part (b) requires candidates to consider the fact that the company accounts may not be comparable and need to be adjusted.

Question Five part (a) asks candidates to advise a manager of the consultative process of producing a new Financial Reporting Standard. Part (b) requires the application of the ASB's SoP to two situations and their impact on the profit and loss account and balance sheet to be identified.

Question Six part (a) requires Accounting Standards to be applied to the creation of an asset with future reinstatement costs. Part (b) requires three different stock items to be considered. Each situation needs to be explained and justified with reference to Accounting Standards.

CIMA

The Examiner's Answers for Financial Accounting - UK Accounting Standards

SECTION A

Answers to Question One

1.1	A	B	(C)	D
1.2	A	B	C	(D)
1.3	A	B	C	(D)
1.4	A	(B)	C	D
1.5	A	(B)	C	D
1.6	A	B	C	(D)
1.7	A	B	(C)	D
1.8	A	(B)	C	D
1.9	A	B	C	(D)
1.10	A	(B)	C	D

Explanations follow for answers to multiple choice questions involving calculations

1.3 EPS 1,700/680 = 2·5
P/E 10/2·5 = 4

Therefore the answer is D

1.5

Balance	*Interest at 7%*	*Instalment*	*Balance*
£	£	£	£
45,000	3,150	10,975	37,175
37,175	2,602	10,975	28,802

Therefore the answer is B

1.6 The greater of value in use or net realisable value is used if they are both below book value.

Property 1 net realisable value, £1,500,000 will be used as it is below book value.

Property 2 book value will remain unchanged as it is below value in use.

Therefore the answer is D

1.8 Stock average days 26/125 x 365 = 75·9
Debtors average days 25/161 x 365 = 56·7
Creditors average days 16/151 x 365 = 38·7
Average working capital cycle is 75·9 + 56·7 - 38·7 = 93·9

Therefore the answer is B

Answer to Question Two

Requirement (a)

Note – Tangible fixed assets

	Land	*Buildings*	*Machinery & equipment*	*Total*
	£000	*£000*	*£000*	*£000*
Cost/valuation				
Cost/valuation balance brought forward	1,500	2,500	1,706	5,706
Disposals	(750)	(400)	(462)	1,612
Cost/valuation balance carried forward	750	2,100	1,244	4,094
Accumulated depreciation				
Balance brought forward		860	415	1,275
Disposals		(220)	(195)	(415)
Charge for the year		105*	256*	361
Balance carried forward		745	476	1,221
Net book value at 30 September 2004	750	1,355	768	2,873
Net book value at 30 September 2003	1,500	1,640	1,291	4,431

* Depreciation charge for the year:
Buildings: 2,100 x 5% = 105
Machinery & equipment: 1,244 - (415 - 195) = 1,024 x 25% = 256

Requirement (b)

ZZ Ltd – Profit and loss account for the year ended 30 September 2004

	£000 *Continuing operations*	£000 *Discontinued operations*	£000 *Total*
Turnover	1,260	42	1,302
Cost of sales (W1)	(874)	(127)	(1,001)
Gross profit	386	(85)	301
Distribution costs	(92)	(12)	(104)
Administrative expenses	(96)	(34)	(130)
Operating profit	198	(131)	67
Exceptional items:			
Gain on sale of fixed assets (W2)		794	794
Closure costs		125	125
Less: Provision brought forward		(100)	(100)
Profit on ordinary activities	198	638	836
Interest payable (W3)			(260)
Profit on ordinary activities before taxation			576
Taxation (W5)			(100)
Profit on ordinary activities after taxation			476
Dividends			(200)
Retained profit for the year			276

ZZ Ltd – Balance Sheet at 30 September 2004

	£000	£000 Net Book Value	£000
Tangible Fixed Assets			
Land		750	
Buildings		1,355	
Machinery & equipment		768	
			2,873
Current Assets			
Stock	210		
Debtors	140		
Cash at bank & in hand (W7)	462		
		812	
Creditors amounts falling due within one year			
Trade creditors	(90)		
Corporation tax	(113)		
Proposed dividends	(200)	(403)	
			409
Total assets less current liabilities			3,282
Provisions for Liabilities and Charges			
Deferred tax			(170)
			3,112
Capital and Reserves			
Ordinary share capital			1,500
Revaluation reserve			450
Profit and loss account (W8)			1,162
			3,112

Workings

(W1) – Cost of sales – A product range	£000	£000
Trial balance	513	
Depreciation	361 (from part (a))	
	874	

(W2) – Disposal of fixed assets		
Brand name	197	
Less: Amortised	(138)	59
Revalued land		750
Buildings	400	
Less: Depreciation	(220)	180
Equipment	462	
Less: Depreciation	(195)	267
Carrying value of assets		1,256
Less: Proceeds		2,050
Gain on disposal		794

(W3) – Interest payable

Interest charge for year:

Trial balance	130
Accrued	130
	260

(W4) – Debenture redemption

Trial balance	2,600
Accrued interest – half year	130
Cash	2,730

(W5) – Taxation

Accrued for year	113
Last year's balance	20
Reduced deferred tax provision	(33)
Tax charge for the year	100

(W6) – Deferred tax

Balance b/fwd	203
Balance c/fwd	170
Reduction	33

(W7) – Bank

Trial balance	3,192
Redemption of debentures	2,730
Balance	462

(W8) – Retained profits

Balance b/fwd	436
Revaluation reserve – realised on disposal	450
Profit for the year	276
	1,162

(W9) – Revaluation reserve

Balance per trial balance	900
Less: Realised on disposal	450
	450

SECTION C

Answer to Question Three

Requirement (a)

An accounting policy defines the process by which events are reflected in the financial statements. For example, the accounting policy for a particular type of expenditure will determine whether an asset or an expense should be recognised in the financial statements.

Estimation techniques put the measurement aspects of accounting policies into practice. For example the different methods of depreciation are estimation techniques used to apply the accounting policy of depreciating tangible fixed assets. It is possible to change the estimation technique without changing the accounting policy. For example changing from reducing balance depreciation to straight line depreciation is a change in estimation technique which will cause a change in the amount of depreciation charged, but the accounting policy of depreciating all tangible fixed assets will remain unchanged. When a change occurs it is important to distinguish between a change in accounting policy and a change in estimation technique as they are treated differently.

Requirement (b)

Change 1

(i) Accounting policy is to depreciate factory machines over their useful economic life. Estimation technique is the method of calculating depreciation. This is a change in estimation technique as U plc is changing its method of calculating depreciation.

(ii) FRS 15 requires the remaining book value to be depreciated over the remaining useful economic life of the assets using the new method of depreciation. A change of estimation technique cannot be treated as a prior year adjustment. Purchased October 2000 the balance at 1 October 2003 is after three years' depreciation, with a useful economic life of six years this means 50% of the cost has been depreciated.

	£000
Cost	1,300
Depreciation to date	650
Net book value 1 October 2003	650
Depreciation for year to 30 September 2004	163
Net book value 30 September 2004	487
Debit Profit and loss account – depreciation	163
Credit Provision for depreciation	163

Change 2

(i) Accounting policy is to make provision for future warranty claims. Estimation technique is the method of estimating the provision. This is a change in estimation technique as U plc is changing its method of calculating the provision.

(ii) The directors want a more scientific approach to calculating the provision, which is to be based on the last three years' actual claims. This will avoid any wide fluctuations caused by one year being abnormally high. A weighted average is calculated and applied to the year's sales.

Year ended 30 September	*2002*	*2003*	*2004*	*Total*
	£000	*£000*	*£000*	*£000*
Sales value	7,500	8,000	9,000	24,500
Warranty claims	375	400	325	1,100

Average warranty claim = 1,100/24,500 x 100 = 4·5%

Provision for warranty claims should be £9,000,000 x 4·5% = £404,082 = £404,000.

The new policy results in a reduction of £496,000 in the provision from £900,000 to £404,000.

	£000
Debit Provision for warranty claims	496
Credit Profit and loss – warranty claims	496

Change 3

(i) Accounting policy now is to capitalise interest directly attributable to the construction of tangible fixed assets into the cost of the asset constructed.

Estimation technique is the method used to identify and calculate the interest that is directly attributable.

This is a change in accounting policy. The original policy was not to include interest; the new policy is to include interest.

(ii) The interest charge should be moved from interest paid in the year to the cost of tangible fixed assets under construction. The total cost will then be transferred to tangible fixed assets.

	£000	*£000*
Debit Assets under construction	56	
Credit Interest paid		56
Debit Tangible fixed assets – cost	1,456	
Credit Assets under construction		1,456

Change 4

(i) U plc has two accounting policies, the treatment of office buildings and the treatment of investment properties. U plc has not changed its accounting policies as buildings and investment properties are still treated in the same way in its accounts.

Estimation technique is the method used to calculate the amount of depreciation of buildings or the basis of valuation of the investment property. There is no change in accounting policy and no change in estimation technique.

The property has been reclassified from tangible fixed assets to investment properties and the accounting policy and estimation technique for investment properties has been applied instead of the fixed asset policy.

(ii) Original cost £250,000 less 10 years' depreciation at 2%, £50,000 leaves £200,000 book value. The buildings cost and depreciation needs to be removed and the revalued property debited to investment properties with a transfer to revaluation reserve of £250,000.

	£000	*£000*
Debit Investment properties	450	
Credit Office buildings at cost		250
Debit Office buildings – accumulated depreciation	50	
Credit Revaluation reserve		250

Answer to Question Four

Report

To: Finance Director

From: Trainee management accountant

Re: Review of candidate organisations for possible business arrangement

Introduction

Two organisations, CDE Ltd and VWX Ltd, are under consideration for a possible long-term business arrangement with JK plc.

I have reviewed the financial statements for both organisations for the year ended 31 October 2004 and have calculated a number of financial ratios for each organisation, see appendix.

Analysis

The review of the financial statements and the calculated ratios reveal the following:

The stated criteria are that the chosen organisation must be in a strong financial position and be able to survive and prosper in the immediate future and medium term.

(i) *Financial position*

Short-term financial position is indicated by liquidity and the medium-term financial position by the gearing.

Liquidity

CDE has a less strong position than VWX in terms of liquidity. VWX has a current ratio of 2 : 1 which is a relatively strong position.

CDE has a current ratio of 1·1 : 1, this is much weaker than VWX.

The reason that CDE has a weaker current ratio is that its current liabilities include a bank loan repayable in 2005. This loan will have to be repaid next year and may cause cash flow problems in the short term.

Gearing

VWX has low gearing with debt to total capital of 28·8%, whereas CDE is very highly geared with debt capital to total capital of 63·8%, (excluding the bank loan). If the bank loan is included in debt the figure increases further to 75·9%. CDE is more vulnerable to increases in interest rates and possible downturn in business. This is illustrated by the interest cover. CDE has interest covered 4·9 times, not too low but much lower than VWX which has its interest covered 13·8 times.

(ii) *Profitability*

To survive and prosper in the medium term all companies must make profits. CDE's high gearing seems to enable it to generate much higher levels of return on its total capital employed than VWX, (44·8% against 27·6%). This large difference is not because of a higher operating profit level in CDE, which is marginally lower at 8·8% than that of VWX at 9·9%. The difference is because of CDE's much higher asset turnover, 5·1 instead of VWX's 2·8. The more intensive use of assets could be caused by CDE having very old assets which are almost fully depreciated or VWX having a number of obsolete assets that are not used, but are still in the balance sheet.

Conclusion
As the stated criteria are that the chosen organisation must be in a strong financial position and be able to survive and prosper in the immediate future and medium term we must give more weighting to liquidity and gearing and less weighting to profitability.

CDE seems to have a much higher return on capital employed, but appears to be under-capitalised. CDE's gearing is very high and needs to be reduced in the medium term. If CDE had a lower gearing it may be the preferred option. There is also concern that CDE may not have sufficient capital to be able to properly fund its element of a business arrangement. CDE appear to be a higher risk and are not therefore recommended as a partner.

VWX is in a strong financial position with a good current ratio and a reasonable level of debt. Although its profitability is lower than CDE, it is profitable and pays reasonable dividends to its shareholders. CDE's profitability will probably increase with the extra turnover resulting from the business arrangement. The advantages of a strong financial position outweigh the lower returns on capital employed as we are looking for a solid partner that will still be around in several years' time.

Recommendation
Start negotiations with VWX regarding the possibility of a joint venture.

Appendix	**CDE Ltd**		**VWX Ltd**	
ROCE	990/2210 x 100 =	44·8%	966/3505 x 100 =	27·6%
Operating profit %	990/11200 x 100 =	8·8%	966/9800 x 100 =	9·9%
Asset turnover	11200/2210	5·1 times	9800/3505	2·8 times
Interest cover	990/202	4·9 times	966/70	13·8 times
Current ratio	1950 : 1740 =	1·1 : 1	1995 : 990 =	2·0 : 1
Gearing (excluding bank loan)	1410/2210 =	63·8%	1010/3505	28·8%
Gearing (including bank loan)	(1410 + 1110)/ (2210 + 1110)	75·9%		

Requirement (b)

The revaluation of tangible fixed assets will cause any ratios that include tangible fixed assets to change. An increase in tangible fixed assets will increase total shareholders' funds and will cause total capital to increase.

The following ratios will all reduce as they are all calculated using capital employed or total capital:

- return on capital employed;
- asset turnover;
- gearing.

Short term liquidity will be unaffected.

CDE Ltd	**Original**	**Revalued**	
ROCE	44·7%	990/(2,210 + 2,750) x 100 =	20·0%
Asset turnover	5·1 times	11,200/(2,210 + 2,750) =	2·3 times
Gearing	63·8%	1,410/(2,210 + 2,750) x 100 =	28·4%

The ROCE and asset turnover have both reduced and are now below VWX's ratios. The gearing has dramatically reduced and is now marginally less than VWX's.

These changes mean that CDE's new gearing is effectively the same as VWX. However it is still higher risk as it has more debt and its interest cover is much lower. CDE's ROCE and asset turnover are now less than VWX, so VWX is still the preferred choice.

Answer to Question Five

Requirement (a)

The Accounting Standards Board (ASB) is responsible for devising and issuing Financial Reporting Standards (FRSs). The ASB issues FRSs on its own authority with a majority of two thirds of the Board being required to approve a new standard.

The ASB can issue a discussion document to test opinions on a topic and, after analysing responses to a discussion document, may decide to publish a Financial Reporting Exposure Draft (FRED) for comment. Occasionally, the ASB will just issue a FRED without first publishing a discussion document. After the exposure time has elapsed, the ASB analyses the responses to the FRED and, if there were few adverse comments, they may decide to issue a FRS, usually taking into account responses to the FRED. If a large number of adverse comments have been received, the ASB may issue a revised FRED for further comment.

Requirement (b)

(i) Initial recognition – on purchase the attributable costs will be recognised.

Delivery vehicles recognised at £29,550 (£9,850 x 3).

Computers: the attributable cost is the cost of acquiring and getting the system ready for use or enabling it to become functional. This can include the initial adaptations, but does not include the in-house programmers as the work was done at a later stage and is regarded as an additional cost incurred. For any additional cost to be capitalised, it must enhance or improve the asset beyond its original specification. The in-house programmers were checking and fixing the software to get it up to its original specification, not enhancing beyond the original specification.

Subsequent remeasurement – the vehicles are subsequently remeasured when they are revalued on 31 October 2003. The computer system has no subsequent remeasurement.

Derecognition – the vehicles are derecognised when they are traded in as E Ltd no longer has access to the risks and rewards of ownership. On derecognition, the value received is deducted from their carrying value to calculate the loss on disposal. The computers are still in use and have not been derecognised.

(ii) FRS 15 – *Tangible fixed assets* requires the cost of the tangible fixed assets to be recognised. Cost includes delivery charge and is net of any trade discount. Annual running costs such as insurance are revenue expenditure and are charged to the profit and loss account. FRS 15 allows tangible fixed assets to be revalued; any increase in value is credited to revaluation reserve.

Balance Sheet (extract) at 31 October 2003

	£
Tangible fixed assets	
Delivery vehicles at valuation (W1)	27,703
Computers (W2)	8,550
Provision for depreciation – computers (W2)	2,138
Revaluation reserve (W1)	5,541

Profit and loss account (extract) for the year ended 31 October 2003

	£
Depreciation – delivery vehicles (W1)	7,388
Depreciation – computers (W2)	2,138
Adjusting software	3,000
Insurance – delivery vehicles	2,100

Balance Sheet (extract) at 31 October 2004

	£
Tangible fixed assets	
Delivery vehicles at cost (18,000 x 3)	54,000
Computers	8,550
Provision for depreciation – delivery vehicles (7/12 x 54,000 x 25%)	7,875
Depreciation – computers	2,138
Revaluation reserve	5,541
(As the revaluation is realised on disposal of the vehicles it can be transferred to profit and loss account)	

Profit and loss account (extract) for the year ended 31 October 2004

	£
Depreciation – delivery vehicles	7,875
Gain on disposal of small delivery vehicles	(2,183)
Depreciation – computers	2,138

Workings

	£
(W1)	
Delivery vehicles – cost	29,550
Depreciation for year – 25%	7,388
	22,162
Gain on revaluation	5,541
31 October 2003 Revalue to 125% of balance	27,703
Less: Five months depreciation	2,886
1 April 2004 Trade in (£9,000 x 3)	27,000
Gain on disposal	2,183

(W2)

Computers at cost	£
Hardware	5,000
Software	950
Adaptation	2,600
Total cost	8,550
Depreciation	2,138

Answer to Question Six

Requirement (a)

The cost will include the initial cost, the licence cost and the cost of reinstatement of the land.

	£m
Initial costs	5
Licence fee	10
Provision for reinstatement	3
Total	18
Depreciation each year (18/25)	0·72

FRS 15 requires all costs of getting the asset into a state where it is ready to use to be included in the cost. The licence cost is therefore added to the other preparation costs as it is not possible to operate the mine without a licence.

FRS 12 requires the full cost of reinstatement to be provided for immediately and added to the cost of the asset. A provision can only be set up where the following criteria are met:

- There is a present obligation arising from past events;
- It is probable that a transfer of economic benefit will be required to settle the obligation;
- A reliable estimate can be made;

The reinstatement meets all of these criteria:

- There is a present obligation; once the mine operation starts it will require to be reinstated when it stops. The past event was the granting of the licence and M plc starting to operate the mine;
- The transfer of economic benefit is certain, as it is contractual, the cost must be incurred;
- The question gives the amount, so it is reasonable to assume that the amount can be reliably estimated.

If the provision causes the value of the asset to become more than its recoverable amount, its balance sheet value may need to be reviewed and written down to its recoverable amount. The provision will remain in the balance sheet until such time as the mine is closed and the costs of reinstatement are incurred.

The provision will be spread over the useful economic life of the mine as it will be charged as part of the depreciation charge each year.

Requirement (b)

Personal cassette tape players: cost £18,000; actual selling price £10,000

The actual selling price in November is the net realisable value of the cassette tape players. SSAP 9 requires stock to be carried in the balance sheet at cost or net realisable value, whichever is the lower. N plc became aware of the reduced value when agreeing the price with the buyer in November 2004; the circumstances already existed at the balance sheet date with N plc obtaining the additional information on value after the balance sheet date. This will be treated as a post balance sheet adjusting event under SSAP 17 and the stock adjusted at the balance sheet date. N plc should write its cassette tape players down from original cost of £18,000 to their net realisable value of £10,000. The loss of £8,000 on the write down of the cassette tape players will be charged to profit and loss account.

The basic CD players are estimated to sell at £10 each. The 5,000 in stock would then be sold for £50,000. This figure is below current selling price, but is above the cost price of £45,000. N plc do not need to make any changes to the stock valuation for the basic CD players as cost is below net realisable value.

The faulty DVD players have an original cost of £10,000 and a scrap value of nil. If they are repaired for £5,000 they can be sold for £12,000. The net realisable value if they are repaired is therefore £7,000 (£12,000 - £5,000). N plc should write down the value of the DVD players to £7,000 and write off £3,000 to the profit and loss account.

Summary

Stock item	*Balance sheet value at 30 September 2004*	*Charge to the profit and loss account for the year ended 30 September 2004*
	£000	*£000*
Personal cassette players	10	8
Basic CD players	45	0
DVD players	7	3

Requirement (c)

(i) **D Ltd – Deferred tax calculation**

	At 30 September		
	2002	*2003*	*2004*
	£	£	£
Depreciation at 20%	144,000	144,000	144,000
Capital allowances at 25% reducing balance	180,000	135,000	101,250
Taxable difference for the year	-36,000	9,000	42,750
Deferred tax for the year at 30%	10,800	2,700	12,825
Cumulative deferred tax balance	-10,800	-8,100	4,725

D Ltd has a deferred tax liability in 2002 of £10,800 which reduces to £8,100 in 2003 and becomes a deferred tax asset of £4,725 in 2004.

(ii) The Statement of Principles definition of a liability is "an obligation to transfer economic benefit in the future as a result of past events". The liability exists in 2002 and 2003 as D Ltd has had tax allowances which have reduced tax in both years, but will cause a higher level of tax in future years when depreciation is higher than deferred tax. There is therefore a future liability.

The Statement of Principles definition of an asset is "access to future economic benefits arising from past events". As long as D Ltd expect to earn future profits, they will be able to claim future tax allowances. The deferred tax balance in 2004 therefore represents access to future economic benefits and is treated as an asset. The future economic benefits are a reduction of tax in the future as a result of having paid more tax now.

CIMA

November 2004 Examinations

Intermediate Level

Financial Accounting – International Standards

(IFAI – Paper 6b)

Question Paper	1
Examiner's Brief Guide to the Paper	17
Examiner's Answers	18

The answers published here have been written by the Examiner and should provide a helpful guide for both lecturers and students.

Published separately on the CIMA website (www.cimaglobal.com/students) from the end of March 2005 is a Post Examination Guide for this paper, which provides much valuable and complementary material including indicative mark information.

CIMA

Intermediate Level

Financial Accounting – International Accounting Standards

6b

IFAI

24 November 2004

Wednesday morning

INSTRUCTIONS TO CANDIDATES

Read this page before you look at the questions

You are allowed three hours to answer this question paper.
This question paper is based on INTERNATIONAL ACCOUNTING STANDARDS. **If you require the paper based on UK Accounting Standards, please speak immediately to the invigilator.**
Answer the ONE question in Section A (this has 10 sub-questions). Answer the ONE question in Section B. Answer TWO questions ONLY from Section C.

SECTION A – 20 MARKS

ANSWER *ALL* TEN SUB-QUESTIONS – 2 MARKS EACH

Question One

1.1 When an external auditor is unable to agree the accounting treatment of a material item with the directors of an enterprise, but the financial statements are not seriously misleading, he will issue

A an unqualified audit report.

B an adverse opinion.

C a qualified audit report using "except for".

D an unqualified audit report using "except for".

1.2 IAS 40 – *Investment property* gives examples of investment properties, which include some of the following:

(i) Property held for long-term capital appreciation
(ii) Property being constructed for use as an investment property
(iii) Property leased to another entity on a finance lease
(iv) Property leased out under one or more operating leases
(v) Owner-occupied property
(vi) Land held for an undetermined future use
(vii) Property occupied by employees

Which of the above are listed by IAS 40 as examples of an investment property?

A (i), (v) and (vi)

B (ii), (v) and (vii)

C (iii), (iv) and (vi)

D (i), (iv) and (vi)

1.3 X, a quoted enterprise, had the following results for the year ended 30 September 2004:

	$m
Profit before tax	2,400
Tax	700
Profit after tax	1,700

X also had the following balances at 30 September 2004:

Equity capital of 680 million shares at a nominal value of $0·50 each
Closing market price per share at 30 September 2004 was $10

X's P/E ratio is:

A 0·25

B 2·0

C 2·9

D 4·0

1.4 In some circumstances, enterprise directors set aside the detailed provisions contained in International Accounting Standards and use their own accounting methods.

This setting aside of detailed regulations could be:

(i) Creative accounting
(ii) Departing from the standard to achieve "fair presentation"
(iii) Illegal manipulation of accounting data

A (i) only

B (ii) only

C (iii) only

D (i) or (iii)

1.5 Z entered into a finance lease agreement on 1 November 2002. The lease was for five years, the fair value of the asset acquired was $45,000 and the interest rate implicit in the lease was 7%. The annual payment was $10,975 in arrears.

The total amount owing under the lease at 31 October 2004 was

A $27,212.

B $28,802.

C $29,350.

D $40,108.

1.6 W owns two properties, property 1 and property 2. As economic circumstances have worsened recently, W has carried out an impairment review of its properties. The values calculated during the review are as follows:

All values are at 31 October 2004:

	Book value	*Market value less disposal costs*	*Value in use*
	$000	*$000*	*$000*
Property 1	1,650	1,500	1,400
Property 2	2,500	2,300	2,600

According to IAS 36 – *Impairment of assets*, the values that W should use in its balance sheet at 31 October 2004 are

	Property 1	*Property 2*
	$000	*$000*
A	1,400	2,300
B	1,400	2,600
C	1,500	2,300
D	1,500	2,500

1.7 Using the requirements set out in IAS 10 – *Events after the Balance Sheet date*, which of the following would be classified as an adjusting post balance sheet event in financial statements ended 31 March 2004 that were approved by the directors on 31 August 2004?

A A reorganisation of the enterprise, proposed by a director on 31 January 2004 and agreed by the Board on 10 July 2004.

B A strike by the workforce which started on 1 May 2004 and stopped all production for 10 weeks before being settled.

C A claim on an insurance policy for damage caused by a fire in a warehouse on 1 January 2004. No provision had been made for the receipt of insurance money at 31 March 2004 as it was uncertain that any money would be paid. The insurance enterprise settled with a payment of $1·5 million on 1 June 2004.

D The enterprise had made large export sales to the USA during the year. The year end receivables included $2 million for amounts outstanding that were due to be paid in US dollars between 1 April 2004 and 1 July 2004. By the time these amounts were received, the exchange rate had moved in favour of the enterprise and the equivalent of $2·5 million was actually received.

1.8 N started business on 1 September 2003. The following balances were extracted from the books of N on 31 August 2004:

	$000	*$000*
Revenue		161
Cost of sales:		
Purchases	151	
Closing inventory	26	
		125
Gross profit		36
Trade receivables		25
Trade payables		16

Assume a 365 day trading year.

Using the information above, N's average working capital cycle for the year ended 31 August 2004 (to the nearest day) was

A 81 days.

B 94 days.

C 113 days.

D 171 days.

1.9 R announced a rights issue of one new share for every four shares currently held. The new shares were sold at a price of $3 per share, all rights were taken up and paid in full. Prior to the rights issue, the quoted market price was $4 per share and there were 8,000,000 shares issued.

R incurred direct issue costs of $40,000.

How much should R credit to the share premium account for the rights issue?

$000

A 3,160

B 3,960

C 4,000

D 5,960

1.10 S revalues its properties to current value each year. One of S's warehouses, in its balance sheet at its September 2003 current value of $1,200,000, is sold on 29 September 2004 for $900,000 with an option to repurchase after four years at $1,093,956 ($900,000 plus compound interest for four years at 5% per annum).

The warehouse's current value at 29 September 2004 was $1,380,000.

How should S treat this transaction in its financial statements for the year ended 30 September 2004?

A As a sale of the warehouse recording a loss on disposal of $300,000.

B Leave the warehouse in its balance sheet at $1,200,000 and record $900,000 as a loan received.

C Revalue the warehouse to $1,380,000 and record a loss on disposal of $480,000.

D Revalue the warehouse to $1,380,000 and record $900,000 as a loan received.

(Total = 20 marks)

End of Section A

SECTION B – 30 MARKS

ANSWER THIS QUESTION

Question Two

ZZ produces two different ranges of products, range A and range B. The range A brand was developed in-house, but the range B brand name was purchased seven years ago.

The B product range has been losing popularity and sales have been in sharp decline for the last two years. By the end of the third quarter of 2002, the level of sales had declined to a point where the directors decided it was no longer viable to produce the B product range. A provision of $100,000 for closure costs was set up in the accounts for the year ended 30 September 2003. The closure was delayed until 1 January 2004 when the production lines ceased production and all the assets relating to the B product range were put up for sale.

ZZ's trial balance at 30 September 2004 is shown below:

	$000	*$000*
10% Loan 2010		2,600
Administration expenses – A product range	96	
Administration expenses – B product range	34	
Bank & Cash	3,192	
Brand name – B product range	197	
Buildings at cost	2,500	
Cash received on disposal of factory		2,000
Cash received on disposal of machinery		50
Closure costs	125	
Cost of goods sold – A product range	513	
Cost of goods sold – B product range	127	
Distribution costs – A product range	92	
Distribution costs – B product range	12	
Equity shares $1 each, fully paid		1,500
Income tax	20	
Inventory at 30 September 2004 – A product range	210	
Land at valuation at 30 September 2003	1,500	
Loan interest paid – half year	130	
Machinery and equipment at cost	1,706	
Provision for amortisation of brand name – B product range at 30 September 2003		138
Provision for closure costs at 30 September 2003		100
Provision for deferred tax at 30 September 2003		203
Provision for depreciation at 30 September 2003:		
Buildings		860
Machinery and equipment		415
Retained earnings at 30 September 2003		436
Revaluation reserve		900
Revenue – A product range		1,260
Revenue – B product range		42
Trade payables		90
Trade receivables	140	
	10,594	10,594

Further information:

(i) The assets relating to the B product range were disposed of as follows:

- The land and the factory buildings were sold on 1 March 2004 for $2,000,000.
- The machinery was sold for $50,000 on the same date.
- All the cash received is included in the trial balance.
- The purchased brand name was deemed to have no value and should be written off. The book values of the assets sold were:

Asset type	*Cost*	*Valuation*	*Accumulated depreciation*
	$000	*$000*	*$000*
Land	300	750	0
Buildings	400		220
Machinery and equipment	462		195

(ii) Buildings are depreciated at 5% per annum on the straight-line basis. Machinery is depreciated at 25% per annum using the reducing balance method. Depreciation is treated as a cost of sales.

(iii) There were no purchases of tangible non-current assets during the year.

(iv) ZZ's accounting policy for amortisation and depreciation is to charge a full year in the year of acquisition and make no charge in the year of disposal.

(v) The directors decided to downsize the enterprise and used the cash received to repay a loan rather than invest in new production facilities. The loan was redeemed on 30 September 2004, a payment equal to the nominal value outstanding plus accrued interest to date was made from the bank account on 30 September 2004. This transaction has not been recorded in the trial balance.

(vi) The directors estimate the income tax charge on the year's profits at $113,000. The balance on the income tax account is the amount remaining after settling the amount due for the year ended 30 September 2003.

(vii) The deferred tax provision needs to be reduced to $170,000.

(viii) No interim dividend was paid during the year.

Required:

(a) Prepare the tangible non-current assets note to the accounts for the year ended 30 September 2004.

(6 marks)

(b) Prepare the income statement of ZZ for the year ended 30 September 2004 and its balance sheet at that date. These should be in a form suitable for publication and in accordance with all current regulations.

(24 marks)

Notes to the financial statements are not required (except as specified in requirement (a)) but all workings must be clearly shown. DO NOT prepare a statement of accounting policies, a statement of recognised gains and losses or a statement of changes in equity.

(Total for Question Two = 30 marks)

End of Section B

SECTION C – 50 MARKS

ANSWER TWO QUESTIONS ONLY

Question Three

Requirement (a)

IAS 1 – *Presentation of financial statements*, distinguishes between accounting policies and accounting estimates.

Required:

Explain the difference between accounting policies and accounting estimates; give an example of each.

(4 marks)

Requirement (b)

The directors of U have recently made four changes to their accounting treatment of certain items, for the year ended 30 September 2004:

Change 1

U has been depreciating its factory machines on the straight-line basis over six years, assuming no residual value. U replaced all of its machines at the same time on 1 October 2000 at a cost of $1,300,000.

The directors of U have decided to change the method of machinery depreciation to the reducing balance method, as they think that it will more accurately reflect usage of the machines and will give a fairer presentation. Effective from 1 October 2003, all machinery will be depreciated at 25% per annum using the reducing balance method.

(5 marks)

Change 2

U manufactures refrigerators and freezers and sells them with a one-year warranty. It applies the requirements of IAS 37 – *Provisions, contingent liabilities and contingent assets* to its financial accounts. U has made a provision for future warranty claims each year.

U did not keep accurate records of previous warranty claims, so when IAS 37 became effective, it estimated future warranty claims based on an estimated 10% of sales turnover. It also started keeping accurate records of warranty claims.

U has decided to change its method of calculating the provision for warranty claims to the weighted average of the last three years' actual claims paid.

A warranty claim provision of $900,000, calculated on the old basis, has already been entered in the accounts for the year ended 30 September 2004.

Year to 30 September	*2002*	*2003*	*2004*
	$000	*$000*	*$000*
Revenue	7,500	8,000	9,000
Actual warranty claims paid	375	400	325

(6 marks)

Change 3
U did not previously capitalise interest incurred in connection with the construction of tangible non-current assets. All interest was charged to the income statement each year. The directors have now decided that, in future, interest incurred on construction contracts will be added to the cost of construction. U's trial balance shows that construction costs of tangible non-current assets completed in the year ended 30 September 2004 were $1,400,000. Interest directly attributable to the construction was $56,000 during the year; this has been included in the trial balance under interest paid.

(5 marks)

Change 4
U owns an office building, which it purchased for $250,000 ten years ago (1 October 1993) for use by its employees. U has charged depreciation on the office building at 2% per annum on the straight line basis.

All of U's employees have now moved to other premises and U has let the office building to a third party on an operating lease. Effective from 1 October 2003, the directors have decided to reclassify the office building as an investment property and to carry it in its balance sheet at valuation without any depreciation, as required by IAS 40 – *Investment property*. The office building was valued at $450,000 on 1 October 2003.

(5 marks)

Required:

For each of the four changes above:

(i) Identify the accounting policy and accounting estimate involved and explain whether U is making a change in accounting policy or a change in accounting estimate or neither.

(ii) Prepare the accounting entries required in U's income statement and balance sheet to implement changes 1 to 4 above for the year ended 30 September 2004 and explain the need for such entries.

(The breakdown of marks is shown against each change detailed above)

(Total for Requirement (b) = 21 marks)

(Total for Question Three = 25 marks)

Question Four

JK is considering entering a long-term business arrangement with another enterprise to provide a full range of contract services for the construction industry.

The selected enterprise must be in a strong financial position and be able to survive and prosper in both the immediate future and the medium term.

JK has two possible candidates for the business arrangement, CDE and VWX. Both candidates have a high reputation for the provision of their services. Neither enterprise carries any significant inventory.

Summarised income statement for the year ended 31 October 2004

	CDE	*VWX*
	$000	*$000*
Revenue	11,200	9,800
Operating profit	990	966
Finance cost	(202)	(70)
Profit before tax	788	896
Income tax expense	(190)	(240)
Profit from operations	598	656

Summarised balance sheets at 31 October 2004

	CDE		*VWX*	
	$000	*$000*	*$000*	*$000*
Tangible non-current assets		2,000		2,500
Current assets		1,950		1,995
		3,950		4,495
Capital and reserves:				
Equity capital		400		1,000
Share premium		100		500
Retained earnings		300		995
Total capital and reserves		800		2,495
Non-current liabilities				
Loans 2010-2015		1,410		1,010
		2,210		3,505
Current liabilities				
Bank loan 2005	1,110		0	
Creditors	630	1,740	990	990
		3,950		4,495

Requirement (a)

As the trainee management accountant you have been asked to prepare a draft report to the finance director, based on the information given above, analysing the financial strengths and weaknesses of each of the candidate enterprises and their suitability for a long-term business arrangement with JK.

(*Note:* You should ignore the further information given in requirement (b) for this draft report.)

(19 marks)

Requirement (b)

VWX regularly revalues all its tangible non-current assets which are carried in its balance sheet at fair value. CDE has not revalued any assets and carries all its assets at depreciated historic cost. If CDE were to revalue its assets at 31 October 2004, its tangible non-current assets would increase by $2,750,000.

All other accounting policies of the two enterprises are substantially the same.

Required:

Explain, with supporting calculations, how the revaluation of CDE's tangible non-current assets will affect its financial ratios and whether this would have any effect on your conclusions regarding CDE's suitability for a long-term business arrangement with JK.

(6 marks)

(Total for Question Four = 25 marks)

Question Five

Requirement (a)

A general manager in your enterprise has recently enrolled on a management course at the local college. She is studying a module on finance and accounting and is having some difficulty understanding the theory. She has asked you, the trainee management accountant, if you could explain the consultative process used to produce a new International Financial Reporting Standard (IFRS).

(5 marks)

Requirement (b)

E, a food retailer, decided to start a home delivery service from 1 November 2002. As E had no vehicles suitable for use by the new service, it purchased three small delivery vehicles to enable them to provide the service.

The invoice for the vehicles included the following details:

	$
Cost price – per vehicle	12,000
Less: Trade discount	(2,400)
	9,600
Delivery charge	250
One vehicle	9,850
Three vehicles	29,550
1 year's insurance for the three vehicles	2,100
Total cost of three vehicles	31,650

By 31 October 2003, there had been a general price increase in all new delivery vehicles of 25%. The directors of E decided to revalue the three delivery vehicles to 125% of their net book value at 31 October 2003.

During the next year, it became apparent that the delivery service was so successful that the delivery vehicles were now too small. On 1 April 2004, E traded in the three delivery vehicles for three new larger vehicles. The new larger delivery vehicles cost $18,000 each and the vendor allowed a trade-in value of $9,000 for each of the old vehicles. E paid the balance of $9,000 per vehicle on 1 May 2004.

All vehicles are depreciated using the reducing balance method at 25% per annum, charged on a time basis.

E purchased new computer equipment, costing $5,000, to assist in running the delivery service. The software required to provide the service was also purchased at the same time. The initial cost of the delivery scheduling software was $950 plus the cost of adapting the software to E's detailed specifications $2,600. The computer equipment and the adapted software were delivered on 1 November 2002, and brought into use at once. During December 2002, the software developed reliability problems, often crashing for no apparent reason. E's in-house programmer spent time resolving these problems at an estimated cost of $2,000 in December 2002 and $1,000 in January 2003. E depreciates all computer equipment and software on a straight line basis over four years, assuming no residual value.

IAS 16 – *Property, plant and equipment* describes the asset recognition process as:

- Initial recognition
- Subsequent remeasurement
- Derecognition

Required:

(i) Apply the IAS 16 asset recognition process to the above situations and explain the relevance of each stage of the process to each of the situations.

(6 marks)

(ii) Prepare income statement and balance sheet extracts for the years ended 31 October 2003 and 31 October 2004 to show how the above transactions would be recorded. Explain your treatment with reference to appropriate International Financial Reporting Standards.

(14 marks)

(Total for Requirement (b) = 20 marks)

(Total for Question Five = 25 marks)

Question Six

Requirement (a)

M operates a copper mine in a remote part of a country which is designated a national park. To obtain the licence to operate the mine, M had to agree to a number of conditions. One condition is that at the end of the useful economic life of the mine, M will remove all above ground buildings and equipment and will reinstate the land on which they were situated. They also agreed to landscape all the waste tips and to plant them with trees normally found in the area. The estimated cost of all of this work is $3 million.

The initial costs of building the required premises, preparing the mine for operation and other set-up costs were $5 million and have been charged to tangible non-current assets – assets under construction.

M paid the government $10 million for a licence to operate the mine for 25 years. This amount has been debited to tangible non-current assets. The mine commenced operations on 1 October 2003.

Required:

Calculate the value of the amounts that M should show in its income statement for the year ended 30 September 2004 and its balance sheet at that date. Justify your treatment of each item by reference to appropriate International Financial Reporting Standards.

(9 marks)

Requirement (b)

N manufactures a range of electrical products for home and portable personal entertainment. Demand for products can fall drastically at very short notice, often due to a product having been superseded by a new product.

At 30 September 2004, N's inventory balance included the following:

	Total cost	*Total normal sales value*
	$000	*$000*
20,000 personal cassette tape players	18	27
5,000 basic CD players	45	90
Damaged DVD players	10	20

At 30 September 2004, the 20,000 personal cassette tape players had been in inventory an average of 18 months. These cassette tape players are no longer manufactured. During November 2004, N found a buyer for its whole inventory of cassette tape players; the total agreed price was $10,000.

The market for the basic CD players has contracted as higher specification models and DVD players have entered the market. N's sales director estimates that the basic CD players will only sell for $10 each.

A quantity of DVD players were found to be damaged and were unable to be sold in their current condition. The DVD players had a zero scrap value. These units could be repaired at a total cost of $5,000; they could then be sold for a total of $12,000.

Required:

Advise N how it should treat the above inventory items in its income statement for the year ended 30 September 2004 and how it should value the inventory in its balance sheet at that date. Your answer should refer to appropriate International Financial Reporting Standards.

(7 marks)

Requirement (c)

D purchased all its tangible non-current assets new three years ago on 1 October 2001. The tangible non-current assets cost $720,000 and all qualified for tax depreciation at 25% per annum on the reducing balance method. D's depreciation policy is to depreciate tangible non-current assets at 20% per annum using the straight-line method and assuming no residual value. D pays income tax at 30%.

Required:

(i) Calculate D's deferred tax balance at the end of each of the years ended 30 September 2002, 2003 and 2004.

(5 marks)

(ii) Using the International Accounting Standards Board's (IASB) *Framework for the Preparation and Presentation of Financial Statements* definitions of assets and liabilities, justify the deferred tax balances at 30 September 2002, 2003 and 2004.

(4 marks)

(Total for requirement (c) = 9 marks)

(Total for Question Six = 25 marks)

End of paper

The Examiner for IFAI offers to future candidates and to lecturers using this booklet for study purposes, the following background and guidance on the questions included in this examination paper.

Section A — compulsory

Question One consists of 10 objective test sub-questions, designed to cover a variety of syllabus topics not covered elsewhere in the paper and addressing a selection of learning outcomes in all sections of the syllabus.

Section B — compulsory

Section B is a single question for 30 marks. **Question Two** requires a specific note to the accounts, which is consistent with the information I presented at the last Lecturers' Conference. As previously stated, I intend using this compulsory question as a final account preparation question in each exam. I said at the Lecturers' Conference that this question will not always be an income statement and balance sheet and could include any published final accounts statement.

The last exam in May 2004 had a cash flow statement, so this one is back to an income statement and balance sheet. The question includes a range of the usual adjustments and a substantial element on closure of a segment and disposal of the assets concerned.

Section C – two questions from four

Question Three is on IAS 1 and accounting policies. The accounting policy and accounting estimate must be identified for a range of situations. Accounting entries then have to be prepared to record the changes.

Question Four part (a) requires the analysis of two entities to be considered for a long-term business arrangement. A range of accounting ratios need to be calculated and analysed. Part (b) requires candidates to consider the fact that the entity accounts may not be comparable and need to be adjusted.

Question Five part (a) asks candidates to advise a manager of the consultative process of producing a new International Financial Reporting Standard. Part (b) requires the application of the IAS 16 asset recognition process to two situations and their impact on the income statement and balance sheet to be identified.

Question Six part (a) requires International Accounting Standards to be applied to the creation of a non-current asset with future reinstatement costs. Part (b) requires three different inventory items to be considered. Each situation needs to be explained and justified with reference to International Financial Reporting Standards.

CIMA

The Examiner's Answers for Financial Accounting - International Accounting Standards

SECTION A

Answers to Question One

1.1	**A**	**B**	**(C)**	**D**
1.2	**A**	**B**	**C**	**(D)**
1.3	**A**	**B**	**C**	**(D)**
1.4	**A**	**(B)**	**C**	**D**
1.5	**A**	**(B)**	**C**	**D**
1.6	**A**	**B**	**C**	**(D)**
1.7	**A**	**B**	**(C)**	**D**
1.8	**A**	**(B)**	**C**	**D**
1.9	**A**	**(B)**	**C**	**D**
1.10	**A**	**B**	**C**	**(D)**

Explanations follow for answers to objective test sub-questions involving calculations

1.3 EPS 1,700/680 = 2·5
P/E 10/2·5 = 4

Therefore the answer is D

1.5

Balance	*Interest at 7·00%*	*Instalment*	*Balance*
$	*$*	*$*	*$*
45,000	3,150	10,975	37,175
37,175	2,602	10,975	28,802

Therefore the answer is B

1.6 The greater of value in use or net realisable value is used if they are both below book value.

Property 1 net realisable value, $1,500,000 will be used as it is below book value.

Property 2 book value will remain unchanged as it is below value in use.

Therefore the answer is D

1.8 Inventory average days 25/125 x 365 = 75·9
Receivables average days 25/161 x 365 = 56·7
Payables average days 16/151 x 365 = 38·7
Average working capital cycle is 75·9 + 56·7 - 38·7 = 93·9 days

Therefore the answer is B

1.9

Shares in issue prior to rights issue	8,000,000
Rights issue 1 for every 4 =	2,000,000
Premium per share	$2
Total premium	$2 x 2,000,000 = 4,000,000
Less issue costs	$40,000
Credit to share premium is	4,000,000 - 40,000 = $3,960,000

Therefore the answer is B

Answer to Question Two

Requirement (a)

Note – Tangible non-current assets

	Land	*Buildings*	*Machinery & equipment*	*Total*
Cost/valuation	*$000*	*$000*	*$000*	*$000*
Balance brought forward	1,500	2,500	1,706	5,706
Disposals	(750)	(400)	(462)	1,612
Balance carried forward	750	2,100	1,244	4,094
Accumulated depreciation				
Balance brought forward		860	415	1,275
Disposals		(220)	(195)	(415)
Charge for the year		105*	256*	361
Balance carried forward		745	476	1,221
Net book value at 30 September 2004	750	1,355	768	2,873
Net book value at 30 September 2003	1,500	1,640	1,291	4,431

* Depreciation charge for the year:
Buildings: 2,100 x 5% = 105
Machinery & equipment: 1,244 - (415 - 195) = 1,024 x 25% = 256

Requirement (b)

ZZ
Income Statement for the year ended 30 September 2004

	$000 Continuing operations	*$000 Discontinued operations*	*$000 Total*
Revenue	1,260	42	1,302
Cost of sales (W1)	874	127	1,001
Gross profit	386	(85)	301
Distribution costs	(92)	(12)	(104)
Administrative expenses	(96)	(34)	(130)
Profit from operations	198	(131)	67
Gain on sale of non-current assets (W2)		794	794
Closure costs		(125)	(125)
Less: Provision brought forward		100	100
Profit on ordinary activities	198	638	836
Finance cost (W3)			(260)
Profit on ordinary activities before taxation			576
Income Tax Expense (W5)			(100)
Profit for the period			476

ZZ
Balance Sheet at 30 September 2004

	$000 Net Book Value	$000
Tangible non-current assets		
Land	750	
Buildings	1,355	
Machinery & equipment	768	
		2,873
Current assets		
Inventory	210	
Trade receivables	140	
Cash at bank & in hand (W7)	462	
		812
		3,685
Capital and reserves		
Share capital		1,500
Revaluation reserve		450
Retained earnings (W8)		1,362
		3,312
Payables amounts falling due after one year		
Deferred tax		170
Payables amounts falling due within one year		
Trade payables	90	
Income tax	113	
		203
		3,685

Workings

(W1) – Cost of sales – A product range	$000	$000
Trial balance	513	
Depreciation	361 (from part (a))	
	874	

(W2) – Disposal of non-current assets		
Brand name	197	
Less: Amortised	(138)	59
Revalued land		750
Buildings	400	
Less: Depreciation	(220)	180
Equipment	462	
Less: Depreciation	(195)	267
		1,256
Less: Proceeds		2,050
Gain on disposal		794

(W3) – Finance cost		
Interest charge for year:		
Trial balance	130	
Accrued	130	
	260	

(W4) – Loan redemption		
Trial balance	2,600	
Accrued interest	130	
Cash	2,730	

	$000
(W5) – Taxation	
Accrued for year	113
Last year's balance	20
Reduced deferred tax provision	(33)
Tax charge for the year	100

(W6) – Deferred Tax	
Balance b/fwd	203
Balance c/fwd	170
Reduction	33

(W7) – Bank	
Trial balance	3,192
Redemption of loans	2,730
Balance	462

(W8) – Retained earnings	
Balance b/fwd	436
Revaluation reserve – realised on disposal	450
Profit for the year	476
	1,362

(W9) – Revaluation reserve	
Balance per trial balance	900
Less: Realised on disposal	450
	450

SECTION C

Answer to Question Three

Requirement (a)

An accounting policy defines the process by which events are reflected in the financial statements. For example, the accounting policy for a particular type of expenditure will determine whether an asset or an expense should be recognised in the financial statements.

Accounting estimates put the measurement aspects of accounting policies into practice. For example, the different methods of depreciation are accounting estimates used to apply the accounting policy of depreciating tangible non-current assets.

It is possible to change the accounting estimate without changing the accounting policy. For example, changing from reducing balance depreciation to straight line depreciation is a change in accounting estimate, which will cause a change in the amount of depreciation charged, but the accounting policy of depreciating all tangible non-current assets will remain unchanged. When a change occurs, it is important to distinguish between a change in accounting policy and a change in accounting estimate as they are treated differently.

Requirement (b)

Change 1

(i) Accounting policy is to depreciate factory machines over their useful economic life. Accounting estimate is the method of calculating depreciation. This is a change in accounting estimate as U is changing its method of calculating depreciation.

(ii) IAS 16 requires the remaining book value to be depreciated over the remaining useful economic life of the assets using the new method of depreciation. A change of accounting estimate cannot be treated as a prior year adjustment.

Purchased October 2000, the balance at 1 October 2003 is after three years' depreciation. With a useful economic life of six years this means 50% of the cost has been depreciated.

	$000
Cost	1,300
Depreciation to date	650
Net book value 1 October 2003	650
Depreciation for year to 30 September 2004	163
Net book value 30 September 2004	487
Debit Income Statement – depreciation	163
Credit Provision for depreciation	163

Change 2

(i) Accounting policy is to make a provision for future warranty claims. Accounting estimate is the method of estimating the provision. This is a change in accounting estimate as U is changing its method of calculating the provision.

(ii) The directors want a more scientific approach to calculating the provision, which is to be based on the last three years' actual claims. This will avoid any wide fluctuations caused by one year's claims being abnormally high. A weighted average is calculated and applied to the year's sales.

Year ended 30 September:	*2002*	*2003*	*2004*	*Total*
	$000	*$000*	*$000*	*$000*
Sales value	7,500	8,000	9,000	24,500
Warranty claims	375	400	325	1,100

Average warranty claim = 1,100/24,500 x 100 = 4·5%
Provision for warranty claims should be $9,000,000 x 4·5% = $404,082 = $404,000
The new policy results in a reduction of $496,000 in the provision from $900,000 to $404,000

	$000
Debit Provision for warranty claims	496
Credit Profit and loss – warranty claims	496

Change 3

(i) Accounting policy now is to capitalise interest directly attributable to the construction of tangible non-current assets into the cost of the asset constructed.

(ii) Accounting estimate is the method used to identify and calculate the interest that is directly attributable.

(iii) This is a change in accounting policy, the original policy was not to include interest, the new policy is to include interest.

(iv) The interest charge should be moved from interest paid in the year to the cost of tangible non-current assets under construction; the total cost will be transferred to tangible non-current assets:

	$000	*$000*
Debit Tangible non-current assets – cost	1,456	
Credit Assets under construction		1,456
Debit Assets under construction – cost	56	
Credit Interest paid		56

Change 4

(i) U has two accounting policies, the treatment of office buildings and the treatment of investment properties. U has not changed its accounting policies as buildings and investment properties are still treated in the same way in its accounts.

Accounting estimate is the method to calculate the amount of depreciation of buildings or the basis of valuation of the investment property.

There is no change in accounting policy and no change in accounting estimate.

The property has been reclassified from tangible non-current assets to investment properties and the accounting policy and accounting estimate for investment properties has been applied instead of the non-current asset policy.

(ii) Original cost $250,000 less 10 years depreciation at 2% $50,000 leaves $200,000 book value. The buildings cost and depreciation need to be removed and the revalued property debited to investment properties with a transfer to revaluation reserve of $250,000.

	$000	*$000*
Debit Investment properties	450	
Credit Office buildings at cost		250
Debit Office buildings – accumulated depreciation	50	
Credit Revaluation reserve		250

Answer to Question Four

Report

To: Finance Director

From: Trainee management accountant

Re: Review of candidate enterprises for possible joint venture

Introduction

Two enterprises, CDE and VWX are under consideration for a possible long-term business arrangement with JK. I have reviewed the financial statements for both enterprises for the year ended 31 October 2004 and have calculated a number of financial ratios for each enterprise, see **appendix**.

The stated criteria are that the chosen enterprise must be in a strong financial position and be able to survive and prosper in the short and medium term.

Analysis
The review of the financial statements and the calculated ratios reveal the following:

(i) *Financial position*
Short-term financial position is indicated by liquidity and the medium-term financial position by the gearing.

Liquidity
CDE has a less strong position than VWX in terms of liquidity. VWX has a current ratio of 2 : 1, which is a relatively strong position.

CDE has a current ratio of 1·1 : 1, this is much weaker than VWX. The reason that CDE has a weaker current ratio is that CDE's current liabilities include a bank loan repayable in 2005. This loan will have to be repaid next year and may cause cash flow problems in the short term.

Gearing
VWX has low gearing with debt to total capital of 28·8% whereas CDE is very highly geared with debt capital to total capital of 63·8%, (excluding the bank loan). If the bank loan is included in debt the figure increases further to 75·9%. CDE is more vulnerable to increases in interest rates and possible downturn in business. This is illustrated by the interest cover. CDE has interest covered 4·9 times, not too low but much lower than VWX which has its interest covered 13·8 times.

(ii) *Profitability*
To survive and prosper in the medium term all enterprises must make profits. CDE's high gearing seems to enable it to generate much higher levels of return on its total capital employed than VWX, (44·8% against 27·6%) This large difference is not due to a higher operating profit level in CDE, which is marginally lower at 8·8% than that of VWX at 9·9%. The difference is due to CDE's much higher asset turnover, 5·1 instead of VWX's 2·8. The more intensive use of assets could be caused by CDE having very old assets which are almost fully depreciated or VWX having a number of obsolete assets that are not used, but are still in the balance sheet.

Conclusion
As the stated criteria are that the chosen enterprise must be in a strong financial position and be able to survive and prosper in the short and medium term we must give more weighting to liquidity and gearing and less weighting to profitability. CDE seems to have a much higher return on capital employed, but appears to be under-capitalised. CDE's gearing is very high and needs to be reduced in the medium term. If CDE had a lower gearing it may be the preferred option.

There is also concern that CDE may not have sufficient capital to be able to properly fund its element of a joint arrangement. CDE appear to be a higher risk and are not therefore recommended as a partner.

VWX are in a strong financial position with a good current ratio and a reasonable level of debt. Although its profitability is lower than CDE, it is profitable. CDE's profitability will probably increase with the extra turnover resulting from the joint arrangement. The advantages of a strong financial position outweigh the lower returns on capital employed as we are looking for a solid partner that will still be around in several years time.

Recommendation
Start negotiations with VWX regarding the possibility of a long-term business arrangement.

Appendix

	CDE		**VWX**	
ROCE	990/2,210 x 100 =	44·8%	966/3,505 x 100 =	27·6%
Operating profit %	990/11,200 x 100 =	8·8%	966/9,800 x 100 =	9·9%
Asset turnover	11,200/2,210	5·1 times	9,800/3,505 =	2·8 times
Interest cover	990/202	4·9 times	966/70 =	13·8 times
Current ratio	1,950 : 1,740 =	1·1 : 1	1,995 : 990 =	2·0 : 1
Gearing	1,410/2,210 =	63·8%	1,010/3,505	28·8%
Gearing (including bank loan)	(1,410 + 1,110)/ (2,210 + 1,110) =	75·9%		

Requirement (b)

The revaluation of tangible non-current assets will cause any ratios that include tangible non-current assets to change. An increase in tangible non-current assets will increase total shareholders' funds and will cause total capital to increase.

The following ratios will all reduce as they are all calculated using capital employed or total capital.

- return on capital employed
- asset turnover
- gearing

Short term liquidity will be unaffected.

CDE	*Original*	*Revalued*	
ROCE	44·7%	990/(2,210 + 2,750) x 100 =	20·0%
Asset turnover	5·1 times	11,200/(2,210 + 2,750) =	2·3 times
Gearing	63·8%	1,410/(2,210 + 2,750) x 100 =	28·4%

The ROCE and asset turnover have both reduced and are now below VWX's ratios. The gearing has dramatically reduced and is now marginally less than VWX's.

These changes mean that CDE's new gearing is effectively the same as VWX. However, it is still higher risk as it has more debt and its interest cover is much lower. CDE's ROCE and asset turnover are now less than VWX, so VWX is still the preferred choice.

Answer to Question Five

Requirement (a)

(i) The International Accounting Standards Board (IASB) is responsible for devising and issuing International Financial Reporting Standards (IFRS). To issue an IFRS, the IASB must have eight of the fourteen members of the Board voting in favour.

The process for the development of an IFRS involves the following:

- During the early stages of the project, the IASB may establish an Advisory Committee to advise on the issues arising in the project. Consultation with this Committee and the Standards Advisory Council occurs throughout the project.
- The IASB may develop and publish a *Discussion Document* for public comment.
- Following receipt and review of comments on the discussion document, the IASB develops and publishes an *Exposure Draft* for public comment.
- Following receipt and review of comments on the exposure draft, the IASB may hold a public hearing or carry out field tests.
- An *International Financial Reporting Standard* is issued along with any dissenting view expressed by an IASB member and a *Basis of Conclusions* to explain how the IASB reached its conclusions.

Requirement (b)

(i) Initial recognition – on purchase the attributable costs will be recognised.
Delivery vehicles recognised at $29,550 ($9,850 x 3).

Computers: the attributable cost is the cost of acquiring and getting the system ready for use or enabling it to become functional. This can include the initial adaptations, but does not include the in-house programmers, as the work was done at a later stage and is regarded as an additional cost incurred. For any additional cost to be capitalised, it must enhance or improve the asset beyond its original specification. The in-house programmers were checking and fixing the software to get it up to its original specification, not enhancing beyond the original specification.

Subsequent remeasurement – the vehicles are subsequently remeasured when they are revalued on 31 October 2003.
The computer system has no subsequent remeasurement.

Derecognition – the vehicles are derecognised when they are traded in as E no longer has access to the risks and rewards of ownership. On derecognition, the value received is deducted from their carrying value to calculate the loss on disposal.
The computers are still in use and have not been derecognised.

(ii) IAS 16 – *Property, plant and equipment* requires the cost of the tangible non-current assets to be recognised. Cost includes delivery charge and is net of any trade discount. Annual running costs such as insurance are revenue expenditure and are charged to the income statement. IAS 16 allows tangible non-current assets to be revalued; any increase in value is credited to revaluation reserve.

Balance sheet (extract) at 31 October 2003

	$
Tangible non-current assets	
Delivery vehicles at valuation (W1)	27,703
Computers (W2)	8,550
Provision for depreciation – computers	2,138
Revaluation reserve (W1)	5,541

Income statement (extract) for the year ended 31 October 2003

	$
Depreciation – delivery vehicles (W1)	7,388
Depreciation – computers (W2)	2,138
Adjusting software	3,000
Insurance – delivery vehicles	2,100

Balance sheet (extract) at 31 October 2004

	$
Tangible non-current assets	
Delivery vehicles at cost (18,000 x 3)	54,000
Computers	8,550
Provision for depreciation – delivery vehicles (7/12 x 54,000 x 25%)	7,875
Depreciation – computers	2,138
Revaluation reserve	5,541

(As the revaluation reserve is realised on disposal of the vehicles, it can be transferred to retained earnings)

Income statement (extract) for the year ended 31 October 2004

	$
Depreciation – delivery vehicles	7,875
Gain on disposal of small delivery vehicles	(2,183)
Depreciation – computers	2,138

Workings

	$
(W1)	
Delivery vehicles – cost	29,550
Depreciation for year – 25%	7,388
	22,162
Gain on revaluation	5,541
31 October 2003 Revalue to 125% of balance	27,703
Less: Five months depreciation	2,886
1 April 2004 Trade in ($9,000 x 3)	27,000
Gain on disposal	2,183

(W2)	
Computers at cost	$
Hardware	5,000
Software	950
Adaptation	2,600
Total cost	8,550
Depreciation	2,138

Answer to Question Six

Requirement (a)

The cost will include the initial cost, the licence cost and the cost of reinstatement of the land.

	$m
Initial costs	5
Licence fee	10
Provision for reinstatement	3
Total	18
Depreciation each year ($^{18}/_{25}$)	0·72

IAS 16 – *Property, plant and equipment* requires all costs of getting the asset into a state where it is ready to use to be included in the cost. The licence fee is therefore added to the other preparation costs as it is not possible to operate the mine without a licence.

IAS 37 – *Provisions, contingent liabilities and contingent assets* requires the full cost of reinstatement to be provided for immediately and added to the cost of the asset. A provision can only be set up where the following criteria are met:

- There is a present obligation arising from past events;
- It is probable that a transfer of economic benefit will be required to settle the obligation
- A reliable estimate can be made;

The reinstatement meets all of these criteria.

- There is a present obligation; once the mine operation starts it will require to be reinstated when it stops. The past event was the granting of the licence and M starting to operate the mine;
- The transfer of economic benefit is certain, as it is contractual, the cost must be incurred;
- The question gives the amount, so it is reasonable to assume that the amount can be reliably estimated.

If the provision causes the value of the asset to become more than its recoverable amount, its balance sheet value may need to be reviewed and written down to its recoverable amount. The provision will remain in the balance sheet until such time as the mine is closed and the costs of reinstatement are incurred.

The provision will be spread over the useful economic life of the mine as it will be charged as part of the depreciation charge each year.

Requirement (b)

Personal cassette tape players: cost $18,000; actual selling price $10,000.

The actual selling price in November is the net realisable value of the cassette tape players. IAS 2 – *Inventories* requires inventory to be carried in the balance sheet at cost or net realisable value, whichever is the lower. N became aware of the reduced value when agreeing the price with the buyer in November 2004; the circumstances were already there at the balance sheet date with N obtaining the additional information on value after the balance sheet date. This will be treated as a post balance sheet adjusting event under IAS 10 – *Events after the balance sheet date* and the inventory adjusted at the balance sheet date. N should write its cassette tape players down from original cost of $18,000 to their net realisable value of $10,000.

The loss of $8,000 on the write down of the cassette tape players will be charged to income statement.

The basic CD players are estimated to sell at $10 each. The 5,000 in inventory would then be sold for $50,000. This figure is below current selling price, but is above the cost price of $45,000. N do not need to make any changes to the inventory valuation for the basic CD players as cost is below net realisable value.

The faulty DVD players have an original cost of $10,000 and a scrap value of $0. If they are repaired for $5,000, they can be sold for $12,000. The net realisable value if they are repaired is therefore $7,000 ($12,000 - $5,000). N should write down the value of the DVD players to $7,000 and write off $3,000 to the income statement.

Summary

Inventory item	*Balance sheet value at 30 September 2004*	*Charge to the income statement for the year ended 30 September 2004*
	$000	*$000*
Personal cassette players	10	8
Basic CD players	45	0
DVD players	7	3

Requirement (c)

(i) **D Deferred tax calculation**

	At 30 September		
	2002	*2003*	*2004*
	$	*$*	*$*
Depreciation at 20%	144,000	144,000	144,000
Capital allowances at 25% reducing balance	180,000	135,000	101,250
Taxable difference for the year	-36,000	9,000	42,750
Deferred tax for the year at 30%	10,800	2,700	12,825
Cumulative deferred tax balance	-10,800	-8,100	4,725

D has a deferred tax liability in 2002 of $10,800, which reduces to $8,100 in 2003, and becomes a deferred tax asset of $4,725 in 2004.

(ii) The IASB's *Framework for the Preparation and Presentation of Financial Statements* defines a liability as "a present obligation of the enterprise arising from past events, the settlement of which is expected to result in an outflow of resources." A liability exists in 2002 and 2003 as D has had tax allowances which have reduced tax in both years, but will cause a higher level of tax in future years when depreciation is higher than deferred tax. There is, therefore, a future liability.

The *Framework's* definition of an asset is "a resource controlled by the enterprise as a result of past events and from which future economic benefits are expected to flow to the enterprise." As long as D expect to earn future profits, it will be able to claim future tax allowances. The deferred tax balance in 2004 therefore represents access to future economic benefits and is treated as an asset. The future economic benefits are a reduction of tax in the future as a result of having paid more tax now.

CIMA

November 2004 Examinations

Intermediate Level

Financial Reporting – UK Standards

(IFRP – Paper 7a)

Question Paper	1
Examiner's Brief Guide to the Paper	20
Examiner's Answers	21

The answers published here have been written by the Examiner and should provide a helpful guide for both lecturers and students.

Published separately on the CIMA website (www.cimaglobal.com/students) from the end of March 2005 is a Post Examination Guide for this paper, which provides much valuable and complementary material including indicative mark information.

CIMA

Intermediate Level

Financial Reporting – UK Accounting Standards

7a

IFRP

24 November 2004

Wednesday morning

INSTRUCTIONS TO CANDIDATES

Read this page before you look at the questions

You are allowed three hours to answer this question paper.
This question paper is based on UK ACCOUNTING STANDARDS. **If you require the paper based upon International Accounting Standards, please speak immediately to the invigilator.**
Answer the ONE question in Section A (this has 10 sub-questions). Answer the ONE question in Section B. Answer TWO questions only from Section C.
Maths Tables and Formulae are provided.

SECTION A – 20 MARKS

ANSWER *ALL* TEN SUB-QUESTIONS – TWO MARKS EACH

Question One

1.1 A plc owns 80% of the equity shares of its subsidiary, B Ltd. The year-ends of both companies are 30 September. On 25 September 2004, A plc sold goods to B Ltd at an invoiced price of £360,000. These goods were included in the stock of B Ltd at 30 September 2004. The goods were invoiced by A plc at cost plus $^{1}/_{3}$.

Assuming this is the first intra-group sale made by either company, what will be the required provision for unrealised profit in the consolidated balance sheet of the A plc group at 30 September 2004?

A £72,000

B £90,000

C £96,000

D £120,000

1.2 On 30 June 2004, C plc purchased 75% of the equity shares of D Ltd for £16 million. The balance sheet of D Ltd showed net assets of £14 million. This was before taking account of the following items:

- The market value of D Ltd's properties at 30 June 2004 [included in the balance sheet of D Ltd at a carrying value of £8 million] was £10 million.
- On 30 June 2004, D Ltd was in the process of negotiating an insurance claim in respect of stock that was damaged before that date. The claim was for £1 million and, although nothing has yet been received, the directors of D Ltd are confident that the claim will be successful.

What is the goodwill on consolidation that will appear in the consolidated balance sheet of C plc at 30 June 2004?

A £3·25 million

B £4 million

C £4·75 million

D £5·5 million

1.3 E plc has made share purchases in F Ltd as follows:

Date	*% of equity shares of F Ltd purchased*	*Balance on P&L reserve of F Ltd at date shares purchased*
		£000
30 June 1997	40	600
30 June 2000	30	800

On 31 March 2004, the profit and loss reserve balance of F Ltd stood at £1·1 million.

Ignoring amortisation of goodwill, what will be included in the consolidated profit and loss reserve of the E plc group in respect of F Ltd at 31 March 2004? All equity shares in F Ltd carry one vote per share.

A £200,000

B £210,000

C £290,000

D £410,000

1.4 The following data relates to the G plc group:

- The opening and closing balances on the minority interest account were £6·6 and £7·2 million respectively.
- The minority interest in the profits for the year was £2·5 million.
- During the year, the group disposed of a 75% owned subsidiary. The net assets of the subsidiary at the date of disposal were £4·4 million. Unamortised goodwill relating to the subsidiary at the date of disposal was £400,000. The subsidiaries of G plc had no dividends payable included in creditors at the start, or at the end, of the year.

What is the dividend paid to the minority shareholders during the year?

A £400,000

B £600,000

C £800,000

D £2,500,000

1.5 H plc owns 40% of the equity shares of its associate J Ltd. Both companies prepare financial statements to 30 September.

On 28 September 2004, H plc sold goods to J Ltd on which H plc recorded a profit of £40,000. All these goods were unsold by J Ltd at 30 September 2004.

What is the consolidation adjustment that will be made in the consolidated accounts of H plc at 30 September 2004 in respect of this inter-company sale?

A	Debit reserves	£16,000	Credit stock	£16,000
B	Debit reserves	£16,000	Credit investment in J Ltd	£16,000
C	Debit reserves	£40,000	Credit stock	£40,000
D	Debit reserves	£40,000	Credit investment in J Ltd	£40,000

1.6 The following statements allegedly refer to the conclusions to be drawn when using ratio analysis to interpret the financial statements of a company:

(i) A company can only increase its gross profit margin by increasing its sales prices or reducing its overall costs of production.

(ii) Revaluing fixed assets upwards would [other things being equal] lead to a reduction in the return on capital employed.

(iii) A company can increase its return on capital employed in the short term by postponing fixed asset replacement.

Which of the statements are true?

A (i) and (ii) only.

B (i) and (iii) only.

C (ii) and (iii) only.

D All of them.

1.7 A public company reported a profit after tax of £25 million for its year ended 30 September 2004. During the year, the following amounts were appropriated to the shareholders:

- £5 million to the non-equity shareholders.
- £12 million to the equity shareholders.

On 1 October 2003, the company had 50 million equity shares in issue. Then, on 1 April 2004, the company made a bonus issue to the equity shareholders of 3 equity shares for every 5 currently held. The company had 40 million non-equity shares in issue for the whole of the year ended 30 September 2004.

What is the earnings per share figure for the year ended 30 September 2004 that will need to be reported in the financial statements in order to comply with FRS 14 – *Earnings per Share* [ignoring comparatives and assuming that no calculations of the diluted earnings per share are needed]?

A 15 pence

B 25 pence

C 30·77 pence

D 31·25 pence

1.8 A parent company is reviewing goodwill arising on a prior acquisition for impairment. The goodwill is in respect of a business that is a single income generating unit. The net assets of the income generating unit immediately before the impairment review were as follows:

Item	*Carrying value prior to impairment review*
	£m
Goodwill on acquisition	20
Production licence	10
Specialist plant	25
Other tangible fixed assets	50
Net current assets	15
	120

The impairment review revealed that the unit had a value in use of £69 million. Further investigations revealed the following:

- The production licence could be assigned to a third party for £6 million.
- The specialist plant had been damaged by a water leak and cannot be used in the business. It can be sold for scrap for £5 million.
- The net current assets are already stated at the lower of cost and net realisable value.

Assuming none of the other tangible fixed assets have a net realisable value that is greater than their carrying value, what is the carrying value of the other tangible fixed assets immediately after the impairment review has been reflected in the financial statements?

A £32 million

B £43 million

C £49 million

D £50 million

1.9 A company prepares financial statements to 30 June each year. On 1 July 2003, the company issued 20 million £1 loan notes at 95 pence. The loan notes attract annual interest at 5% and are redeemable on 30 June 2008 at £1·20. Alternatively, the notes can be redeemed [at the option of the note-holder] on 30 June 2006 at £1·08. The company paid professional fees of £200,000 in connection with the issue and estimates that the cost of staff time in connection with the issue was £100,000.

Under the principles of FRS 4 – *Capital Instruments* – which of the following statements regarding the loan notes is true?

A The issue costs are £200,000 and the term of the loan is 3 years.

B The issue costs are £200,000 and the term of the loan is 5 years.

C The issue costs are £300,000 and the term of the loan is 3 years.

D The issue costs are £300,000 and the term of the loan is 5 years.

1.10 A company contributes to a defined benefit pension scheme and has fully complied with FRS 17 – *Retirement Benefits* – since its issue in 2000. On 1 July 2003, the net pension liability [before deferred tax] that was included in its balance sheet was £30 million. This liability was re-measured at 30 June 2004 at £35 million.

You are given the following information relevant to the pension scheme for the year ended 30 June 2004:

- The current service cost was £52 million.
- The expected return on assets was £25 million.
- The unwinding of discount on the pension liability was £10 million.
- The company closed down a division and the pension scheme paid a lump sum of £15 million in settlement of the accrued pension rights of employees affected by the closure. This figure was based on the actuarially determined liability to the relevant employees at the date of the closure.
- The company paid contributions of £30 million into the scheme.

What is the actuarial gain or loss that will be recognised in the Statement of Total Recognised Gains and Losses for the year ended 30 June 2004?

A A gain of £2 million

B A gain of £17 million

C A loss of £2 million

D A loss of £13 million

(Total = 20 marks)

End of Section A

SECTION B – 30 MARKS

ANSWER THIS QUESTION

Question Two

East plc is a company incorporated in the United Kingdom. East plc has a subsidiary, West Ltd that is located in Africa and prepares its financial statements under local accounting standards. West Ltd prepares its financial statements in African Francs (AFr). Financial information relating to the two companies for the financial year ended 30 September 2004 is given below:

Balance sheets at 30 September 2004	*East plc*		*West Ltd*	
	£m	*£m*	*AFrm*	*AFrm*
Fixed assets:				
Intangible assets [*Note 1*]	-		20	
Tangible assets [*Note 2*]	100		120	
Investments [*Note 3*]	27		-	
		127		140
Current assets:				
Stocks [*Note 4*]	40		50	
Debtors	45		60	
Cash and bank balances	15		-	
	100		110	
Creditors falling due within one year:				
Trade creditors	25		30	
Tax payable	10		15	
Bank overdraft	-		20	
	35		65	
Net current assets		65		45
Creditors falling due after more than one year:				
Long term loans		(50)		(60)
Provisions for liabilities and charges:				
Deferred tax		(15)		(12)
		127		113
Capital and reserves:				
Called-up share capital [£1/AFr1 shares]		75		60
Profit and loss account		52		53
		127		113

Profit and loss accounts for the year ended 30 September 2004	*East plc*	*West Ltd*
	£m	*AFrm*
Turnover	200	240
Cost of sales	(120)	(145)
Gross profit	80	95
Other operating expenses	(35)	(40)
Operating profit	45	55
Intra-group investment income	4·5	-
Interest payable	(7·5)	(10)
Profit before tax	42	45
Tax	(10)	(15)
Profit after tax	32	30
Dividends paid	(16)	(15)
Retained profit for the year	16	15
Retained profit – 1 October 2003	36	38
Retained profit – 30 September 2004	52	53

Notes to the financial statements

Note 1 The intangible assets of West Ltd comprise internally developed brands that have no ascertainable market value. At the date of acquisition of West Ltd by East plc (see *note 3* below) the carrying value of such brands was AFr12 million. The brands are not amortised and no change occurred in their carrying value during the year ended 30 September 2004.

Note 2 When East plc acquired West Ltd (see *note 3* below) the fair value of the tangible fixed assets of West Ltd was AFr20 million higher than their carrying value in West Ltd's balance sheet. These assets were being depreciated over their estimated useful economic lives and at the date of acquisition the directors estimated that the future useful lives of these assets was 4 years. This depreciation is recognised as part of cost of sales.

Note 3 On 1 October 2001, when the profit and loss reserve of West Ltd showed a credit balance of AFr25 million, East plc purchased 45 million shares in West Ltd for AFr1·80 each. East plc amortises purchased goodwill over 10 years, presenting the amortisation under other operating expenses. East plc has not provided West Ltd with any loan finance.

Note 4 On 1 September 2004, East plc sold a supply of components to West Ltd for £12 million. These components had cost East plc £10 million to manufacture. All of these components were included in the stock of West Ltd at 30 September 2004. West Ltd had paid for half of the consignment before the year-end and the balance of the liability was included in its creditors. Apart from this transaction, and the payment of a dividend by West Ltd on 30 June 2004, there were no other intra-group transactions.

Note 5 Exchange rates on relevant dates were:

Date	*Exchange rate AFr to £1*
1 October 2001	3·00
30 September 2003	2·70
30 June 2004	2·50
1 September 2004	2·45
30 September 2004	2·40

The weighted average exchange rate for the year ended 30 September 2004 was AFr2·5 = £1.

Note 6 In preparing the consolidated financial statements, the directors of East plc treat fair value adjustments and purchased goodwill as part of the net investment in West Ltd and so both are subject to exchange fluctuations. The closing rate [or net investment] method is appropriate for translating the financial statements of West Ltd for consolidation purposes, using the weighted average exchange rate for the year to translate the profit and loss account.

Required:

(a) Translate the balance sheet of West Ltd at 30 September 2004 into £ Sterling and prepare the consolidated balance sheet of East plc at 30 September 2004.

(18 marks)

(b) Translate the profit and loss account of West Ltd for the year ended 30 September 2004 into £ Sterling and prepare the consolidated profit and loss account of East plc for the year ended 30 September 2004. You should start with "Turnover" and end with "Retained profit for the year".

(12 marks)

(Total = 30 marks)

You should prepare all computations to the nearest £100,000.

End of Section B

SECTION C – 50 MARKS

ANSWER TWO QUESTIONS ONLY

Question Three

Investor plc is a company that seeks to grow by acquisition. The company is cash rich and is therefore more concerned about the profitability of potential investments than their cash generating ability. Earnings per share is regarded as a key corporate performance indicator.

The directors have identified two possible targets for takeover – Alpha Ltd and Beta Ltd. Alpha Ltd is a subsidiary of another UK company, while the shares in Beta Ltd are held by its directors. The most recent audited accounts of Alpha Ltd and Beta Ltd have been obtained. Both companies disclose earnings per share on a voluntary basis. The directors of Investor plc have noted that the earnings per share of Alpha Ltd is higher than that of Beta Ltd and have concluded that the performance of Alpha Ltd must therefore be superior.

Profit and loss accounts of the two companies – year ended 31 March 2004

	Alpha Ltd	*Beta Ltd*
	£000	*£000*
Turnover	42,000	44,000
Cost of sales	(20,000)	(24,500)
Gross profit	22,000	19,500
Other operating expenses	(15,000)	(14,000)
Operating profit	7,000	5,500
Interest payable	(290)	(980)
Profit before tax	6,710	4,520
Tax	(2,000)	(1,300)
Profit for the year	4,710	3,220
Earnings per share	157 pence	107 pence

Other relevant information concerning the two companies:

1 – Interests in property
Alpha Ltd and Beta Ltd both acquired interests in very similar properties 20 years ago. Beta Ltd purchased its property for £15 million. The useful economic life of the property was estimated as 50 years at the date of purchase and Beta Ltd is charging depreciation of £150,000 each year to cost of sales on the depreciable amount. The purchase was funded with a long-term loan and £420,000 of the interest charge of Beta Ltd is in respect of this loan.

Alpha Ltd acquired a 50 year leasehold interest in a very similar property, paying a premium of £12 million and annual rentals of £160,000. This lease has been treated as an operating lease with the amortisation of the premium and annual rentals charged to cost of sales. However, the auditors have always been sceptical as to the classification of the lease as operating. If the directors of Alpha Ltd had classified the lease as a finance lease, then the charges to the profit and loss account in respect of depreciation and finance charges would have been very similar to the equivalent profit and loss account charges made by Beta Ltd.

2 – Alpha Ltd's terms of trade

- Alpha Ltd has loan capital of £7 million provided by a company that is part of the same group. Alpha Ltd pays interest at 3% per annum on these loans whereas the current market rate is 6% per annum.
- Included in the turnover of Alpha Ltd is £15 million representing sales to a fellow subsidiary, Gamma Ltd. Alpha Ltd earns a profit margin of 60% on these intra-group sales. The profit margin that Alpha Ltd earns on sales of similar products outside the group is 50%.
- Alpha Ltd receives administrative services from its parent, but no charge is made for the services. The directors of Alpha Ltd estimate that the market value of such services in the year ended 31 March 2004 was £1·5 million. Similar charges borne by Beta Ltd are presented in other operating expenses.

3 – Rates of tax
Both companies pay corporation tax at a rate of 30%. All adjustments made to profit (see requirement *(b)*) are subject to tax at this rate.

4 – Issued share capital
Both companies have an issued share capital of £3 million in £1 shares. This issued capital has not changed during the year ended 31 March 2004.

Required:

(a) Identify the factors that should be considered when comparing the financial statements of different companies when the acquisition of one of the companies is being considered.

(5 marks)

(b) Explain and compute any adjustments you consider should be made to the earnings per share of Alpha Ltd, so that the directors of Investor plc can validly compare this figure with that of Beta Ltd.

YOU SHOULD RECOMPUTE THE EARNINGS PER SHARE OF ALPHA LTD, BUT YOU DO NOT NEED TO WRITE OUT THE ADJUSTED PROFIT AND LOSS ACCOUNT OF ALPHA LTD.

(10 marks)

(c) Write a report to the directors of Investor plc identifying the underlying differences between the earnings per share of Alpha Ltd and Beta Ltd. You should clearly indicate any limitations in your conclusions based on the information available to you.

(10 marks)

(Total = 25 marks)

Question Four

You are the management accountant of Flexible plc, a UK company that has business interests all around the world. The financial statements for the year ended 31 October 2004 are currently in the course of preparation. The directors have sought your advice on the financial reporting implications of the following issues.

(1) On 30 September 2004, the directors decided to close down a business segment that had been making losses for a few years. The closure commenced on 15 November 2004 and was due to be completed on 31 December 2004. On 10 October 2004, letters were sent to employees offering voluntary redundancy or redeployment in other sectors of the business. On 13 October 2004, negotiations commenced with relevant parties with a view to terminating existing contracts of the business segment. Latest estimates of the financial implications of the closure are as follows:

- Redundancy costs will total £20 million.
- The pension scheme will make a lump sum payment totalling £10 million to the employees who accept voluntary redundancy in termination of their rights under the scheme. Flexible plc will pay this amount into the scheme on 31 January 2005.
- The cost of redeploying and retraining staff who do not accept redundancy will total £6 million.
- The costs of terminating existing contracts, including professional fees, will total £5 million.
- Plant having a net book value of £12 million at 31 October 2004 will be sold for £1 million.
- A freehold property having a net book value of £10 million at 31 October 2004 will be sold for £15 million.
- The operating losses of the business segment for November and December 2004 will total £8 million.

(12 marks)

(2) In 2005, Flexible plc is planning a major investment in Europe. Latest indications are that this investment will cost 50 million Euros and that the funds will be required on 28 February 2005. In order to provide a measure of certainty regarding the cost of the investment in £ Sterling on 31 August 2004, the directors entered into a contract to purchase 50 million Euros for £35 million, with a delivery date of 28 February 2005. On 31 October 2004, the rate of exchange was such that this contract had a fair value of £800,000.

(5 marks)

(3) Flexible plc has a subsidiary located in Taxland, which has its own tax jurisdiction. No other group company is located within it. The subsidiary regularly sells goods to Flexible plc and the stock of Flexible plc at 31 October 2004 included goods purchased from its subsidiary on which its subsidiary had made a profit of £1 million (after translation at the appropriate rate). The subsidiary had made a loss adjusted for tax purposes for the year ended 31 October 2004 that was equivalent to £4 million. Local tax legislation only allows tax losses to be carried forward for relief against future trading profits. The directors of Flexible plc consider that the loss of the subsidiary is due to identifiable non-recurring causes and that the subsidiary will record a taxable profit for the foreseeable future. Both Flexible plc and its subsidiary pay tax at 30%.

(8 marks)

Required:

Advise the directors on the financial reporting implications of the three issues for the year ended 31 October 2004. Where the primary financial statements are affected (excluding the cashflow statement), you should indicate the amounts that would be included where possible. In each case, you should indicate the nature of any disclosures that might be appropriate in the notes to the financial statements.

You should justify your conclusion with reference to appropriate Accounting Standards and include any other explanations you consider relevant.

The allocation of marks to the three issues is indicated after each issue.

(Total = 25 marks)

Question Five

The profit and loss accounts of Hansen plc and its subsidiary companies Williams Ltd and Charvis Ltd for the year ended 30 September 2004 are given below:

	Hansen plc	*Williams Ltd*	*Charvis Ltd*
	£000	*£000*	*£000*
Turnover	60,000	45,000	35,000
Cost of sales	(30,000)	(25,000)	(19,000)
Gross profit	30,000	20,000	16,000
Other operating expenses	(15,000)	(10,000)	(8,000)
Operating profit	15,000	10,000	8,000
Investment income	2,800	-	-
Interest payable	(5,000)	(4,000)	(3,000)
Profit before tax	12,800	6,000	5,000
Tax	(3,500)	(2,000)	(1,800)
Profit after tax	9,300	4,000	3,200
Dividends paid 31 January 2004	(4,500)	(2,000)	(1,600)
Retained profit for the year	4,800	2,000	1,600
Retained profit 1 October 2003	20,000	12,000	10,000
Retained profit 30 September 2004	24,800	14,000	11,600

Note 1 – Investments by Hansen plc

- On 1 October 1996, when the profit and loss account of Williams Ltd showed a credit balance of £6 million, Hansen plc purchased 4 million of Williams plc's five million £1 issued equity shares. Hansen paid £10·8 million for these shares.
- On 1 October 1997, when the profit and loss account of Charvis Ltd showed a credit balance of £4 million, Hansen plc purchased 4·5 million of Charvis Ltd's six million £1 issued equity shares. Hansen paid £8·7 million for these shares.
- All shares in Williams Ltd and Charvis Ltd have equal voting rights. Neither company has any other reserves apart from its profit and loss reserve.
- No fair value adjustments were necessary in respect of either company when it was first consolidated by Hansen plc.
- Goodwill on both acquisitions is written off on a straight line basis over 240 months [20 years]. Hansen plc presents the amortisation of goodwill on acquisition of subsidiaries in other operating expenses.

Note 2 – Sale of shares in Charvis Ltd

On 1 April 2004, Hansen plc sold a total of three million shares in Charvis Ltd for £3·50 per share. The sale was made to help finance organic growth and Hansen plc retained a significant influence over the operating and financial policies of Charvis Ltd following the sale. Under UK tax legislation, no tax is payable on the disposal.

Note 3 – Intra-group trading

Hansen plc levies a management charge [included in its turnover] of £1 million per annum on each of its subsidiaries. The subsidiaries presented this charge under other operating expenses. In the case of Charvis Ltd, this charge ceased with effect from 1 April 2004. However, Charvis Ltd was obliged to incur equivalent costs from 1 April 2004 in order to replace the service formerly supplied by Hansen plc.

Note 4 – Profits of Charvis Ltd
All the profits of Charvis Ltd accrued evenly over the year ended 30 September 2004.

Required:

(a) Explain how the disposal of shares in Charvis Ltd will affect the method of consolidation of its profits by Hansen plc. You should make reference to appropriate Accounting Standards, but are NOT required to describe the consolidation method(s) in detail.

(5 marks)

(b) Prepare the consolidated profit and loss account of Hansen plc for the year ended 30 September 2004, starting with "Turnover" and ending with "Retained profit for the year".

(20 marks)

(Total = 25 marks)

Question Six

You are the assistant to the finance director of Rex plc. Rex plc is a UK parent company whose shares are listed on a number of different Stock Exchanges across the world. The finance director has had to take unexpected compassionate leave and before leaving he handed you a memorandum from the Chief Executive [who is not an accountant]. The Chief Executive has recently joined Rex plc from a similar position in the USA.

The memorandum contains three questions relating to three separate issues:

Issue One
I have recently heard that we should be preparing our financial statements in accordance with International Financial Reporting Standards. Surely this isn't right for a UK company! Aren't UK Standards more relevant to us? I vaguely remember someone saying that a change may occur in 2005 or 2007, but this is 2004. Please explain the latest position to me.

(9 marks)

Issue Two
You have probably read that we want to acquire a new subsidiary soon after our next year-end [31 December 2004]. I am worried about the impact this acquisition will have on our consolidated financial statements in the short term. Although the long-term prospects are good, the new subsidiary will almost certainly make losses in 2005 and maybe in 2006. Perhaps we can set up a provision for these losses when we first consolidate next year? I know this will increase the goodwill figure, but I know of companies who just leave their goodwill in the balance sheet and never write it off. Surely we could do the same? This would make the 2005 and 2006 earnings look much more acceptable to our shareholders.

(8 marks)

Issue Three
We are in the final stages of arranging the financing for the acquisition in 2004. It looks like we will have to use debt finance since shareholder confidence is low and share issues would be prohibitively expensive. However, I am concerned at the potential effect of the interest payments on cash flows and earnings. Therefore, I propose issuing debt that is repayable in 10 years' time at a substantial premium. As an alternative to repayment, we will offer the subscribers the option of converting their debt into equity shares – I am confident that shareholder confidence will have returned in 10 years' time. The dual effect of a large potential premium on repayment, together with the option to take shares instead, should mean that the investors will accept a very low coupon rate of interest. An additional benefit is that the convertible debt will be classified in the equity interests section of the balance sheet, with a consequential reduction in our borrowing ratios. Do you agree that this proposal will have the implications that I have predicted?

(8 marks)

Required:
Draft a reply to the memorandum sent by the Chief Executive. Where appropriate you should refer to Accounting Standards and any current developments to support your arguments.

The allocation of marks to the three issues is indicated after each issue.

(Total = 25 marks)

End of paper

Maths Tables and Formulae follow

TABLES AND FORMULAE

TABLES

Present value table

Present value of £1, that is $(1 + r)^{-n}$ where r = interest rate; n = number of periods until payment or receipt.

Periods	Interest rates (r)									
(n)	1%	2%	3%	4%	5%	6%	7%	8%	9%	10%
1	0.990	0.980	0.971	0.962	0.952	0.943	0.935	0.926	0.917	0.909
2	0.980	0.961	0.943	0.925	0.907	0.890	0.873	0.857	0.842	0.826
3	0.971	0.942	0.915	0.889	0.864	0.840	0.816	0.794	0.772	0.751
4	0.961	0.924	0.888	0.855	0.823	0.792	0.763	0.735	0.708	0.683
5	0.951	0.906	0.863	0.822	0.784	0.747	0.713	0.681	0.650	0.621
6	0.942	0.888	0.837	0.790	0.746	0705	0.666	0.630	0.596	0.564
7	0.933	0.871	0.813	0.760	0.711	0.665	0.623	0.583	0.547	0.513
8	0.923	0.853	0.789	0.731	0.677	0.627	0.582	0.540	0.502	0.467
9	0.914	0.837	0.766	0.703	0.645	0.592	0.544	0.500	0.460	0.424
10	0.905	0.820	0.744	0.676	0.614	0.558	0.508	0.463	0.422	0.386
11	0.896	0.804	0.722	0.650	0.585	0.527	0.475	0.429	0.388	0.350
12	0.887	0.788	0.701	0.625	0.557	0.497	0.444	0.397	0.356	0.319
13	0.879	0.773	0.681	0.601	0.530	0.469	0.415	0.368	0.326	0.290
14	0.870	0.758	0.661	0.577	0.505	0.442	0.388	0.340	0.299	0.263
15	0.861	0.743	0.642	0.555	0.481	0.417	0.362	0.315	0.275	0.239
16	0.853	0.728	0.623	0.534	0.458	0.394	0.339	0.292	0.252	0.218
17	0.844	0.714	0.605	0.513	0.436	0.371	0.317	0.270	0.231	0.198
18	0.836	0.700	0.587	0.494	0.416	0.350	0.296	0.250	0.212	0.180
19	0.828	0.686	0.570	0.475	0.396	0.331	0.277	0.232	0.194	0.164
20	0.820	0.673	0.554	0.456	0.377	0.312	0.258	0.215	0.178	0.149

Periods	Interest rates (r)									
(n)	11%	12%	13%	14%	15%	16%	17%	18%	19%	20%
1	0.901	0.893	0.885	0.877	0.870	0.862	0.855	0.847	0.840	0.833
2	0.812	0.797	0.783	0.769	0.756	0.743	0.731	0.718	0.706	0.694
3	0.731	0.712	0.693	0.675	0.658	0.641	0.624	0.609	0.593	0.579
4	0.659	0.636	0.613	0.592	0.572	0.552	0.534	0.516	0.499	0.482
5	0.593	0.567	0.543	0.519	0.497	0.476	0.456	0.437	0.419	0.402
6	0.535	0.507	0.480	0.456	0.432	0.410	0.390	0.370	0.352	0.335
7	0.482	0.452	0.425	0.400	0.376	0.354	0.333	0.314	0.296	0.279
8	0.434	0.404	0.376	0.351	0.327	0.305	0.285	0.266	0.249	0.233
9	0.391	0.361	0.333	0.308	0.284	0.263	0.243	0.225	0.209	0.194
10	0.352	0.322	0.295	0.270	0.247	0.227	0.208	0.191	0.176	0.162
11	0.317	0.287	0.261	0.237	0.215	0.195	0.178	0.162	0.148	0.135
12	0.286	0.257	0.231	0.208	0.187	0.168	0.152	0.137	0.124	0.112
13	0.258	0.229	0.204	0.182	0.163	0.145	0.130	0.116	0.104	0.093
14	0.232	0.205	0.181	0.160	0.141	0.125	0.111	0.099	0.088	0.078
15	0.209	0.183	0.160	0.140	0.123	0.108	0.095	0.084	0.079	0.065
16	0.188	0.163	0.141	0.123	0.107	0.093	0.081	0.071	0.062	0.054
17	0.170	0.146	0.125	0.108	0.093	0.080	0.069	0.060	0.052	0.045
18	0.153	0.130	0.111	0.095	0.081	0.069	0.059	0.051	0.044	0.038
19	0.138	0.116	0.098	0.083	0.070	0.060	0.051	0.043	0.037	0.031
20	0.124	0.104	0.087	0.073	0.061	0.051	0.043	0.037	0.031	0.026

Cumulative present value of £1 per annum, Receivable or Payable at the end of each year for *n* years

$$\frac{1-(1+r)^{-n}}{r}$$

Periods (*n*)	Interest rates (*r*) 1%	2%	3%	4%	5%	6%	7%	8%	9%	10%
1	0.990	0.980	0.971	0.962	0.952	0.943	0.935	0.926	0.917	0.909
2	1.970	1.942	1.913	1.886	1.859	1.833	1.808	1.783	1.759	1.736
3	2.941	2.884	2.829	2.775	2.723	2.673	2.624	2.577	2.531	2.487
4	3.902	3.808	3.717	3.630	3.546	3.465	3.387	3.312	3.240	3.170
5	4.853	4.713	4.580	4.452	4.329	4.212	4.100	3.993	3.890	3.791
6	5.795	5.601	5.417	5.242	5.076	4.917	4.767	4.623	4.486	4.355
7	6.728	6.472	6.230	6.002	5.786	5.582	5.389	5.206	5.033	4.868
8	7.652	7.325	7.020	6.733	6.463	6.210	5.971	5.747	5.535	5.335
9	8.566	8.162	7.786	7.435	7.108	6.802	6.515	6.247	5.995	5.759
10	9.471	8.983	8.530	8.111	7.722	7.360	7.024	6.710	6.418	6.145
11	10.368	9.787	9.253	8.760	8.306	7.887	7.499	7.139	6.805	6.495
12	11.255	10.575	9.954	9.385	8.863	8.384	7.943	7.536	7.161	6.814
13	12.134	11.348	10.635	9.986	9.394	8.853	8.358	7.904	7.487	7.103
14	13.004	12.106	11.296	10.563	9.899	9.295	8.745	8.244	7.786	7.367
15	13.865	12.849	11.938	11.118	10.380	9.712	9.108	8.559	8.061	7.606
16	14.718	13.578	12.561	11.652	10.838	10.106	9.447	8.851	8.313	7.824
17	15.562	14.292	13.166	12.166	11.274	10.477	9.763	9.122	8.544	8.022
18	16.398	14.992	13.754	12.659	11.690	10.828	10.059	9.372	8.756	8.201
19	17.226	15.679	14.324	13.134	12.085	11.158	10.336	9.604	8.950	8.365
20	18.046	16.351	14.878	13.590	12.462	11.470	10.594	9.818	9.129	8.514

Periods (*n*)	Interest rates (*r*) 11%	12%	13%	14%	15%	16%	17%	18%	19%	20%
1	0.901	0.893	0.885	0.877	0.870	0.862	0.855	0.847	0.840	0.833
2	1.713	1.690	1.668	1.647	1.626	1.605	1.585	1.566	1.547	1.528
3	2.444	2.402	2.361	2.322	2.283	2.246	2.210	2.174	2.140	2.106
4	3.102	3.037	2.974	2.914	2.855	2.798	2.743	2.690	2.639	2.589
5	3.696	3.605	3.517	3.433	3.352	3.274	3.199	3.127	3.058	2.991
6	4.231	4.111	3.998	3.889	3.784	3.685	3.589	3.498	3.410	3.326
7	4.712	4.564	4.423	4.288	4.160	4.039	3.922	3.812	3.706	3.605
8	5.146	4.968	4.799	4.639	4.487	4.344	4.207	4.078	3.954	3.837
9	5.537	5.328	5.132	4.946	4.772	4.607	4.451	4.303	4.163	4.031
10	5.889	5.650	5.426	5.216	5.019	4.833	4.659	4.494	4.339	4.192
11	6.207	5.938	5.687	5.453	5.234	5.029	4.836	4.656	4.486	4.327
12	6.492	6.194	5.918	5.660	5.421	5.197	4.988	7.793	4.611	4.439
13	6.750	6.424	6.122	5.842	5.583	5.342	5.118	4.910	4.715	4.533
14	6.982	6.628	6.302	6.002	5.724	5.468	5.229	5.008	4.802	4.611
15	7.191	6.811	6.462	6.142	5.847	5.575	5.324	5.092	4.876	4.675
16	7.379	6.974	6.604	6.265	5.954	5.668	5.405	5.162	4.938	4.730
17	7.549	7.120	6.729	6.373	6.047	5.749	5.475	5.222	4.990	4.775
18	7.702	7.250	6.840	6.467	6.128	5.818	5.534	5.273	5.033	4.812
19	7.839	7.366	6.938	6.550	6.198	5.877	5.584	5.316	5.070	4.843
20	7.963	7.469	7.025	6.623	6.259	5.929	5.628	5.353	5.101	4.870

FORMULAE

Annuity

Present value of an annuity of £1 per annum, receivable or payable for *n* years, commencing in one year, discounted at *r*% per annum:

$$PV = \frac{1}{r}\left[1 - \frac{1}{[1+r]^n}\right]$$

Perpetuity

Present value of £1 per annum, payable or receivable in perpetuity, commencing in one year, discounted at *r*% per annum:

$$PV = \frac{1}{r}$$

Growing perpetuity

Present value of £1 per annum, receivable or payable, commencing in one year, growing in perpetuity at a constant rate of *g*% per annum, discounted at *r*% per annum:

$$PV = \frac{1}{r - g}$$

The Examiner for IFRP offers to future candidates and to lecturers using this booklet for study purposes, the following background and guidance on the questions included in this examination paper.

Section A – compulsory

Question One provides a selection of 10 multiple-choice sub-questions, designed to cover the whole of the IFRP syllabus and to test candidates' knowledge, understanding and application.

Section B – compulsory

Question Two: The preparation of consolidated financial statements will always be a key component of this question paper. This question tests the following learning outcomes:

- *Explain the difference between the closing rate/net investment method and the temporal method.*
- *Prepare a consolidated balance sheet and a consolidated profit and loss account for a group of companies.*
- *Explain and apply foreign currency translation principles.*
- *Explain and apply the concept of fair value at the point of acquisition.*

Section C – two questions from four

Question Three requires candidates to assess the extent to which financial statements provide a reliable source of comparison between two companies, and to identify appropriate adjustments that might be made to render comparison more meaningful. The question tests the following learning outcomes:

- *Evaluate financial statements and prepare a concise report on the results of the analysis.*
- *Identify the limitations of analysis based on financial statements.*
- *Explain the weaknesses of the financial report which reduce ifs effectiveness in communicating meaningful information to users.*

Question Four tests the ability of candidates to identify the appropriate accounting treatment for three complex transactions. The question tests the following learning outcome:

- *Explain the principle of profit measurement and alternative approaches to asset valuations.*

Question Five: As candidates have spent a considerable part of their study time on consolidated accounts, there will usually be an optional question on this topic in Section C to supplement the compulsory question in Section B. This question tests the following learning outcomes:

- *Explain the conditions required for an undertaking to be a subsidiary or an associate of a group.*
- *Prepare a consolidated profit and loss account for a group of companies.*

Question Six requires candidates to communicate the financial reporting implications of three key issues to a superior. An ability to do this is an important skill for a chartered management accountant at this level. The question tests the following learning outcomes:

- *Identify major differences between UK GAAP, IASs and US GAAP.*
- *Explain and apply the concept of fair value at the point of acquisition.*
- *Explain the problems of profit measurement and alternative approaches to asset valuations.*
- *Discuss the principle of substance over form to a range of transactions.*
- *Discuss emerging developments in financial reporting evidenced by discussion and exposure drafts issued by Regulatory bodies.*

CIMA

The Examiner's Answers for Financial Reporting – UK Accounting Standards

SECTION A

Answers to Question One

1.1	A	(B)	C	D
1.2	(A)	B	C	D
1.3	A	B	(C)	D
1.4	A	B	(C)	D
1.5	A	(B)	C	D
1.6	A	B	(C)	D
1.7	A	(B)	C	D
1.8	A	(B)	C	D
1.9	(A)	B	C	D
1.10	(A)	B	C	D

Answers to Objective Test Questions requiring calculations

1.1 The unrealised profit is made by the parent, so there is no minority interest. The correct amount is £360,000 x $^{33}/_{133}$ = £90,000.

Therefore the correct answer is B

1.2 The goodwill on consolidation would be £16 million - 75% [£14 million + (£10 million - £8 million) + £1 million].

Therefore the correct answer is A

1.3 The amount of profit that would be included is 40% [£1,100,000 - £600,000] + 30% [£1,100,000 - £800,000] = £290,000.

Therefore the correct answer is C

1.4 The reconciliation of the movement in the minority interest account is as follows:

	£000
Opening balance	6,600
Profit for the year	2,500
Disposal [25% x £4·4 million]	(1,100)
Dividend paid [balancing figure]	(800)
Closing balance	7,200

Therefore the correct answer is C

1.7 The earnings attributable to the equity shareholders are £20 million [£25 million - £5 million]. The number of shares to be used in the calculation is 80 million [the closing number of shares]. Therefore the earnings per share figure is 25 pence.

Therefore the correct answer is B

1.8 The total impairment loss is £51 million [£120 million - £69 million]. It is allocated in the following order:

- To the obviously impaired plant £20 million [£25 million - £5 million].
- To the goodwill £20 million.
- To the licence £4 million [£10 million - £6 million].
- To the other tangible fixed assets £7 million [the balance, since the net current assets are already at the lower of cost and net realisable value].

Therefore the new carrying value of the fixed assets is £43 million [£50 million - £7 million].

Therefore the correct answer is B

1.10 A reconciliation of the net pension liability is as follows:

	£m
Opening balance	30
Current service cost	52
Unwinding of discount	10
Expected return on assets	(25)
Contributions payable	(30)
Actuarial gain [balancing figure]	(2)
Closing balance	35

The curtailment is ignored since it has no overall effect on the net pension liability.

Therefore the correct answer is A

SECTION B

Answer to Question Two

Requirement (a)

Translation of Balance Sheet of West Ltd

Description		*Monetary amount*	
	AFrm	*Rate*	*£m*
Intangible fixed assets (W1)	–	N/A	–
Tangible fixed assets (W1)	125	2·4	52·1
Stocks	50	2·4	20·8
Debtors	60	2·4	25·0
Trade creditors	(30)	2·4	(12·5)
Tax payable	(15)	2·4	(6·3)
Bank overdraft	(20)	2·4	(8·3)
Long term loans	(60)	2·4	(25·0)
Deferred tax	(12)	2·4	(5·0)
	98		40·8
Share capital	60	2·4	25·0
Profit and loss account:			
Pre-acquisition (W1)	33	2·4	13·7
Post-acquisition (W1)	5	2·4	2·1
	98		40·8

Consolidated Balance Sheet of East plc at 30 September 2004

	£m	*£m*
Fixed assets:		
Intangible assets [W4]	3·3	
Tangible assets [100 million + 52·1 million]	152·1	
		155·4
Current assets:		
Stocks [40 million + 20·8 million - 2 million (W2)]	58·8	
Debtors [45 million + 25 million - 6 million (W2)]	64·0	
Cash and bank balances	15·0	
	137·8	
Creditors falling due within one year:		
Trade creditors [25 million + 12·5 million - 6 million (W2)]	31·5	
Tax payable [10 million + 6·3 million]	16·3	
Bank overdraft	8·3	
	56·1	
Net current assets		81·7
Creditors falling due after more than one year:		
Long term loans [50 million + 25 million]		(75·0)
Provisions for liabilities and charges:		
Deferred tax [15 million + 5 million]		(20·0)
		142·1

Capital and reserves:

Called up share capital [£1 shares]	75·0
Profit and loss account [W5]	56·9
	131·9
Minority interest [W3]	10·2
	142·1

Workings

[W1] – *Net assets table*	*Date of acquisition AFrm*	*Balance sheet date AFrm*
Share capital	60	60
Profit and loss account:		
Per accounts of West Ltd	25	53
Accounting policy adjustment	(12)	(20)
Fair value adjustment	20	5
Net assets for the consolidation	93	98

[W2] – *Adjustment for intra-group sales*

- Reduce stocks and consolidated reserves by £2 million.
- Reduce trade debtors and trade creditors by £6 million.

[W3] – *Minority interest*

- East plcowns 45 million out of 60 million shares so the minority interest is 25%.
- The minority interest at 30 September 2004 is 25% x £40·8 million = **£10·2 million**

[W4] – *Goodwill on consolidation*

- The cost of investment in West Ltd (in AFr) is 81 million (45 million x 1·8).
- So the total goodwill in AFr is 81 million – 75% x 93 million (W1) = **11·3 million**
- Translated into £s at AFr 2·4 to £1 gives £4·7 million.
- The unamortised amount at 30 September 2004 is $^{7}/_{10}$ x £4·7 million = **£3·3 million**

[W5] – *Consolidated reserves*	*£m*
Reserves of East plc– per draft financial statements	52·0
Exchange gain on investment in West Ltd [W6]	6·7
75% of post-acquisition reserves of West Ltd in £s	1·6
Amortisation of goodwill [$^{3}/_{10}$ x £4·7 million (W4)]	(1·4)
Unrealised profit in stock [W2]	(2·0)
	56·9

[W6] – *Exchange gain on investment in West Ltd*	*£m*
AFr 81 million (W4) translated at AFr 3 to £1	27·0
AFr 81 million translated at AFr 2·4 to £1	33·7
Exchange gain	6·7

Requirement (b)

Translation of profit and loss account of West Ltd

Description		*Monetary amount*	
	AFrm	*Rate*	*£m*
Turnover	240	2·5	96
Cost of sales	(145)	2·5	(58)
Gross profit	95	2·5	38
Other operating expenses	(40)	2·5	(16)
Operating profit	55	2·5	22
Interest payable	(10)	2·5	(4)
Profit before tax	45	2·5	18
Tax	(15)	2·5	(6)
Profit after tax	30	2·5	12
Dividends	(15)	2·5	(6)
Retained profit	15	2·5	6

Consolidated profit and loss account of North plc

	£m
Turnover [200 million + 96 million - 12 million (W1)]	284
Cost of sales [Balancing figure]	(170)
Gross profit [80 million + 38 million - 4 million (W2)]	114
Other operating expenses [35 million + 16 million + 0·5 million (W3)]	(51·5)
Operating profit	62·5
Interest payable [7·5 million + 4 million]	(11·5)
Profit before tax	51
Tax [10 million + 6 million]	(16)
Profit after tax	35
Minority interest [W4]	(2·5)
Group profit	32·5
Dividends [East plc only]	(16)
Retained profit	16·5

Workings

[W1] – *Intra-group sales*

- Sales and purchases are reduced by £12 million
- Closing stock is reduced by £2 million so the net effect on cost of sales is to reduce it by £10 million.

[W2] – *Gross profit*

- Reduced by £2 million unrealised profit [W1].
- Reduced by one year's extra depreciation of £2 million [(20 million x ¼)/2·5]
- Total reduction £4 million.

[W3] – *Other operating expenses*

- Total goodwill on consolidation is AFr 11·3 million [W4 to BS].
- One year's amortisation [in £s] is (11·3 x $^1/_{10}$)/2·5 = **£0·5 million**

[W4] – *Minority Interest*

- The profit after tax of West Ltd in AFr is 30 million.
- The extra depreciation necessary due to the fair value adjustment is 5 million (see [W2] above.
- So the MI in AFr is 25% [30 million - 5 million] = 6·25 million.
- The MI in £ is 6·25/2·5 = £2·5 million.

SECTION C

Answer to Question Three

Requirement (a)

A key factor that needs to be borne in mind before making decisions based on the financial statements of two companies is the extent to which the companies and the financial statements can be validly compared with each other. Factors that need to be considered can be divided into two:

1 – Differences in operating environments
Before comparing the performance of companies, it is essential to consider the extent to which the businesses they are engaged in are similar. A number of aspects of financial performance will depend on the business sector. One example would be the profit margin of a company. If the company operates in a sector where customers are prepared to pay a high price for high quality goods, then a high profit margin would be expected. On the other hand, if the company operated in a sector where price competition is intense, then a lower margin would be expected, with perhaps a higher sales volume to compensate.

A further aspect relating to the operating environments might be the ownership structure of the company. If the company is part of a group, it might have a ready market for its product through fellow subsidiaries that are required by the parent to do business with the company. This would put such a company at a competitive advantage compared with a company that was not able to secure such a "ready market" for its products.

2 – Differences in financial statement preparation
Despite the regulatory framework that exists, many of the amounts included in financial statements can vary depending on the accounting policies followed by the directors. This is partly because of the fact that some Accounting Standards allow for alternative treatments and partly because there still exist areas of accounting that are not subject to Accounting Standards. Furthermore, where Accounting Standards do exist they tend to be principles-based and, as such, subject to interpretation when they are applied. Even where companies are following the same accounting policies, there are many figures in the financial statements [depreciation of fixed assets for example] that are based on the estimates of management. These estimates can vary considerably from company to company, even where the operating environments are similar and so ought to be the same.

Requirement (b)

First change – leasehold interest in property
The leasehold interest of Alpha Ltd could easily have been classified as a finance lease and were this classification to be adopted the financial statements of the two companies would be more comparable. Suggested adjustments are to:

- Reduce cost of sales by £250,000 [£160,000 + £240,000 (£12 million x $^{1}/_{50}$) - £150,000].
- Increase interest payable by £420,000.
- Net reduction in profit £170,000.

Second change – interest on long term loans
- Charging the profit and loss account of Alpha Ltd with loan interest based on market rates would make the financial statements of the two companies more comparable.
- This change would increase the interest payable of Alpha Ltd by £210,000 [£7 million x (6 - 3)%].

Third change – intra-group sales at inflated prices

- Showing the sales revenue that Alpha Ltd would earn on the sale of such products outside the group would make the financial statements more comparable.
- The goods that Alpha Ltd sold to Beta Ltd in the year to 31 March 2004 cost £6 million [40% x £15 million]. A more normal selling price for these goods would have been £12 million [$^{100}/_{50}$ x £6 million]. The gross profit on these goods would have been £6 million [50% x £12 million] rather than the actual figure of £9 million [60% x £15 million]
- Therefore decrease the pre-tax profits of Alpha Ltd by £3 million [£9 million - £6 million].

Fourth change – administration expenses

- Since Beta Ltd would have paid £1·5 million for these services it makes sense to adjust the profits of Alpha Ltd by this amount to make them comparable.

Summary – reduction in pre- and post-tax profits and EPS calculation

	£000
Leasehold	(170)
Loan interest	(210)
Intra-group sale	(3,000)
Management fee	(1,500)
Pre-tax effect	(4,880)
Tax effect (30%)	1,464
Post-tax effect	(3,416)
Published post-tax profit	4,710
Revised post-tax profit	1,294
Number of shares in issue ('000)	3,000
So revised EPS =	**43·1p**

Requirement (c)

Report

To: The Directors of Investor plc

From: Management Accountant

Since both companies have the same number of shares in issue throughout the year, then an analysis of the earnings per share figures of the two companies can be based on their relative profitabilities. In the absence of balance sheet information for the two companies, the analysis needs to be restricted to a comparison of their profit margins. A meaningful comparison is only possible after adjustments have been made to render the financial statements of Alpha Ltd comparable with those of Beta Ltd. The comments that follow are based on an analysis of the **adjusted** financial statements of Alpha Ltd.

The appendix shows that all the margins of Beta Ltd are superior to those of Alpha Ltd, but the most significant factor is the much higher net profit margin of Beta Ltd relative to Alpha Ltd. This, in turn, is caused by the higher operating costs of Alpha Ltd. In fact the gross profit margin of Alpha Ltd [even after adjustments] is superior to that of Beta Ltd. All in all, the performance of Alpha Ltd is inferior to that of Beta Ltd, and this fact is hidden in the audited financial statements.

Appendix – relevant accounting ratios

	Alpha Ltd	*Beta Ltd*
Net profit margin	2,750/(42,000 - 3,000) = **7·1%**	5,500/44,000 = **12·5%**
Gross profit margin	19,250/39,000 = **49·4%**	19,500/44,000 = **44·3%**
Other operating expenses/sales	(15,000 + 1,500/39,000) = **42·3%**	14,000/44,000 = **31·8%**

Workings – adjustments to Alpha Ltd figures

[W1] – *profit before interest*	*£000*
Per accounts	7,000
Effect of leasehold adjustment	250
Effect of favourable terms of trade	(3,000)
Effect of management fee	(1,500)
Revised for comparability	2,750

[W2] – *gross profit*	*£000*
Per accounts:	22,000
Effect of leasehold adjustment	250
Effect of favourable terms of trade	(3,000)
Revised for comparability	19,250

Answer to Question Four

First issue

It is necessary to make a provision for the financial effects of the closure in the current year's financial statements. This is because FRS 12 – *Provisions, Contingent Liabilities and Contingent Assets* – requires provisions to be made for the unavoidable consequences of events occurring before the balance sheet date. In this case, the steps taken before the balance sheet date have effectively committed the company to the closure.

The basic principle laid down in FRS 12 is that provision should be made for the direct costs associated with the closure. On this basis, the expected redundancy costs and the contract termination costs [total £20 million + £5 million = £25 million] should be provided for. A further cost associated with the closure is the cost of terminating the pension rights of the employees who accept redundancy [£10 million]. FRS 17 – *Retirement Benefits* – requires that the costs of settlement or curtailment of pension rights are a one-off amount that should be recognised in the profit and loss account of a contributing company. Given that a provision is appropriate, then this cost should be recognised.

The costs of redeployment and retraining are an ongoing cost associated with the continuing business and FRS 12 specifically states that restructuring provisions should not include those items.

The anticipated losses on the sale of plant are not part of the provision as such, but provide *prima facie* evidence of impairment in value and so the fixed assets should probably be written down to their recoverable amount of £1 million. The provision should not be reduced by the anticipated profit on sale of the property.

The treatment of expected operating losses is a little unclear. FRS 12 states that a provision is inappropriate unless the losses are anticipated to arise on an onerous contract. This is because they basically relate to future events rather than past events. However, FRS 3 – *Reporting Financial Performance* – states that where a binding commitment has been made to sell or terminate an operation any provision should include future expected operating losses. It may be that the more specific mention of the issue in FRS 3 overrides the general prohibition that is contained in FRS 12.

Given the fact that the provision is likely to be material and non-recurring, then FRS 3 would require that it be separately disclosed on the face of the profit and loss account as an exceptional item.

A further issue to consider is the reporting of the results of the business segment. The closure of the segment is due to be completed within two months of the year end. Provided the closure constitutes a major change in the nature and focus of operations for Flexible then it would appear that, under the provisions of FRS 3, the results of the business segment for the year to October 2004 need to be separately disclosed on the face of the profit and loss account as a discontinued operation.

Second issue

It is not yet appropriate to record the planned investment that is due to take place in 2005, unless the company has entered into irrevocable obligations by the balance sheet date. Based on the evidence provided this does not appear to be the case. The only commitment that the company has entered into prior to the balance sheet date is to purchase 50 million Euros for £35 million. Based on the exchange rate at 31 October 2004, this is a financial asset that has been acquired at no cost. Current UK Accounting Standards do not require such financial instruments [known as derivative financial instruments] to be recognised in financial statements. However, FRS 13 – *Financial Instruments – Disclosure* – does require disclosure both of the use of derivatives as a risk management tool and their market value at the year end.

Third issue

The unrealised profit of £1 million would need to be eliminated from the consolidated stock figure and charged against the ownership interests in the consolidated balance sheet. Since the profit is made by a subsidiary, the charge to ownership interests would be allocated between the parent and the minority unless the subsidiary is wholly owned.

The adjustment for unrealised profit creates a timing difference because the current tax position of the group is unaffected by the provision, or by its reversal, when the stock is sold outside the group. The same applies to the tax loss because no tax relief has yet been given, but relief will be available in the future against taxable profits. The total timing difference is £5 million [£1 million + £4 million] and the potential deferred tax is £1·5 million [30% x £5 million].

Since the deferred tax amount is a deferred tax asset, then the question of recoverability arises. FRS 19 – *Deferred Taxation* – states that deferred tax assets can be carried forward where recovery is assured beyond reasonable doubt. In this case, recoverability depends on the availability of taxable profits in the future to absorb the timing differences. It would appear from the information given that these will be available for the subsidiary. The deferred tax asset will be shown in current assets and should not be offset against deferred tax credit balances unless they relate to the same tax jurisdiction.

Answer to Question Five

Requirement (a)

The initial purchase of shares in Charvis Ltd in 1997 made Hansen plc a 75% shareholder. Since all shares carry the same voting rights, then this gave Hansen plc voting control over Charvis Ltd and under the provisions of FRS 2 – *Subsidiary undertakings* – Charvis Ltd would be regarded as a subsidiary of Hansen plc and line by line consolidated.

On 1 April 2004, the sale of 3 million shares reduced the shareholding in Charvis Ltd to 25%. Unless Hansen plc was able to continue to exercise a dominant influence over Charvis Ltd, then this disposal would result in Charvis Ltd ceasing to be a subsidiary of Hansen plc. The circumstances appear to indicate that Hansen plc exercises a significant influence over the operating and financial policies of Charvis Ltd from 1 April 2004 and so under the provisions of FRS 9 – *Associates and joint ventures* – Charvis Ltd would be regarded as an associate from that date. This means that for the second half of the current year Charvis Ltd would be consolidated under the equity method of accounting.

Requirement (b)

Consolidated profit and loss account – year ended 30 September 2004

	£000	*£000*
Turnover [60,000 + 45,000 + 35,000 x $^{6}/_{12}$ - 1,500 (W1)]		121,000
Cost of sales [30,000 + 25,000 + 19,000 x $^{6}/_{12}$]		(64,500)
Gross profit		56,500
Other operating expenses [15,000 + 10,000 + 8,000 x $^{6}/_{12}$ - 1,500 (W1) + (100 + 60 x $^{6}/_{12}$ - (W2)]		(27,630)
Operating profit		28,870
Share of operating profit of associate [W5]		990
Interest payable:		
Group [5,000 + 4,000 + 3,000 x $^{6}/_{12}$]	10,500	
Associate [3,000 x $^{6}/_{12}$ x 25%]	375	
		(10,875)
Gain on sale of shares in Charvis Ltd [W3]		1,960
Profit before tax		20,945
Tax:		
Group [3,500 + 2,000 + 1,800 x $^{6}/_{12}$]	6,400	
Associate [1,800 x $^{6}/_{12}$ x 25%]	225	
		(6,625)
Profit after tax		14,320
Minority interest [4,000 x 20% + 3,200 x $^{6}/_{12}$ x 25%]		(1,200)
Group profit		13,120
Dividends paid [Hansen plc only]		(4,500)
Retained profit		8,620

Workings

[W1] – *Intra-group turnover and costs (£000)*
£1,000 + £1,000 x $^{0}/_{12}$ = **£1,500**

[W2] – *Goodwill on acquisition*	*Williams Ltd*		*Charvis Ltd*	
	£000	*£000*	*£000*	*£000*
Cost of investment		10,800		8,700
Net assets at date of acquisition:				
Share capital	5,000		6,000	
Profit and loss account	6,000		4,000	
	11,000		10,000	
Group share [80%/75%]		(8,800)		(7,500)
So total goodwill [amortised over 20 years]		2,000		1,200
So one year's amortisation equals		100		60

[W3] – *Gain on sale of shares in Charvis Ltd*	*£000*
Disposal proceeds [£3·50 x 3 million]	10,500
Reduction in carrying value of net assets [W4]	(8,000)
Unamortised goodwill relating to the disposal [£1,200 x $^{13.5}/_{20}$ x $^{2}/_{3}$ [W4]]	(540)
So gain on sale equals	1,960

[W4] – *Reduction in carrying value of net assets of Charvis Ltd at the date of sale*	*£000*
Share capital	6,000
Profit and loss reserve:	
At 1 October 2003	10,000
$^{6}/_{12}$ x profit after tax for the current year	1,600
Dividends paid prior to date of disposal	(1,600)
	16,000
Relating to disposal [75% - 25% = 50%]	8,000

NB: $^{50}/_{75}$ of the unamortised goodwill relates to the disposal

[W5] – *share of operating profit of Charvis Ltd as an associate*	*£000*
8,000 x 25% x $^{6}/_{12}$	1,000
Amortisation of goodwill [£1,200 x $^{1}/_{20}$ x $^{25}/_{75}$ x $^{6}/_{12}$]	(10)
	990

Answer to Question Six

Issue 1

You are correct that our 2004 financial statements should comply with UK Financial Reporting Standards [FRSs]. For UK companies, compliance with UK FRSs provides *prima facie* evidence that financial statements show a true and fair view, a legal requirement under the UK Companies Act. The current position is that if a UK FRS differs in its requirements from an international FRS, then the requirement of the UK FRS prevails for UK companies.

All this will change from 2005 because, from this date, all companies that are incorporated in the European Union and that file consolidated accounts will have to prepare those financial statements in accordance with International Financial Reporting Standards [IFRSs]. This regulation applies first to accounting periods ending on 31 December 2005. This does have implications for 2004, because the 2005 financial statements will need to have comparative figures for 2004 that are IFRS compliant. Therefore, a balance sheet under IFRSs is required for 1 January 2004 – this is not a future issue, but a current one. The implications of 2007 are that EU member states who currently file financial statements under US GAAP are permitted to postpone application of IFRS's until 2007 if they wish, but it does not appear that the UK will exercise this option.

As a consequence of the European Union regulation, the UK Accounting Standards Board is currently engaged in an exercise that compares its existing Standards to the International equivalents. Attempts are being made to converge the two sets of Standards and recent output from the ASB suggests that, in many cases, changes will be made to existing UK Standards to align them more closely with their international counterparts.

A further reason for IFRS's being relevant to our group is that a number of stock exchanges around the world allow filed financial statements to be in compliance with IFRS's. The facility is not of particular value to us in the UK, but if we seek listings in other jurisdictions then using IFRS compliant financial statements is likely to save us time and money. However, not all jurisdictions offer this facility, for example the US Securities and Exchange Commission currently requires that all companies seeking a listing file financial statements that are compliant with US GAAP.

Issue 2

You are correct in your conclusion that any allowable provisions have the effect of increasing the purchased goodwill figure. This is because provisions, being liabilities, have the effect of reducing the net assets at the date of acquisition that are used to compare with the cost of acquisition. However, under FRS 7 – *Fair values in acquisition accounting* – provisions for future operating losses cannot be included as pre-acquisition liabilities because they relate to post-acquisition events and so should reduce post-acquisition earnings. More generally, FRS 12 – *Provisions and contingencies* – only allows provisions for future operating losses where they arise under an onerous contract. This requirement is based on the principle that future losses relate to future events and provisions should be made only for the consequences of past events.

As far as purchased goodwill is concerned, the normal accounting treatment under UK GAAP [FRS 10] is to amortise it over its useful economic life. There is a presumption in FRS 10 that this will be no more than 20 years, but the presumption can be rebutted if the durability of the acquired business can be demonstrated. In fact, FRS 10 allows for the possibility that purchased goodwill has an infinite useful economic life and can be left in the balance sheet of the acquiring company or group as a permanent item. If purchased goodwill is amortised over a period of longer than 20 years [or not amortised at all] then FRS 10 requires that it be reviewed annually for impairment. The International Accounting Standards Board has published a proposal that non-amortisation of goodwill with an annual impairment test be regarded as the standard treatment. This proposal, if adopted, would affect our future financial statements for the reasons outlined in *Issue 1*.

Issue 3

There are two separate matters to consider here. The first is the finance cost that is reported in the profit and loss account. FRS 4 – *Capital Instruments* – states that the total finance cost is the total amount payable to the providers of the finance minus the net amount receivable from them. Therefore the finance cost includes the premium payable on repayment as well as the actual interest. The finance cost needs to be recognised over the term of the relevant instrument – the period from the date of issue to the date of repayment. FRS 4 further states that the recognition of the finance cost on convertible instruments, like the one you are describing, should be on the same basis as non-convertible instruments and take no account whatever of the likelihood, or otherwise, of conversion.

The second issue is the classification of the instrument. FRS 4 states that capital instruments should be classified as liabilities, if they carry an obligation for the issuer to transfer economic benefits to the investor. Unless, or until, the holders of the convertible stock exercise their option to convert, this obligation exists and so the instrument should be shown as a borrowing rather than in equity. However, the UK ASB has issued an exposure draft that proposes regarding convertible loans as a combination of two simpler instruments:

- A non-convertible loan, shown as a liability.
- An option to purchase shares, shown as equity.

This is in line with current international practice.

CIMA

November 2004 Examinations

Intermediate Level

Financial Reporting – International Standards

(IFRI – Paper 7b)

Question Paper	1
Examiner's Brief Guide to the Paper	20
Examiner's Answers	21

The answers published here have been written by the Examiner and should provide a helpful guide for both lecturers and students.

Published separately on the CIMA website (www.cimaglobal.com/students) from the end of March 2005 is a Post Examination Guide for this paper, which provides much valuable and complementary material including indicative mark information.

INTERNATIONAL STANDARDS INTERNATIONAL STANDARDS INTERNATIONAL

CIMA

Intermediate Level

Financial Reporting – International Accounting Standards

7b

IFRI

24 November 2004

Wednesday morning

INSTRUCTIONS TO CANDIDATES

Read this page before you look at the questions

You are allowed three hours to answer this question paper.
This question paper is based on INTERNATIONAL ACCOUNTING STANDARDS. **If you require the paper based on UK Accounting Standards, please speak immediately to the invigilator.**
Answer the ONE question in Section A (this has 10 sub-questions). Answer the ONE question in Section B. Answer TWO questions only from Section C.
Maths Tables and Formulae are provided.

SECTION A — 20 MARKS

ANSWER *ALL* TEN SUB-QUESTIONS – TWO MARKS EACH

Question One

1.1 A owns 80% of the equity shares of its subsidiary, B. The year-ends of both entities are 30 September. On 25 September 2004, A sold goods to B at an invoiced price of $360,000. These goods were included in the inventory of B at 30 September 2004. The goods were invoiced by A at cost plus $^1/_3$.

Assuming this is the first intra-group sale made by either entity, what will be the required provision for unrealised profit in the consolidated balance sheet of the A group at 30 September 2004?

A $72,000

B $90,000

C $96,000

D $120,000

1.2 On 30 June 2004, C purchased 75% of the equity shares of D for $16 million. The balance sheet of D showed net assets of $14 million. This was before taking account of the following items:

- The market value of D's properties at 30 June 2004 [included in the balance sheet of D at a carrying value of $8 million] was $10 million.
- On 30 June 2004, D was in the process of negotiating an insurance claim in respect of inventory that was damaged before that date. The claim was for $1 million and, although nothing has yet been received, the directors of D are confident that the claim will be successful.

What is the goodwill on consolidation that will appear in the consolidated balance sheet of C at 30 June 2004?

A $3·25 million

B $4 million

C $4·75 million

D $5·5 million

1.3 E has made share purchases in F as follows:

Date	*% of equity shares of F purchased*	*Balance on accumulated profits of F at date shares purchased*
		$000
30 June 1997	40	600
30 June 2000	30	800

On 31 March 2004, the accumulated profits balance of F stood at $1·1 million.

Ignoring amortisation of goodwill what will be included in the consolidated accumulated profits of the E group in respect of F at 31 March 2004? All equity shares in F carry one vote per share.

A $200,000

B $210,000

C $290,000

D $410,000

1.4 The following data relates to the G group:

- The opening and closing balances on the minority interest account were $6·6 and $7·2 million respectively.
- The minority interest in the profits for the year was $2·5 million.
- During the year the group disposed of a 75% owned subsidiary. The net assets of the subsidiary at the date of disposal were $4·4 million. Unamortised goodwill relating to the subsidiary at the date of disposal was $400,000. The subsidiaries of G had no dividends payable included in payables at the start, or at the end, of the year.

What is the dividend paid to the minority shareholders during the year?

A $400,000

B $600,000

C $800,000

D $2,500,000

1.5 H owns 40% of the equity shares of its associate J. Both entities prepare financial statements to 30 September.

On 28 September 2004, H sold goods to J on which H recorded a profit of $40,000. All these goods were unsold by J at 30 September 2004.

What is the consolidation adjustment that will be made in the consolidated accounts of H at 30 September 2004 in respect of this inter-entity sale?

A	Debit reserves $16,000	Credit inventory	$16,000
B	Debit reserves $16,000	Credit investment in J	$16,000
C	Debit reserves $40,000	Credit inventory	$40,000
D	Debit reserves $40,000	Credit investment in J	$40,000

1.6 The following statements allegedly refer to the conclusions to be drawn when using ratio analysis to interpret the financial statements of an entity using ratio analysis:

(i) An entity can only increase its gross profit margin by increasing its sales prices or reducing its overall costs of production.

(ii) Revaluing non-current assets upwards would [other things being equal] lead to a reduction in the return on capital employed.

(iii) An entity can increase its return on capital employed in the short term by postponing replacement of non-current assets.

Which of the statements are true?

A (i) and (ii) only.

B (i) and (iii) only.

C (ii) and (iii) only.

D All of them.

1.7 A public entity reported a profit after tax of $25 million for its year ended 30 September 2004. During the year, the following amounts were appropriated to the shareholders:

- $5 million to the non-equity shareholders.
- $12 million to the equity shareholders.

On 1 October 2003, the entity had 50 million equity shares in issue. Then, on 1 April 2004, the entity made a bonus issue to the equity shareholders of 3 equity shares for every 5 currently held. The entity had 40 million non-equity shares in issue for the whole of the year ended 30 September 2004.

What is the earnings per share figure for the year ended 30 September 2004 that will need to be reported in the financial statements in order to comply with IAS 33 – *Earnings per Share* [ignoring comparatives and assuming that no calculations of the diluted earnings per share are needed]?

A 15 cents

B 25 cents

C 30·77 cents

D 31·25 cents

1.8 A public entity is reviewing goodwill arising on a prior acquisition for impairment. The goodwill is in respect of a business that is a single cash generating unit. The net assets of the cash generating unit immediately before the impairment review were as follows:

Item	*Carrying value prior to impairment review*
	$m
Goodwill on acquisition	20
Production licence	10
Specialist plant	25
Other tangible non-current assets	50
Net current assets	15
	120

The impairment review revealed that the unit had a value in use of $69 million. Further investigations revealed the following:

- The production licence has no market value, but is expected to generate future economic benefits for the entity.
- The specialist plant had been damaged by a water leak and cannot be used in the business. It can be sold for scrap for $5 million.
- The net current assets are already stated at the lower of cost and net realisable value.

Assuming none of the other tangible non-current assets has a net realisable value that is greater than their carrying value, what is the carrying value of the other tangible non-current assets immediately after the impairment review has been reflected in the financial statements?

A $31·76 million

B $40·84 million

C $49 million

D $50 million

1.9 An entity prepares financial statements to 30 June each year. On 1 July 2003, the entity issued 20 million $1 loan notes at 95 cents. The loan notes attract annual interest at 5% and are redeemable on 30 June 2008 at $1·20. Alternatively, the notes can be converted into equity shares [at the option of the note-holder] on 30 June 2008. The entity paid professional fees of $200,000 in connection with the issue and estimate that the cost of staff time in connection with the issue was $100,000.

Under the principles of IAS 39 – *Financial Instruments: Recognition and Measurement* – which of the following statements regarding the loan notes is true?

A The issue costs are $200,000 and in the financial statements the loan would be presented partly as a payable and partly as equity.

B The issue costs are $200,000 and in the financial statements the loan would be presented as a payable.

C The issue costs are $300,000 and in the financial statements the loan would be presented as a payable.

D The issue costs are $300,000 and in the financial statements the loan would be presented partly as a payable and partly as equity.

1.10 An entity contributes to a defined benefit pension scheme. On 1 July 2003, the net pension liability that was included in its balance sheet was $30 million. This liability was re-measured at 30 June 2004 at $35 million [before allowing for actuarial gains or losses arising in the year ended 30 June 2004].

You are given the following information relevant to the pension scheme for the year ended 30 June 2004:

- The current service cost was $52 million.
- The expected return on assets was $25 million.
- The unwinding of discount on the pension liability was $10 million.
- The entity closed down a division and the pension scheme paid a lump sum of $15 million in settlement of the accrued pension rights of employees affected by the closure. This figure was based on the actuarially determined liability to the relevant employees at the date of the closure.
- The entity paid contributions of $30 million into the scheme.
- No amortisation of unrecognised actuarial gains and losses was required for the year ended 30 June 2004.

What is the actuarial gain or loss on the scheme for the year ended 30 June 2004?

A A gain of $2 million

B A gain of $17 million

C A loss of $2 million

D A loss of $13 million

(Total = 20 marks)

End of Section A

SECTION B – 30 MARKS

ANSWER THIS QUESTION

Question Two

East is an entity incorporated in Asia. East has a subsidiary, West, that is located in Africa and prepares its financial statements under local accounting standards. West prepares its financial statements in African Francs (AFr). Financial information relating to the two entities for the financial year ended 30 September 2004 is given below:

Balance sheets at 30 September 2004	*East*		*West*	
	$m	*$m*	*AFrm*	*AFrm*
ASSETS				
Non-current assets:				
Property, plant and equipment [Note 1]	100		120	
Intangible assets [Note 2]	-		20	
Investments [Note 3]	27		-	
		127		140
Current assets:				
Inventories [Note 4]	40		50	
Receivables	45		60	
Cash and bank balances	15		-	
		100		110
		227		250
EQUITY AND LIABILITIES				
Capital and reserves:				
Called up share capital [$1/AFr1 shares]	75		60	
Accumulated profits	52		53	
		127		113
Non-current liabilities:				
Interest bearing borrowings	50		60	
Deferred tax	15		12	
		65		72
Current liabilities:				
Trade and other payables	35		45	
Short-term borrowings	-		20	
		35		65
		227		250

Income statements for the year ended 30 September 2004	*East*	*West*
	$m	*AFrm*
Revenue	200	240
Cost of sales	(120)	(145)
Gross profit	80	95
Other operating expenses	(35)	(40)
Profit from operations	45	55
Intra-group investment income	4·5	-
Finance cost	(7·5)	(10)
Profit before tax	42	45
Income tax expense	(10)	(15)
Net profit for the period after tax	32	30

Statements of changes in equity for the year ended 30 September 2004	*East*	*West*
	$m	*AFrm*
Balance at 1 October 2003	111	98
Net profit for the period	32	30
Dividends paid	(16)	(15)
Balance at 30 September 2004	127	113

Notes to the financial statements

Note 1 When East acquired West (see *note 3* below) the fair value of the plant and equipment of West was AFr20 million higher than its carrying value in West's balance sheet. These assets were being depreciated over their estimated useful economic lives and, at the date of acquisition, the directors estimated that the future useful lives of these assets was 4 years. This depreciation is recognised as part of cost of sales.

Note 2 The intangible assets of West comprise internally developed brands that have no ascertainable market value. At the date of acquisition of West by East (see *note 3* below) the carrying value of such brands was AFr12 million. The brands are not amortised and no change occurred in their carrying value during the year ended 30 September 2004.

Note 3 On 1 October 2001, when the accumulated profits of West showed a credit balance of AFr25 million, East purchased 45 million shares in West for AFr1·80 each. East amortises purchased goodwill over 10 years, presenting the amortisation under other operating expenses. East has not provided West with any loan finance.

Note 4 On 1 September 2004, East sold a supply of components to West for $12 million. These components had cost East $10 million to manufacture. All of these components were included in the inventory of West at 30 September 2004. West had paid for half of the consignment before the year-end and the balance of the liability was included in its payables. Apart from this transaction, and the payment of a dividend by West on 30 June 2004, there were no other intra-group transactions.

Note 5 Exchange rates on relevant dates were:

Date	*Exchange rate AFr to $1*
1 October 2001	3·00
30 September 2003	2·70
30 June 2004	2·50
1 September 2004	2·45
30 September 2004	2·40

The weighted average exchange rate for the year ended 30 September 2004 was AFr2·5 = $1.

Note 6 In preparing the consolidated financial statements, the directors of East treat fair value adjustments and purchased goodwill as part of the net investment in West and so both are subject to exchange fluctuations. The closing rate [or net investment] method is appropriate for translating the financial statements of West for consolidation purposes.

Required:

(a) Translate the balance sheet of West at 30 September 2004 into $s and prepare the consolidated balance sheet of East at 30 September 2004.

(18 marks)

(b) Translate the income statement of West for the year ended 30 September 2004 into $s and prepare the consolidated income statement of East for the year ended 30 September 2004.

(12 marks)

(Total = 30 marks)

You should prepare all computations to the nearest $100,000.

End of Section B

SECTION C – 50 MARKS

ANSWER TWO QUESTIONS ONLY

Question Three

Investor is an entity that seeks to grow by acquisition. The entity is cash rich and is therefore more concerned about the profitability of potential investments than their cash generating ability. Earnings per share is regarded as a key corporate performance indicator.

The directors have identified two possible targets for takeover – Alpha and Beta. Alpha is a subsidiary of another entity, while the shares in Beta are held by its directors. The most recent audited accounts of Alpha and Beta have been obtained. Both entities disclose earnings per share on a voluntary basis. The directors of Investor have noted that the earnings per share of Alpha is higher than that of Beta and have concluded that the performance of Alpha must therefore be superior.

Income statements of the two entities – year ended 31 March 2004

	Alpha	*Beta*
	$000	*$000*
Revenue	42,000	44,000
Cost of sales	(20,000)	(24,500)
Gross profit	22,000	19,500
Other operating expenses	(15,000)	(14,000)
Profit from operations	7,000	5,500
Finance cost	(290)	(980)
Profit before tax	6,710	4,520
Income tax expense	(2,000)	(1,300)
Net profit for the year	4,710	3,220
Earnings per share	157 cents	107 cents

Other relevant information concerning the two entities:

1 – Interests in property

Alpha and Beta both acquired interests in very similar properties 20 years ago. Beta purchased its property for $15 million. The useful economic life of the property was estimated as 50 years at the date of purchase and Beta is charging depreciation of $150,000 each year to cost of sales on the depreciable amount. The purchase was funded with a long-term loan and $420,000 of the finance cost of Beta is in respect of this loan.

Alpha acquired a 50 year leasehold interest in a very similar property, paying a premium of $12 million and annual rentals of $160,000. This lease has been treated as an operating lease with the amortisation of the premium and annual rentals charged to cost of sales. However, the auditors have always been sceptical as to the classification of the lease as operating. If the directors of Alpha had classified the lease as a finance lease, then the charges to the income statement in respect of depreciation and finance charges would have been very similar to the equivalent income statement charges made by Beta.

2 – Alpha's terms of trade

- Alpha has loan capital of $7 million provided by an entity that is part of the same group. Alpha pays interest at 3% per annum on these loans whereas the current market rate is 6% per annum.
- Included in the revenue of Alpha is $15 million representing sales to a fellow subsidiary, Gamma. Alpha earns of profit margin of 60% on these intra-group sales. The profit margin that Alpha earns on sales of similar products outside the group is 50%.
- Alpha receives administrative services from its parent, but no charge is made for the services. The directors of Alpha estimate that the market value of such services in the year ended 31 March 2004 was $1·5 million. Similar charges borne by Beta are presented in other operating expenses.

3 – Rates of tax
Both entities pay tax at a rate of 30% on profits. All adjustments made to profit (see requirement *(b)*) are subject to tax at this rate.

4 – Issued capital
Both entities have an issued share capital of $3 million in $1 shares. This issued capital has not changed during the year ended 31 March 2004.

Required:

(a) Identify the factors that should be considered when comparing the financial statements of two entities for the purposes of decision making.

(5 marks)

(b) Explain and compute any adjustments you consider should be made to the earnings per share of Alpha, so that the directors of Investor can validly compare this figure with that of Beta.

YOU SHOULD RECOMPUTE THE EARNINGS PER SHARE OF ALPHA, BUT YOU DO NOT NEED TO WRITE OUT THE ADJUSTED INCOME STATEMENT OF ALPHA.

(10 marks)

(c) Write a report to the directors of Investor identifying the underlying differences between the earnings per share of Alpha and Beta. You should clearly indicate any limitations in your conclusions based on the information available to you.

(10 marks)

(Total = 25 marks)

Question Four

You are the management accountant of Flexible, an entity that has business interests all around the world. The financial statements for the year ended 31 October 2004 are currently in the course of preparation. The directors have sought your advice on the financial reporting implications of the following issues:

(1) On 30 September 2004, the directors decided to close down a business segment that had been making losses for a few years. The closure commenced on 15 November 2004 and was due to be completed on 31 December 2004. On 10 October 2004, letters were sent to employees offering voluntary redundancy or redeployment in other sectors of the business. On 13 October 2004, negotiations commenced with relevant parties with a view to terminating existing contracts of the business segment. Latest estimates of the financial implications of the closure are as follows:

- Redundancy costs will total $20 million.
- The pension scheme will make a lump sum payment totalling $10 million to the employees who accept voluntary redundancy in termination of their rights under the scheme. Flexible will pay this amount into the scheme on 31 January 2005.
- The cost of redeploying and retraining staff who do not accept redundancy will total $6 million.
- The costs of terminating existing contracts, including professional fees, will total $5 million.
- Plant having a net book value of $12 million at 31 October 2004 will be sold for $1 million.
- A freehold property having a net book value of $10 million at 31 October 2004 will be sold for $15 million.
- The operating losses of the business segment for November and December 2004 will total $8 million.

(12 marks)

(2) In 2005, Flexible is planning a major investment in Europe. Latest indications are that this investment will cost 50 million Euros and that the funds will be required on 28 February 2005. In order to provide a measure of certainty regarding the cost of the investment in $s on 31 August 2004, the directors entered into a contract to purchase 50 million Euros for $35 million, with a delivery date of 28 February 2005. On 31 October 2004, the rate of exchange was such that this contract had a fair value of $800,000.

(5 marks)

(3) Flexible has a subsidiary located in Taxland, which has its own tax jurisdiction. No other group entity is located within it. The subsidiary regularly sells goods to Flexible and the inventory of Flexible at 31 October 2004 included goods purchased from its subsidiary on which its subsidiary had made a profit of $1 million [after translation at the appropriate rate]. The subsidiary had made a loss adjusted for tax purposes for the year ended 31 October 2004 that was equivalent to $4 million. Local tax legislation only allows tax losses to be carried forward for relief against future trading profits. The directors of Flexible consider that the loss of the subsidiary is due to identifiable non-recurring causes and that the subsidiary will record a taxable profit for the foreseeable future. Both Flexible and its subsidiary pay tax at 30%.

(8 marks)

Required:

Advise the directors on the financial reporting implications of the three issues for the year ended 31 October 2004. Where the primary financial statements are affected (excluding the cashflow statement), you should indicate the amounts that would be included where possible. In each case, you should indicate the nature of any disclosures that might be appropriate in the notes to the financial statements.

You should justify your conclusion with reference to appropriate International Financial Reporting Standards and include any other explanations you consider relevant.

The allocation of marks to the three issues is indicated after each issue.

(Total = 25 marks)

Question Five

The income statements and statements of changes in equity of Hansen and its subsidiary entities Williams and Charvis for the year ended 30 September 2004 are given below:

Income statement – year ended 30 September 2004	*Hansen*	*Williams*	*Charvis*
	$000	*$000*	*$000*
Revenue	60,000	45,000	35,000
Cost of sales	(30,000)	(25,000)	(19,000)
Gross profit	30,000	20,000	16,000
Other operating expenses	(15,000)	(10,000)	(8,000)
Profit from operations	15,000	10,000	8,000
Investment income	2,800		
Finance cost	(5,000)	(4,000)	(3,000)
Profit before income tax	12,800	6,000	5,000
Income tax expense	(3,500)	(2,000)	(1,800)
Net profit for the period	9,300	4,000	3,200

Statement of changes in equity – year ended 30 September 2004	*Hansen*	*Williams*	*Charvis*
	$000	*$000*	*$000*
Balance at 1 October 2003	30,000	17,000	16,000
Net profit for the year	9,300	4,000	3,200
Dividends paid 31 January 2004	(4,500)	(2,000)	(1,600)
Balance at 30 September 2004	34,800	19,000	17,600

Note 1 – Investments by Hansen

- On 1 October 1996, when the accumulated profits of Williams showed a credit balance of $6 million, Hansen purchased 4 million of Williams' 5 million $1 issued equity shares. Hansen paid $10·8 million for these shares.
- On 1 October 1997, when the accumulated profits of Charvis showed a credit balance of $4 million, Hansen purchased 4·5 million of Charvis' 6 million $1 issued equity shares. Hansen paid $8·7 million for these shares.
- All shares in Williams and Charvis have equal voting rights. Neither entity has any other reserves apart from its accumulated profits.
- No fair value adjustments were necessary in respect of either entity when it was first consolidated by Hansen.
- Goodwill on both acquisitions is written off on a straight line basis over 240 months [20 years]. Hansen presents the amortisation of goodwill on acquisition of subsidiaries in other operating expenses.

Note 2 – Sale of shares in Charvis

On 1 April 2004, Hansen sold a total of 3 million shares in Charvis for $3·50 per share. The sale was made to help finance organic growth and Hansen retained a significant influence over the operating and financial policies of Charvis following the sale. Under local tax legislation no tax is payable on the disposal.

Note 3 – Intra-group trading
Hansen levies a management charge [included in its revenue] of $1 million per annum on each of its subsidiaries. The subsidiaries presented this charge under other operating expenses. In the case of Charvis this charge ceased with effect from 1 April 2004. However, Charvis was obliged to incur equivalent costs from 1 April 2004 in order to replace the service formerly supplied by Hansen.

Note 4 – Profits of Charvis
All the profits of Charvis accrued evenly over the year ended 30 September 2004.

Required:

(a) Explain how the disposal of shares in Charvis will affect the method of consolidation of its profits by Hansen. You should make reference to appropriate International Financial Reporting Standards, but are NOT required to describe the consolidation method(s) in detail.

(5 marks)

(b) Prepare the consolidated income statement of Hansen for the year ended 30 September 2004.

(20 marks)

(Total = 25 marks)

Question Six

You are the assistant to the finance director of Rex. Rex is an entity based in a jurisdiction that allows financial statements to be prepared in accordance with International Financial Reporting Standards. The shares of Rex are listed in a number of different securities markets across the world, but Rex does not currently have a listing on any stock exchange located in the United States of America [USA]. However, Rex may be seeking such a listing in the near future. The finance director has had to take unexpected compassionate leave and before leaving he handed you a memorandum from the Chief Executive [who is not an accountant].

The memorandum contains three questions relating to three separate issues:

Issue One
I have recently heard that if we seek a listing in the USA we will need to prepare financial statements in accordance with US Accounting Standards. Surely this can't be right! I thought that International Financial Reporting Standards were replacing domestic standards quite soon. Please explain the latest position to me.

(9 marks)

Issue Two
You have probably read that we want to acquire a new subsidiary soon after our next year-end [31 December 2004]. I am worried about the impact this acquisition will have on our consolidated financial statements in the short term. Although the long-term prospects are good, the new subsidiary will almost certainly make losses in 2005 and maybe in 2006. Perhaps we can set up a provision for these losses when we first consolidate next year? I know this will increase the goodwill figure, but I know of entities who just leave their goodwill in the balance sheet and never write it off. Surely we could do the same? This would make the 2005 and 2006 earnings look much more acceptable to our shareholders.

(8 marks)

Issue Three
We are in the final stages of arranging the financing for the acquisition in 2004. It looks like we will have to use debt finance since shareholder confidence is low and share issues would be prohibitively expensive. However I am concerned at the potential effect of the interest payments on cash flows and earnings. Therefore I propose issuing debt that is repayable in 10 years' time at a substantial premium. As an alternative to repayment we will offer the subscribers the option of converting their debt into equity shares – I am confident that shareholder confidence will have returned in 10 years' time. The dual effect of a large potential premium on repayment, together with the option to take shares instead, should mean that the investors will accept a very low coupon rate of interest. An additional benefit is that the convertible debt will be classified in the equity interests section of the balance sheet, with a consequential reduction in our borrowing ratios. Do you agree that this proposal will have the implications that I have predicted?

(8 marks)

Required:

Draft a reply to the memorandum sent by the Chief Executive. Where appropriate you should refer to International Financial Reporting Standards and any current developments to support your arguments.

The allocation of marks to the three issues is indicated after each issue.

(Total = 25 marks)

End of paper
Maths Tables and Formulae follow

MATHS TABLES AND FORMULAE

TABLES

Present value table

Present value of $1, that is $(1 + r)^{-n}$ where r = interest rate; n = number of periods until payment or receipt.

Periods	Interest rates (*r*)									
(*n*)	1%	2%	3%	4%	5%	6%	7%	8%	9%	10%
1	0.990	0.980	0.971	0.962	0.952	0.943	0.935	0.926	0.917	0.909
2	0.980	0.961	0.943	0.925	0.907	0.890	0.873	0.857	0.842	0.826
3	0.971	0.942	0.915	0.889	0.864	0.840	0.816	0.794	0.772	0.751
4	0.961	0.924	0.888	0.855	0.823	0.792	0.763	0.735	0.708	0.683
5	0.951	0.906	0.863	0.822	0.784	0.747	0.713	0.681	0.650	0.621
6	0.942	0.888	0.837	0.790	0.746	0705	0.666	0.630	0.596	0.564
7	0.933	0.871	0.813	0.760	0.711	0.665	0.623	0.583	0.547	0.513
8	0.923	0.853	0.789	0.731	0.677	0.627	0.582	0.540	0.502	0.467
9	0.914	0.837	0.766	0.703	0.645	0.592	0.544	0.500	0.460	0.424
10	0.905	0.820	0.744	0.676	0.614	0.558	0.508	0.463	0.422	0.386
11	0.896	0.804	0.722	0.650	0.585	0.527	0.475	0.429	0.388	0.350
12	0.887	0.788	0.701	0.625	0.557	0.497	0.444	0.397	0.356	0.319
13	0.879	0.773	0.681	0.601	0.530	0.469	0.415	0.368	0.326	0.290
14	0.870	0.758	0.661	0.577	0.505	0.442	0.388	0.340	0.299	0.263
15	0.861	0.743	0.642	0.555	0.481	0.417	0.362	0.315	0.275	0.239
16	0.853	0.728	0.623	0.534	0.458	0.394	0.339	0.292	0.252	0.218
17	0.844	0.714	0.605	0.513	0.436	0.371	0.317	0.270	0.231	0.198
18	0.836	0.700	0.587	0.494	0.416	0.350	0.296	0.250	0.212	0.180
19	0.828	0.686	0.570	0.475	0.396	0.331	0.277	0.232	0.194	0.164
20	0.820	0.673	0.554	0.456	0.377	0.312	0.258	0.215	0.178	0.149

Periods	Interest rates (*r*)									
(*n*)	11%	12%	13%	14%	15%	16%	17%	18%	19%	20%
1	0.901	0.893	0.885	0.877	0.870	0.862	0.855	0.847	0.840	0.833
2	0.812	0.797	0.783	0.769	0.756	0.743	0.731	0.718	0.706	0.694
3	0.731	0.712	0.693	0.675	0.658	0.641	0.624	0.609	0.593	0.579
4	0.659	0.636	0.613	0.592	0.572	0.552	0.534	0.516	0.499	0.482
5	0.593	0.567	0.543	0.519	0.497	0.476	0.456	0.437	0.419	0.402
6	0.535	0.507	0.480	0.456	0.432	0.410	0.390	0.370	0.352	0.335
7	0.482	0.452	0.425	0.400	0.376	0.354	0.333	0.314	0.296	0.279
8	0.434	0.404	0.376	0.351	0.327	0.305	0.285	0.266	0.249	0.233
9	0.391	0.361	0.333	0.308	0.284	0.263	0.243	0.225	0.209	0.194
10	0.352	0.322	0.295	0.270	0.247	0.227	0.208	0.191	0.176	0.162
11	0.317	0.287	0.261	0.237	0.215	0.195	0.178	0.162	0.148	0.135
12	0.286	0.257	0.231	0.208	0.187	0.168	0.152	0.137	0.124	0.112
13	0.258	0.229	0.204	0.182	0.163	0.145	0.130	0.116	0.104	0.093
14	0.232	0.205	0.181	0.160	0.141	0.125	0.111	0.099	0.088	0.078
15	0.209	0.183	0.160	0.140	0.123	0.108	0.095	0.084	0.079	0.065
16	0.188	0.163	0.141	0.123	0.107	0.093	0.081	0.071	0.062	0.054
17	0.170	0.146	0.125	0.108	0.093	0.080	0.069	0.000	0.052	0.045
18	0.153	0.130	0.111	0.095	0.081	0.069	0.059	0.051	0.044	0.038
19	0.138	0.116	0.098	0.083	0.070	0.060	0.051	0.043	0.037	0.031
20	0.124	0.104	0.087	0.073	0.061	0.051	0.043	0.037	0.031	0.026

Cumulative present value of $1 per annum, Receivable or Payable at the end of each year for *n* years

$$\frac{1-(1+r)^{-n}}{r}$$

Periods	Interest rates (*r*)									
(*n*)	1%	2%	3%	4%	5%	6%	7%	8%	9%	10%
1	0.990	0.980	0.971	0.962	0.952	0.943	0.935	0.926	0.917	0.909
2	1.970	1.942	1.913	1.886	1.859	1.833	1.808	1.783	1.759	1.736
3	2.941	2.884	2.829	2.775	2.723	2.673	2.624	2.577	2.531	2.487
4	3.092	3.808	3.717	3.630	3.546	3.465	3.387	3.312	3.240	3.170
5	4.853	4.713	4.580	4.452	4.329	4.212	4.100	3.993	3.890	3.791
6	5.795	5.601	5.417	5.242	5.076	4.917	4.767	4.623	4.486	4.355
7	6.728	6.472	6.230	6.002	5.786	5.582	5.389	5.206	5.033	4.868
8	7.652	7.325	7.020	6.733	6.463	6.210	5.971	5.747	5.535	5.335
9	8.566	8.162	7.786	7.435	7.108	6.802	6.515	6.247	5.995	5.759
10	9.471	8.983	8.530	8.111	7.722	7.360	7.024	6.710	6.418	6.145
11	10.368	9.787	9.253	8.760	8.306	7.887	7.499	7.139	6.805	6.495
12	11.255	10.575	9.954	9.385	8.863	8.384	7.943	7.536	7.161	6.814
13	12.134	11.348	10.635	9.986	9.394	8.853	8.358	7.904	7.487	7.103
14	13.004	12.106	11.296	10.563	9.899	9.295	8.745	8.244	7.786	7.367
15	13.865	12.849	11.938	11.118	10.380	9.712	9.108	8.559	8.061	7.606
16	14.718	13.578	12.561	11.652	10.838	10.106	9.447	8.851	8.313	7.824
17	15.562	14.292	13.166	12.166	11.274	10.477	9.763	9.122	8.544	8.022
18	16.398	14.992	13.754	12.659	11.690	10.828	10.059	9.372	8.756	8.201
19	17.226	15.679	14.324	13.134	12.085	11.158	10.336	9.604	8.950	8.365
20	18.046	16.351	14.878	13.590	12.462	11.470	10.594	9.818	9.129	8.514

Periods	Interest rates (*r*)									
(*n*)	11%	12%	13%	14%	15%	16%	17%	18%	19%	20%
1	0.901	0.893	0.885	0.877	0.870	0.862	0.855	0.847	0.840	0.833
2	1.713	1.690	1.668	1.647	1.626	1.605	1.585	1.566	1.547	1.528
3	2.444	2.402	2.361	2.322	2.283	2.246	2.210	2.174	2.140	2.106
4	3.102	3.037	2.974	2.914	2.855	2.798	2.743	2.690	2.639	2.589
5	3.696	3.605	3.517	3.433	3.352	3.274	3.199	3.127	3.058	2.991
6	4.231	4.111	3.998	3.889	3.784	3.685	3.589	3.498	3.410	3.326
7	4.712	4.564	4.423	4.288	4.160	4.039	3.922	3.812	3.706	3.605
8	5.146	4.968	4.799	4.639	4.487	4.344	4.207	4.078	3.954	3.837
9	5.537	5.328	5.132	4.946	4.772	4.607	4.451	4.303	4.163	4.031
10	5.889	5.650	5.426	5.216	5.019	4.833	4.659	4.494	4.339	4.192
11	6.207	5.938	5.687	5.453	5.234	5.029	4.836	4.656	4.486	4.327
12	6.492	6.194	5.918	5.660	5.421	5.197	4.988	7.793	4.611	4.439
13	6.750	6.424	6.122	5.842	5.583	5.342	5.118	4.910	4.715	4.533
14	6.982	6.628	6.302	6.002	5.724	5.468	5.229	5.008	4.802	4.611
15	7.191	6.811	6.462	6.142	5.847	5.575	5.324	5.092	4.876	4.675
16	7.379	6.974	6.604	6.265	5.954	5.668	5.405	5.162	4.938	4.730
17	7.549	7.120	6.729	6.373	6.047	5.749	5.475	5.222	4.990	4.775
18	7.702	7.250	6.840	6.467	6.128	5.818	5.534	5.273	5.033	4.812
19	7.839	7.366	6.938	6.550	6.198	5.877	5.584	5.316	5.070	4.843
20	7.963	7.469	7.025	6.623	6.259	5.929	5.628	5.353	5.101	4.870

FORMULAE

Annuity

Present value of an annuity of $1 per annum, receivable or payable for *n* years, commencing in one year, discounted at *r*% per annum:

$$PV = \frac{1}{r}\left[1 - \frac{1}{[1+r]^n}\right]$$

Perpetuity

Present value of $1 per annum, payable or receivable in perpetuity, commencing in one year, discounted at *r*% per annum:

$$PV = \frac{1}{r}$$

Growing perpetuity

Present value of $1 per annum, receivable or payable, commencing in one year, growing in perpetuity at a constant rate of *g*% per annum, discounted at *r*% per annum:

$$PV = \frac{1}{r - g}$$

The Examiner for IFRI offers to future candidates and to lecturers using this booklet for study purposes, the following background and guidance on the questions included in this examination paper.

Section A – compulsory

Question One provides a selection of 10 multiple-choice sub-questions, designed to cover the whole of the IFRI syllabus and to test candidates' knowledge, understanding and application.

Section B – compulsory

Question Two: The preparation of consolidated financial statements will always be a key component of this question paper. This question tests the following learning outcomes:

- *Explain the difference between the closing rate/net investment method and the temporal method.*
- *Prepare a consolidated balance sheet and a consolidated income statement for a group of enterprises.*
- *Explain and apply foreign currency translation principles.*
- *Explain and apply the concept of fair value at the point of acquisition.*

Section C – two questions from four

Question Three requires candidates to assess the extent to which financial statements provide a reliable source of comparison between two enterprises, and to identify appropriate adjustments that might be made to render comparison more meaningful. The question tests the following learning outcomes:

- *Evaluate financial statements and prepare a concise report on the results of the analysis.*
- *Identify the limitations of analysis based on financial statements.*
- *Explain the weaknesses of the financial report which reduce its effectiveness in communicating meaningful information to users.*

Question Four tests the ability of candidates to identify the appropriate accounting treatment for three complex transactions. The question tests the following learning outcome:

- *Explain the principle of profit measurement and alternative approaches to asset valuations.*

Question Five: As candidates have spent a considerable part of their study time on consolidated accounts, there will usually be an optional question on this topic in Section C to supplement the compulsory question in Section B. This question tests the following learning outcomes:

- *Explain the conditions required for an undertaking to be a subsidiary or an associate of a group.*
- *Prepare a consolidated income statement for a group of enterprises.*

Question Six requires candidates to communicate the financial reporting implications of three key issues to a superior. An ability to do this is an important skill for a chartered management accountant at this level. The question tests the following learning outcomes:

- *Identify major differences between IASs, UK GAAP and US GAAP.*
- *Explain and apply the concept of fair value at the point of acquisition.*
- *Explain the problems of profit measurement and alternative approaches to asset valuations.*
- *Discuss the principle of substance over form to a range of transactions.*
- *Discuss emerging developments in financial reporting evidenced by discussion and exposure drafts issued by Regulatory bodies.*

CIMA

The Examiner's Answers for Financial Reporting – International Accounting Standards

SECTION A

Answers to Question One

1.1	A	Ⓑ	C	D
1.2	Ⓐ	B	C	D
1.3	A	B	Ⓒ	D
1.4	A	B	Ⓒ	D
1.5	A	Ⓑ	C	D
1.6	A	B	Ⓒ	D
1.7	A	Ⓑ	C	D
1.8	A	Ⓑ	C	D
1.9	Ⓐ	B	C	D
1.10	Ⓐ	B	C	D

Answers to Objective Test Questions requiring calculations

1.1 The unrealised profit is made by the parent, so there is no minority interest. The correct amount is $360,000 x $^{33}/_{133}$ = $90,000.

Therefore the correct answer is B

1.2 The goodwill on consolidation would be $16 million - 75% [$14 million + ($10 million - $8 million) + $1 million].

Therefore the correct answer is A

1.3 The amount of profit that would be included is 40% [$1,100,000 - $600,000] + 30% [$1,100,000 - $800,000] = $290,000.

Therefore the correct answer is C

1.4 The reconciliation of the movement in the minority interest account is as follows:

	$000
Opening balance	6,600
Profit for the year	2,500
Disposal [25% x $4·4 million]	(1,100)
Dividend paid [balancing figure]	(800)
Closing balance	7,200

Therefore the correct answer is C

1.7 The earnings attributable to the equity shareholders are $20 million [$25 million – $5 million]. The number of shares to be used in the calculation is 80 million [the closing number of shares]. Therefore the earnings per share figure is 25 cents.

Therefore the correct answer is B

1.8 The total impairment loss is $51 million [$120 million - $69 million]. It is allocated in the following order:

- To the obviously impaired plant $20 million [$25 million - $5 million].
- To the goodwill $20 million.
- The residue [$11 million] to the other non-current assets on a pro-rata basis [the next current assets are already at the lower of cost and net realisable value].
- This means an impairment loss of $11 million x 50/(50 + 10) = $9·16 million is allocated to the other tangible non-current assets and their new carrying value is $40·84 million.

Therefore the correct answer is B

1.10 A reconciliation of the net pension liability is as follows:

	$m
Opening balance	30
Current service cost	52
Unwinding of discount	10
Expected return on assets	(25)
Contributions payable	(30)
Actuarial gain [balancing figure]	(2)
Closing balance	35

The curtailment is ignored since it has no overall effect on the net pension liability.

Therefore the correct answer is A

SECTION B

Answer to Question Two

Requirement (a)

Translation of Balance Sheet of West

Description	*AFm*	*Monetary amount* *Rate*	*$m*
Intangible non-current assets [W1]	–	N/A	–
Tangible non-current assets [W1]	125	2·4	52·1
Inventories	50	2·4	20·8
Receivables	60	2·4	25·0
	235		97·9
Issued capital	60	2·4	25·0
Accumulated profits:			
Pre-acquisition [W1]	33	2·4	13·7
Post-acquisition [W1]	5	2·4	2·1
	98		40·8
Interest bearing borrowings	60	2·4	25·0
Deferred tax	12	2·4	5·0
Trade and other payables	45	2·4	18·8
Short-term borrowings	20	2·4	8·3
	235		97·9

Consolidated Balance Sheet of East at 30 September 2004

	$m	*$m*
ASSETS		
Non-current assets:		
Intangible assets [W4]	3·3	
Property, plant and equipment [100 million + 52·1 million]	152·1	
		155·4
Current assets:		
Inventories [40 million + 20·8 million - 2 million (W2)]	58·8	
Debtors [45 million + 25 million - 6 million (W2)]	64·0	
Cash and bank balances	15.0	
		137·8
		293·2
EQUITY AND LIABILITIES		
Capital and reserves:		
Issued capital [$1 shares]	75·0	
Accumulated profits [W5]	56·9	
		131·9
Minority interest [W3]		10·2
		142·1
Non-current liabilities:		
Interest bearing borrowings [50 million + 25 million]	75·0	
Deferred tax [15 million + 5 million]	20·0	
		95·0

Current liabilities:

Trade and other payables [35 million + 18·8 million - 6 million (W2)]	47·8	
Short term borrowings	8·3	
		56·1
		293·2

Workings

[W1] – *Net assets table*	*Date of acquisition AFrm*	*Balance sheet date AFrm*
Issued capital	60	60
Accumulated profits:		
Per accounts of West	25	53
Accounting policy adjustment	(12)	(20)
Fair value adjustment	20	5
Net assets for the consolidation	93	98

[W2] – *Adjustment for intra-group sales*

- Reduce inventories and consolidated reserves by $2 million.
- Reduce trade receivables and trade payables by $6 million.

[W3] – *Minority interest*

- East owns 45 million out of 60 million shares so the minority interest is 25%.
- The minority interest at 30 September 2004 is 25% x $40·8 million = **$10·2 million**.

[W4] – *Goodwill on consolidation*

- The cost of investment in West (in AFr) is 81 million (45 million x 1·8).
- So the total goodwill in AFr is 81 million - 75% x 93 million (W1) = **11·3 million**.
- Translated into $s at AFr 2·4 to $1 gives $4·7 million.
- The unamortised amount at 30 September 2004 is $^{7}/_{10}$ x $4·7 million = **$3·3 million**.

[W5] – *Consolidated reserves*	*$m*
Reserves of East – per draft financial statements	52·0
Exchange gain on investment in West [W6]	6·7
75% of post-acquisition reserves of West in $s	1·6
Amortisation of goodwill [$^{3}/_{10}$ x $4·7 million (W4)]	(1·4)
Unrealised profit on inventory [W2]	(2·0)
	56·9

[W6] – *Exchange gain on investment in West*	*$m*
AFr 81 million (W4) translated at AFr 3 to $1	27·0
AFr 81 million translated at AFr 2·4 to $1	33·7
Exchange gain	6·7

Requirement (b)

Translation of Income Statement of West

Description		*Monetary amount*	
	AFrm	*Rate*	*$m*
Revenue	240	2·5	96
Cost of sales	(145)	2·5	(58)
Gross profit	95	2·5	38
Other operating expenses	(40)	2·5	(16)
Profit from operations	55	2·5	22
Finance cost	(10)	2·5	(4)
Profit before tax	45	2·5	18
Tax	(15)	2·5	(6)
Net profit for the period	30	2·5	12

Consolidated Income Statement of East

	$m
Revenue [200 million + 96 million - 12 million (W1)]	284
Cost of sales [Balancing figure]	(170)
Gross profit [80 million + 38 million - 4 million (W2)]	114
Other operating expenses [35 million + 16 million + 0·5 million (W3)]	(51·5)
Profit from operations	62·5
Finance cost [7·5 million + 4 million]	(11·5)
Profit before tax	51
Tax [10 million + 6 million]	(16)
Profit after tax	35
Minority interest [W4]	(2·5)
Group profit for the period	32.5

Workings

[W1] – *Intra-group sales*

- Sales and purchases are reduced by $12 million.
- Closing inventory is reduced by $2 million so the net effect on cost of sales is to reduce it by $10 million.

[W2] – *Gross profit*

- Reduced by $2 million unrealised profit [W1].
- Reduced by one year's extra depreciation of $2 million [(20 million x ¼)/2·5].
- Total reduction $4 million.

[W3] – *Other operating expenses*

- Total goodwill on consolidation is AFr 11·3 million [W4 to BS].
- One year's amortisation [in $s] is (11·3 x $^{1}/_{10}$)/2·5 = **$0·5 million**.

[W4] – *Minority Interest*

- The profit after tax of West in AFr is 30 million.
- The extra depreciation necessary due to the fair value adjustment is 5 million (see [W2] above).
- So the MI in AFr is 25% [30 million - 5 million] = 6·25 million.
- The MI in $ is 6·25/2·5 = $2·5 million.

SECTION C

Answer to Question Three

Requirement (a)

A key factor that needs to be borne in mind before making decisions based on the financial statements of different entities is the extent to which the entities and the financial statements can be validly compared with each other. Factors that need to be considered can be divided into two:

1 – Differences in operating environments
Before comparing the performance of entities it is essential to consider the extent to which the businesses they are engaged in are similar. A number of aspects of financial performance will depend on the business sector. One example would be the profit margin of an entity. If the entity operates in a sector where customers are prepared to pay a high price for high quality goods, then a high profit margin would be expected. On the other hand, if the entity operated in a sector where price competition is intense, then a lower margin would be expected, with perhaps a higher sales volume to compensate.

A further aspect relating to the operating environments might be the ownership structure of the entity. If the entity is part of a group, it might have a ready market for its product through fellow subsidiaries that are required by the parent to do business with the entity. This would put such an entity at a competitive advantage compared with an entity that was not able to secure such a "ready market" for its products.

2 – Differences in financial statement preparation
Despite the regulatory framework that exists, many of the amounts included in financial statements can vary depending on the accounting policies followed by the directors. This is partly because of the fact that some Accounting Standards allow for alternative treatments and partly because there still exist areas of accounting that are not subject to Accounting Standards. Furthermore, where Accounting Standards do exist they tend to be principles-based and so subject to interpretation when they are applied. Even where entities are following the same accounting policies, there are many figures in the financial statements [depreciation of fixed assets for example] that are based on the estimates of management. These estimates can vary considerably from entity to entity, even where the operating environments are similar and so ought to be the same.

Requirement (b)

First change – leasehold interest in property
The leasehold interest of Alpha could easily have been classified as a finance lease and were this classification to be adopted, the financial statements of the two entities would be more comparable. Suggested adjustments are to:

- Reduce cost of sales by $250,000 [$160,000 + $240,000 ($12 million x $^1/_{50}$) - $150,000].
- Increase Interest payable by $420,000.
- Net reduction in profit $170,000.

Second change – interest on long term loans

- Charging the income statement of Alpha with loan interest based on market rates would make the financial statements of the two entities more comparable.
- This change would increase the interest payable of Alpha by $210,000 [$7 million x (6 - 3)%].

Third change – intra-group sales at inflated prices

- Showing the sales revenue that Alpha would earn on the sale of such products outside the group would make the financial statements more comparable.
- The goods that Alpha sold to Beta in the year to 31 March 2004 cost $6 million [40% x $15 million]. A more normal selling price for these goods would have been $12 million [$^{100}/_{50}$ x $6 million]. The gross profit on these goods would have been $6 million [50% x $12 million] rather than the actual figure of $9 million [60% x $15 million].
- Therefore decrease the pre-tax profits of Alpha by $3 million [$9 million - $6 million].

Fourth change – administration expenses

- Since Beta would have paid $1·5 million for these services it makes sense to adjust the profits of Alpha by this amount to make them comparable.

Summary – reduction in pre- and post-tax profits and EPS calculation

	$000
Leasehold	(170)
Loan interest	(210)
Intra-group sale	(3,000)
Management fee	(1,500)
Pre-tax effect	(4,880)
Tax effect (30%)	1,464
Post-tax effect	(3,416)
Published post-tax profit	4,710
Revised post-tax profit	1,294
Number of shares in issue ('000)	3,000
So revised EPS =	**43·1c**

Requirement (c)

Report

To: The Directors of Investor

From: Management Accountant

Since both entities have the same number of shares in issue throughout the year, then an analysis of the earnings per share figures of the two entities can be based on their relative profitabilities. In the absence of balance sheet information for the two entities, the analysis needs to be restricted to a comparison of their profit margins. A meaningful comparison is only possible after adjustments have been made to render the financial statements of Alpha comparable with those of Beta. The comments that follow are based on an analysis of the **adjusted** financial statements of Alpha.

The appendix shows that all the margins of Beta are superior to those of Alpha, but the most significant factor is the much higher net profit margin of Beta relative to Alpha. This, in turn, is caused by the higher operating costs of Alpha. In fact the gross profit margin of Alpha [even after adjustments] is superior to that of Beta. All in all, the performance of Alpha is inferior to that of Beta, and this fact is hidden in the audited financial statements.

Appendix – relevant accounting ratios

	Alpha	*Beta*
Net profit margin	2,750/(42,000 - 3,000) = **7·1%**	5,500/44,000 = **12·5%**
Gross profit margin	19,250/39,000 = **49·4%**	19,500/44,000 = **44·3%**
Other operating expenses/sales	(15,000 + 1,500/39,000) = **42·3%**	14,000/44,000 = **31·8%**

Workings – adjustments to Alpha figures

[W1] – *profit before interest*	*$000*
Per accounts	7,000
Effect of leasehold adjustment	250
Effect of favourable terms of trade	(3,000)
Effect of management fee	(1,500)
Revised for comparability	2,750

[W2] – *gross profit*	*$000*
Per accounts:	22,000
Effect of leasehold adjustment	250
Effect of favourable terms of trade	(3,000)
Revised for comparability	19,250

Answer to Question Four

First issue

It is necessary to make a provision for the financial effects of the closure in the current year's financial statements. This is because IAS 37 – *Provisions, Contingent Liabilities and Contingent Assets* – requires provisions to be made for the unavoidable consequences of events occurring before the balance sheet date. In this case, the steps taken before the balance sheet date have effectively committed the entity to the closure.

The basic principle laid down in IAS 37 is that provision should be made for the direct costs associated with the closure. On this basis, the expected redundancy costs and the contract termination costs [total $20 million + $5 million = $25 million] should be provided for. A further cost associated with the closure is the cost of terminating the pension rights of the employees who accept redundancy [$10 million] IAS 19 – *Accounting for Employee Benefits* – requires that the costs of settlement or curtailment of pension rights are a one-off amount that should be recognised in the income statement of a contributing entity. Given that a provision is appropriate, then this cost should be recognised.

The costs of redeployment and retraining are an ongoing cost associated with the continuing business and IAS 37 specifically states that restructuring provisions should not include those items.

The anticipated losses on the sale of plant are not part of the provision as such, but provide *prima facie* evidence of impairment in value and so the fixed assets should probably be written down to their recoverable amount of $1 million. The provision should not be reduced by the anticipated profit on sale of the property.

The treatment of expected operating losses is also dealt with in IAS 37 which states that a provision is inappropriate, unless the losses are anticipated to arise on an onerous contract. Given the fact that the provision is likely to be material and non-recurring, then IAS 8 – *Net profit or loss for the period, fundamental errors and changes* – would require that it be separately disclosed in the financial statements.

A further issue to consider is the reporting of the results of the business segment. Provided the closure constitutes a separate major line of business or geographical area of operations then, under the provisions of IAS 35 – *Discontinuing Operations* – the business segment would appear to be a discontinuing operation. This means that the results of the business segment for the year to October 2004 need to be separately disclosed on the face of the income statement.

Second issue

It is not yet appropriate to record the planned investment that is due to take place in 2005, unless the entity has entered into irrevocable obligations by the balance sheet date. Based on the evidence provided this does not appear to be the case. The only commitment that the entity has entered into prior to the balance sheet date is to purchase 50 million Euros for $35 million. This is a derivative financial instrument and under the provisions of IAS 39 – *Financial Instruments: Recognition and Measurement* – the derivative need to be recognised in the income statement, but in this case the derivative seems to be an instrument that hedges a net investment in a foreign entity. Therefore, it qualifies for treatment under the hedging accounting rules of IAS 39. Under these rules exchange differences on hedging instruments are taken to equity. IAS 21 – *The effects of changes in foreign exchange rates* – states that the exchange differences will be recognised as income when the relevant investment is disposed of. In addition, IAS 32 – *Financial Instruments – Disclosure and Presentation* requires disclosure of the use of derivatives as a risk management tool.

Third issue

The unrealised profit of $1 million would need to be eliminated from the consolidated inventory figure and charged against the ownership interests in the consolidated balance sheet. Since the profit is made by a subsidiary, the charge to ownership interests would be allocated between the parent and the minority unless the subsidiary is wholly owned.

The adjustment for unrealised profit creates a temporary difference because the current tax position of the group is unaffected by the provision, or by its reversal, when the inventory is sold outside the group. The same applies to the tax loss because no tax relief has yet been given, but relief will be available in the future against taxable profits. The total temporary difference is $5 million [$1 million + $4 million] and the potential deferred tax is $1·5 million [30% x $5 million].

Since the deferred tax amount is a deferred tax asset, then the question of recoverability arises. IAS 12 – *Income Taxes* – states that deferred tax assets can be carried forward where recovery is assured beyond reasonable doubt. In this case, recoverability depends on the availability of taxable profits in the future to absorb the temporary differences. It would appear from the information given that these will be available for the subsidiary. The deferred tax asset will be shown in current assets and should not be offset against deferred tax credit balances unless they relate to the same tax jurisdiction.

Answer to Question Five

Requirement (a)

The initial purchase of shares in Charvis in 1997 made Hansen a 75% shareholder. Since all shares carry the same voting rights, then this gave Hansen voting control over Charvis and under the provisions of IAS 27 – *Accounting for Investment in Subsidiaries* – Charvis would be regarded as a subsidiary of Hansen and line by line consolidated.

On 1 April 2004, the sale of 3 million shares reduced the shareholding in Charvis to 25%. Unless Hansen was able to continue to exercise a dominant influence over Charvis, then this disposal would result in Charvis ceasing to be a subsidiary of Hansen. The circumstances appear to indicate that Hansen exercises a significant influence over the operating and financial policies of Charvis from 1 April 2004 and so under the provisions of IAS 28 – *Accounting for investments in associates* – Charvis would be regarded as an associate from that date. This means that for the second half of the current year Charvis would be consolidated under the equity method of accounting.

Requirement (b)

Consolidated income statement – year ended 30 September 2004

	$000	*$000*
Revenue [60,000 + 45,000 + 35,000 x $^{6}/_{12}$ - 1,500 (W1)]		121,000
Cost of sales [30,000 + 25,000 + 19,000 x $^{6}/_{12}$]		(64,500)
Gross profit		56,500
Other operating expenses [15,000 + 10,000 + 8,000 x $^{6}/_{12}$ - 1,500 (W1) + (100 + 60 x $^{6}/_{12}$ - (W2)]		(27,630)
Profit from operations		28,870
Share of operating profit of associate [W5]		990
Finance cost:		
Group [5,000 + 4,000 + 3,000 x $^{6}/_{12}$]	10,500	
Associate [3,000 x $^{6}/_{12}$ x 25%]	375	
		(10,875)
Gain on sale of shares in Charvis [W3]		1,960
Profit before tax		20,945
Tax:		
Group [3,500 + 2,000 + 1,800 x $^{6}/_{12}$]	6,400	
Associate [1,800 x $^{6}/_{12}$ x 25%]	225	
		(6,625)
Profit after tax		14,320
Minority interest [4,000 x 20% + 3,200 x $^{6}/_{12}$ x 25%]		(1,200)
Group profit for the period		13,120

Workings

[W1] – *Intra-group revenue and costs ($000)*
$1,000 + $1,000 x $^{6}/_{12}$ = **$1,500**

[W2] – *Goodwill on acquisition*

	Williams		*Charvis*	
	$000	*$000*	*$000*	*$000*
Cost of investment		10,800		8,700
Net assets at date of acquisition:				
Issued capital	5,000		6,000	
Accumulated profits	6,000		4,000	
	11,000		10,000	
Group share [80%/75%]		(8,800)		(7,500)
So total goodwill [amortised over 20 years]		2,000		1,200
So one year's amortisation equals		100		60

[W3] – *Gain on sale of shares in Charvis*

	$000
Disposal proceeds [$3·50 x 3 million]	10,500
Reduction in carrying value of net assets [W4]	(8,000)
Unamortised goodwill relating to the disposal [$1,200 x 13·5/20 x $^2/_3$ [W4]]	(540)
So gain on sale equals	1,960

[W4] – *Reduction in carrying value of net assets of Charvis at the date of sale*

	$000
At 1 October 2003	16,000
$^6/_{12}$ x profit after tax for the current year	1,600
Dividends paid prior to date of disposal	(1,600)
	16,000
Relating to disposal [75% - 25% = 50%]	8,000

NB: $^{50}/_{75}$ of the unamortised goodwill relates to the disposal

[W5] – *share of operating profit of Charvis as an associate*

	$000
8,000 x 25% x $^6/_{12}$	1,000
Amortisation of goodwill [$1,200 x $^1/_{20}$ x $^{25}/_{75}$ x $^6/_{12}$]	(10)
	990

Answer to Question Six

Issue 1

The current position is that International Financial Reporting Standards [IFRSs] are increasing in importance compared with a few years ago. Many jurisdictions [for example Europe and Australia] are either allowing or requiring IFRS compliant financial statements for local reporting purposes. In addition, IOSCO [the international organisation that represents stock exchanges on a global basis] has encouraged its members to allow foreign entities that are seeking a listing on a local stock exchange to file IFRS compliant financial statements for listing purposes.

Unfortunately, IOSCO's conclusions had no mandatory force for any individual stock exchange and, in any event, the IOSCO conclusions suggested that individual exchanges may wish to require additional disclosures to be given. The US exchanges have basically interpreted this as allowing them to continue to require all foreign entities seeking listings in the US to produce reconciliations of key figures in their financial statements to the equivalent figures under US standards.

The outlook for the future is slightly more optimistic. The International Accounting Standards Board [IASB] is working with the US Financial Accounting Standards Board [FASB] to identify and seek to reduce differences between IFRSs and US standards. Many European stock exchanges currently allow US entities access to their markets using financial statements based on US standards. There must be a concern that if the US stock exchanges do not reciprocate the European exchanges will introduce a "tit for tat" measure that will require US entities to reconcile to IFRSs. Therefore, in future, it may well be possible to access US capital markets using IFRS-based financial statements.

Issue 2

You are correct in your conclusion that any allowable provisions have the effect of increasing the purchased goodwill figure. This is because provisions, being liabilities, have the effect of reducing the net assets at the date of acquisition that are used to compare with the cost of acquisition. However, under IAS 22 – *Business combinations* – provisions for future operating losses cannot be included as pre-acquisition liabilities because they relate to post-acquisition events and so should reduce post-acquisition earnings. More generally, IAS 37 – *Provisions and contingencies* – only allows provisions for future operating losses where they arise under an onerous contract. This requirement is based on the principle that future losses relate to future events and provisions should be made only for the consequences of past events.

As far as purchased goodwill is concerned, the current accounting treatment under IFRSs [IAS 22] is to amortise it over its useful economic life. However, the IASB has recently published an exposure draft that proposes ending the automatic amortisation of goodwill and replacing this with an annual impairment test. This proposal is very likely to be reflected in an IFRS in the near future.

Examiner's Note:

Candidates who answered this question by citing the provisions of IFRS 3 – *Business Combinations* – issued in early 2004, but not examinable legislation for November 2004 – were given full credit.

Issue 3

There are two separate matters to consider here. The first issue is the classification of the instrument. IAS 32 – *Financial Instruments – Disclosure and Presentation* regards convertible loans as a combination of two simpler instruments:

- A non-convertible loan, shown as a liability.
- An option to purchase shares, shown as equity.

The practice under IAS 32 would be to measure the easier of these two amounts and show the other amount as the residual figure. It will usually be easier to measure the amount attributable to a non-convertible loan than to measure the value of a share option.

The second is the finance cost that is reported in the income statement in respect of the liability element. IAS 39 – *Financial Instruments: Recognition and Measurement* – states financial liabilities other than derivatives and those held for trading be measured using the amortised cost method. This involves recognising the total amount payable to the providers of finance [minus the net amount received from them] in the income statement over the period from the start of the loan to its maturity.

CIMA

November 2004 Examinations

Intermediate Level

Management Accounting – Performance Management

(IMPM – Paper 8)

Question Paper	1
Examiner's Brief Guide to the Paper	17
Examiner's Answers	18

The answers published here have been written by the Examiner and should provide a helpful guide for both lecturers and students.

Published separately on the CIMA website (www.cimaglobal.com/students) from the end of March 2005 is a Post Examination Guide for this paper, which provides much valuable and complementary material including indicative mark information.

CIMA

Intermediate Level

Management Accounting – Performance Management

8

IMPM

24 November 2004

Wednesday afternoon

INSTRUCTIONS TO CANDIDATES

Read this page before you look at the questions

You are allowed three hours to answer this question paper.
Answer the ONE question in Section A (this has 10 sub-questions). Answer the ONE question in Section B. Answer ONE question ONLY from Section C. Answer ONE question ONLY from Section D.
Maths Tables and Formulae are provided.

SECTION A – 20 MARKS

ANSWER *ALL* TEN SUB-QUESTIONS – 2 MARKS EACH

Question One

1.1 E has received a job enquiry from a prospective customer and wishes to provide a very competitive quotation in the hope that this job may lead to future orders.

One of the items needed for this job would be a material regularly used by E. The job requires 3,400 kgs of this material. E has 5,000 kgs of the material in stock that were bought for £2·40 per kg. The material is also used on other jobs which earn a contribution of £1·30 per kg of material. The material is readily available at a cost of £2·60 per kg.

The relevant cost of the material to be used for the quotation is

A £8,160.

B £8,840.

C £10,200.

D £12,580.

1.2 F provides three different consultancy services using a high specification computer. The processing hours available on this computer are limited to 50 per week and incur variable processing costs of £40 per hour.

Data relating to the services provided by F are as follows:

Service	*P1* *£/service*	*P2* *£/service*	*P3* *£/service*
Sales value	600	430	400
Variable processing costs	200	160	120
Variable consultant costs	180	40	80
Fixed costs	100	50	75
Profit	120	180	125

The rank order, derived from determining the most profitable use of the scarce processing hours is:

	P1	*P2*	*P3*
A	1st	2nd	3rd
B	2nd	1st	3rd
C	3rd	1st	2nd
D	3rd	2nd	1st

---

*The following data are to be used to answer questions **1.3** and **1.4** below*

G operates a standard absorption costing system. The fixed production overhead absorption rate is based on machine hours. Data for October was as follows:

	Budget	*Actual*
Number of units produced	5,000	4,800
Number of machine hours worked	10,000	10,300
Fixed overhead expenditure	£100,000	£96,400

1.3 The fixed overhead capacity variance for October was

A £3,600 F

B £3,000 F

C £4,000 A

D £7,000 A

1.4 The fixed overhead efficiency variance for October was

A £3,600 F

B £3,000 F

C £4,000 A

D £7,000 A

1.5 J provides three different payroll services to businesses that cannot justify operating their own payroll departments. The following contribution and sales values have been determined for each of these services:

Service	*X*	*Y*	*Z*
Sales value per service (£)	100	200	100
Contribution per service (£)	40	70	25

If equal quantities of X, Y and Z are to be sold and fixed costs are £100,000 per month, the monthly sales value that would result in a profit of £40,000 is nearest to

A £311,000.

B £336,000.

C £415,000.

D £420,000.

1.6 M is preparing its budgets for next year and has collected the following data concerning its vehicle running costs:

Cost	*Kilometres*
£000	*000*
100	400
96	380
148	640

If cost price levels and cost structures are expected to be unchanged, the budget cost allowance for 490,000 kilometres is nearest to

A £98,000.

B £113,000.

C £118,000.

D £122,000.

1.7 When deciding whether or not to further process a joint product after the separation point the information required is

(i) the costs of the joint process;

(ii) the costs of further processing;

(iii) the quantity of losses expected from further processing and their sales value;

(iv) the sales value prior to further processing;

(v) the sales value after further processing;

(vi) the quantity of losses that occurred during the joint process and their sales value.

A (i), (ii) and (vi) only.

B (ii), (iii), (iv) and (v) only.

C (ii), (iii), (iv) and (vi) only.

D All of the above.

1.8 In a period when finished stock levels increase, the profit and closing stock valuations shown under marginal costing and absorption costing would be

	Profit	*Closing stock valuations*
A	Marginal higher than absorption costing	Marginal lower than absorption costing
B	Marginal lower than absorption costing	Marginal higher than absorption costing
C	Marginal higher than absorption costing	Marginal higher than absorption costing
D	Marginal lower than absorption costing	Marginal lower than absorption costing

---

The following data are to be used to answer questions ***1.9*** *and* ***1.10***

P manufactures product PS3 by mixing together two raw materials, PF4 and SE5. An extract from the relevant section of the standard cost card for 1,000 litres of PS3 was as follows:

600 litres of PF4 @ £8·00 per litre	£4,800
500 litres of SE5 @ £6·00 per litre	£3,000

During October, the actual output was 123,500 litres using the following materials:

81,800 litres of PF4 costing £7·00 per litre
55,400 litres of SE5 costing £6·50 per litre

1.9 The material mix variance for October was

A £3,482 A

B £9,269 A

C £9,571 A

D £13,928 A

1.10 The material yield variance for October was

A £3,482 A

B £9,269 A

C £9,571 A

D £13,928 A

(Total = 20 marks)

End of Section A

SECTION B – 30 MARKS

ANSWER THIS QUESTION, showing supporting calculations where appropriate

---

Question Two

LMN produces a compound T5, which is used to manufacture tyres. The compound, which earns a contribution of £6 per tonne, is produced by mixing two materials, R1 and R2, in a common process. The process causes the production of a by-product Z, which can be sold without further processing for £5 per tonne. The process is inefficient and large losses occur. The losses can currently only be identified at the completion of the process.

Process details

In addition to the costs of materials R1 and R2, variable and fixed processing costs are incurred.

The expected inputs and outputs of the process are as follows:

Input:	equal quantities of R1 and R2
Outputs:	T5: 60% of weight of new input Z: 10% of weight of new input Loss: 30% of weight of new input

Data for October

Opening work in progress	200 tonnes of T5 fully complete in respect of materials, but only 30% converted. This stock was valued at £450.
Inputs: Materials:	24,000 tonnes of R1 costing £60,480 24,000 tonnes of R2 costing £24,000
Conversion costs:	Variable £36,125 Fixed £39,015
Outputs	T5: 28,800 tonnes Z: 4,800 tonnes
Closing work in progress	200 tonnes of T5 fully complete in respect of materials, but only 80% converted.

Note:
By-product Z is not considered to be a major source of income and consequently the revenue generated by its sale is credited to the process account.

Required:

(a) Prepare the process account for LMN for the month of October using a First In, First Out (FIFO) basis of valuation. Show all your workings.

(10 marks)

(b) The production director of LMN has been investigating alternative production methods to reduce the loss that arises in the process. Two alternatives have been identified:

(i) to change the mix of input materials R1 and R2, such that twice as much R1 is used compared to R2. Conversion costs would not be affected and trials have suggested that this would reduce the expected loss to 15% of the materials input during a period with no effect on the output of the by-product.

(ii) to introduce a quality control procedure that would enable any loss to be identified and the units rejected after 60% of the conversion costs had been incurred. It is expected that the quantity of the normal loss will remain at 30% of the input to the process. There would be no capital expenditure costs associated with this quality control procedure, but other costs would comprise £0·20 for every tonne of input materials processed together with a fixed cost of £1,000 per month. The quantity of the by-product produced and its continued saleability would not be affected by this proposed inspection process.

Required:

Evaluate each of the SEPARATE alternatives (i) and (ii) above and recommend which, if either, should be adopted by LMN. Show all your workings.

(10 marks)

(c) As a management accountant, prepare a report addressed to the Board of Directors of LMN that explains the costs and benefits that would arise following the adoption of a Quality Control Programme. Your answer should refer to the different quality cost classifications that would be used and also to non-financial factors.

(10 marks)

(Total = 30 marks)

End of Section B

SECTION C – 25 MARKS

ANSWER ONE QUESTION ONLY [EITHER question three OR question four, BUT NOT BOTH], showing supporting calculations where appropriate

---

Question Three

TBS produces two products in a single factory. The following details have been extracted from the standard marginal cost cards of the two products:

Product	*S3* *$/unit*	*S5* *$/unit*
Selling price	100	135
Variable costs:		
Material X ($3 per kg)	30	39
Liquid Z ($4·50 per litre)	27	45
Direct labour ($6 per hour)	18	24
Overheads	12	16

TBS uses a standard marginal costing system linked with budgets.

Budgeted data for the month of October included:

	S3	*S5*	
Sales (units)	10,000	10,000	
Production (units)	12,000	13,500	
Fixed costs:			
Production			$51,000
Administration			$34,000

Actual data for the month of October was as follows:

	S3	*S5*
Sales (units)	12,200	8,350
Production (units)	13,000	9,400
Selling prices per unit	$96	$145

Variable costs:

Material X	270,000 kgs costing	$786,400
Liquid Z	150,000 litres costing	$763,200
Direct labour	73,200 hours costing	$508,350
Overheads		$347,000

Fixed costs:

Production	$47,550
Administration	$36,870

Required:

(a) Calculate the budgeted profit/loss for October.

(2 marks)

(b) Calculate the actual profit/loss for October.

(3 marks)

(c) As a management accountant in TBS you will be attending the monthly management team meeting. In preparation for that meeting you are required to:

(i) Prepare a statement that reconciles the budgeted and actual profit/loss for October, showing the variances in as much detail as is possible from the data provided.

(15 marks)

(ii) State, and then briefly explain, the main issues in your profit reconciliation statement.

(5 marks)

(Total = 25 marks)

Question Four

The management team of WZX is about to start preparing the budgets for the year ending 31 December 2005. Relevant information is given below:

Sales

The predicted sales for 2005 are as follows:

Quarter	*1*	*2*	*3*	*4*	*Total*
Sales (units)	25,799	24,078	34,763	39,820	124,460

Sales demand is the principal budget factor.

Costs

The production costs have been predicted to be:

Materials £15 per unit, but if production exceeds 30,000 units in a quarter a discount of 5% will be allowed on all units in the quarter.

Labour £25 per unit in normal time. However, if production exceeds 30,000 units in a quarter, overtime will have to be worked and costs will rise to £38 per unit for those in excess of 30,000 in the quarter.

Overheads

Variable £10 per unit at all levels of activity.

Fixed £100,000 per quarter for up to 30,000 units produced, but rising by 20% if output exceeds 30,000 units.

Stocks

WZX uses a Just in Time (JIT) system for raw materials.

It is company policy that there should be no stock of finished goods at the start of any year.

Finished goods are valued at the budgeted average annual marginal production cost per unit.

Production schedule

The total annual production requirement will be scheduled to be produced in equal amounts in the four quarters.

Costing system

WZX uses a marginal costing system based on the budgeted average annual cost per unit.

Required:

(a) Prepare the production cost of sales budget for WZX for 2005 on the basis of its current purchasing, production and stock holding policies and its use of marginal costing. You should show the costs of each quarter and the total for the year.

(7 marks)

(b) The management of WZX is thinking of extending its use of a JIT approach to include finished goods and production.

Prepare the production cost of sales budget for 2005 on the basis of this policy change. You should show the costs of each quarter and the total for the year.

(8 marks)

(c) Explain the reasons for the differences in materials, labour and fixed overhead costs in your answers to parts *(a)* and *(b)* above.

(6 marks)

(d) Sales demand in 2006 is expected to be subject to seasonal fluctuations, as it has been in previous years. These seasonal variations are expected to be as follows:

Quarter	*1*	*2*	*3*	*4*
% variation	-10	-20	+10	+20

Assume that sales for Quarter 3 of 2005 will be 34,763 units and will continue to show an underlying growth of 5% per quarter. This trend of underlying growth is expected to continue throughout 2006.

Prepare a forecast of the sales volumes expected for each quarter of 2006.

(4 marks)

(Total = 25 marks)

End of Section C

SECTION D – 25 MARKS

ANSWER ONE QUESTION ONLY [EITHER question five OR question six, BUT NOT BOTH]

Question Five

HJL provides consultancy services to companies considering improving their telephone and communication systems, including those operated using computer technology. HJL employs a number of consultants and measures its performance based on profitability and the number of chargeable hours. Performance measures make comparisons between actual and budget performance using budgets that are developed on an incremental approach which adds 5% to the budget of the previous year.

The Managing Director has returned from a management training conference which provided her with a basic understanding of the use of alternative performance measures. Two of these were The Balanced Scorecard and Benchmarking. She has asked you, as a management accountant, to prepare a report to be discussed at the next meeting of the Board of Directors. The report should explain these terms and how the performance of the company may improve if HJL were to introduce these new performance measures.

Required:

Prepare a report, to be discussed at the next meeting of the Board of Directors, that:

(a) Reviews the suitability of the existing performance measures used by HJL;

(7 marks)

(b) Explains "The Balanced Scorecard" and recommends, with reasons, performance measures that could be used if it were introduced in HJL;

(12 marks)

(c) Explains "Benchmarking" and the potential impact on operations within HJL if it were to be introduced.

(6 marks)

(Total = 25 marks)

Question Six

DFR operates a number of retail outlets selling a range of audio-visual products. These products range in size and value from small items such as portable radios that are easily displayed on shelves, to large and expensive equipment such as widescreen televisions. Some of these products take up considerable amounts of retail staff time advising customers at the point of sale.

DFR has a warehouse that it uses for storage of its products before they are delivered to its retail outlets using its own transport fleet. The warehouse and the retail outlets are all based in one country, but some of the outlets are significantly closer to the warehouse than others.

At present, warehousing costs are analysed between storage costs and distribution costs and these are then apportioned to retail outlets on the basis of the sales value of orders delivered. Retail outlet costs (including rent, heating and staff costs) are attributed to individual products based on their sales values.

For some time, the management of DFR has been considering the introduction of an Activity Based Costing (ABC) system. The management team has heard that this is a more accurate system of costing than that which is currently used, particularly since some of DFR's products require more involvement of staff in the retail outlets in advising customers of the meaning of the product specifications.

Required:

You have been appointed as a management accountant by DFR to introduce an ABC system. Prepare a report addressed to the Board of Directors of DFR that

(a) explains the weaknesses of the present method used by DFR when attributing costs to products and its implications for cost control and product profitability.

(9 marks)

(b) states the principles of ABC.

(4 marks)

(c) explains, with suitable examples, how DFR's warehouse storage and distribution costs and retail outlet costs could be attributed to individual products using an ABC system.

(8 marks)

(d) explains how DFR will benefit from the introduction of an ABC system.

(4 marks)

(Total = 25 marks)

End of paper

Maths Tables and Formulae follow

Maths Tables and Formulae

Tables

LOGARITHMS

	0	1	2	3	4	5	6	7	8	9	1	2	3	4	5	6	7	8	9
10	0000	0043	0086	0128	0170						4	9	13	17	21	26	30	34	38
						0212	0253	0294	0334	0374	4	8	12	16	20	24	28	32	37
11	0414	0453	0492	0531	0569						4	8	12	15	19	23	27	31	35
						0607	0645	0682	0719	0755	4	7	11	15	19	22	26	30	33
12	0792	0828	0864	0899	0934	0969					3	7	11	14	18	21	25	28	32
							1004	1038	1072	1106	3	7	10	14	17	20	24	27	31
13	1139	1173	1206	1239	1271						3	7	10	13	16	20	23	26	30
						1303	1335	1367	1399	1430	3	7	10	12	16	19	22	25	29
14	1461	1492	1523	1553							3	6	9	12	15	18	21	24	28
					1584	1614	1644	1673	1703	1732	3	6	9	12	15	17	20	23	26
15	1761	1790	1818	1847	1875	1903					3	6	9	11	14	17	20	23	26
							1931	1959	1987	2014	3	5	8	11	14	16	19	22	25
16	2041	2068	2095	2122	2148						3	5	8	11	14	16	19	22	24
						2175	2201	2227	2253	2279	3	5	8	10	13	15	18	21	23
17	2304	2330	2355	2380	2405	2430					3	5	8	10	13	15	18	20	23
							2455	2480	2504	2529	2	5	7	10	12	15	17	19	22
18	2553	2577	2601	2625	2648						2	5	7	9	12	14	16	19	21
						2672	2695	2718	2742	2765	2	5	7	9	11	14	16	18	21
19	2788	2810	2833	2856	2878						2	4	7	9	11	13	16	18	20
						2900	2923	2945	2967	2989	2	4	6	8	11	13	15	17	19
20	3010	3032	3054	3075	3096	3118	3139	3160	3181	3201	2	4	6	8	11	13	15	17	19
21	3222	3243	3263	3284	3304	3324	3345	3365	3385	3404	2	4	6	8	10	12	14	16	18
22	3424	3444	3464	3483	3502	3522	3541	3560	3579	3598	2	4	6	8	10	12	14	15	17
23	3617	3636	3655	3674	3692	3711	3729	3747	3766	3784	2	4	6	7	9	11	13	15	17
24	3802	3820	3838	3856	3874	3892	3909	3927	3945	3962	2	4	5	7	9	11	12	14	16
25	3979	3997	4014	4031	4048	4065	4082	4099	4116	4133	2	3	5	7	9	10	12	14	15
26	4150	4166	4183	4200	4216	4232	4249	4265	4281	4298	2	3	5	7	8	10	11	13	15
27	4314	4330	4346	4362	4378	4393	4409	4425	4440	4456	2	3	5	6	8	9	11	13	14
28	4472	4487	4502	4518	4533	4548	4564	4579	4594	4609	2	3	5	6	8	9	11	12	14
29	4624	4639	4654	4669	4683	4698	4713	4728	4742	4757	1	3	4	6	7	9	10	12	13
30	4771	4786	4800	4814	4829	4843	4857	4871	4886	4900	1	3	4	6	7	9	10	11	13
31	4914	4928	4942	4955	4969	4983	4997	5011	5024	5038	1	3	4	6	7	8	10	11	12
32	5051	5065	5079	5092	5105	5119	5132	5145	5159	5172	1	3	4	5	7	8	9	11	12
33	5185	5198	5211	5224	5237	5250	5263	5276	5289	5302	1	3	4	5	6	8	9	10	12
34	5315	5328	5340	5353	5366	5378	5391	5403	5416	5428	1	3	4	5	6	8	9	10	11
35	5441	5453	5465	5478	5490	5502	5514	5527	5539	5551	1	2	4	5	6	7	9	10	11
36	5563	5575	5587	5599	5611	5623	5635	5647	5658	5670	1	2	4	5	6	7	8	10	11
37	5682	5694	5705	5717	5729	5740	5752	5763	5775	5786	1	2	3	5	6	7	8	9	10
38	5798	5809	5821	5832	5843	5855	5866	5877	5888	5899	1	2	3	5	6	7	8	9	10
39	5911	5922	5933	5944	5955	5966	5977	5988	5999	6010	1	2	3	4	5	7	8	9	10
40	6021	6031	6042	6053	6064	6075	6085	6096	6107	6117	1	2	3	4	5	6	8	9	10
41	6128	6138	6149	6160	6170	6180	6191	6201	6212	6222	1	2	3	4	5	6	7	8	9
42	6232	6243	6253	6263	6274	6284	6294	6304	6314	6325	1	2	3	4	5	6	7	8	9
43	6335	6345	6355	6365	6375	6385	6395	6405	6415	6425	1	2	3	4	5	6	7	8	9
44	6435	6444	6454	6464	6474	6484	6493	6503	6513	6522	1	2	3	4	5	6	7	8	9
45	6532	6542	6551	6561	6571	6580	6590	6599	6609	6618	1	2	3	4	5	6	7	8	9
46	6628	6637	6646	6656	6665	6675	6684	6693	6702	6712	1	2	3	4	5	6	7	7	8
47	6721	6730	6739	6749	6758	6767	6776	6785	6794	6803	1	2	3	4	5	5	6	7	8
48	6812	6821	6830	6839	6848	6857	6866	6875	6884	6893	1	2	3	4	4	5	6	7	8
49	6902	6911	6920	6928	6937	6946	6955	6964	6972	6981	1	2	3	4	4	5	6	7	8

LOGARITHMS

	0	1	2	3	4	5	6	7	8	9	1	2	3	4	5	6	7	8	9
50	6990	6998	7007	7016	7024	7033	7042	7050	7059	7067	1	2	3	3	4	5	6	7	8
51	7076	7084	7093	7101	7110	7118	7126	7135	7143	7152	1	2	3	3	4	5	6	7	8
52	7160	7168	7177	7185	7193	7202	7210	7218	7226	7235	1	2	2	3	4	5	6	7	7
53	7243	7251	7259	7267	7275	7284	7292	7300	7308	7316	1	2	2	3	4	5	6	6	7
54	7324	7332	7340	7348	7356	7364	7372	7380	7388	7396	1	2	2	3	4	5	6	6	7
55	7404	7412	7419	7427	7435	7443	7451	7459	7466	7474	1	2	2	3	4	5	5	6	7
56	7482	7490	7497	7505	7513	7520	7528	7536	7543	7551	1	2	2	3	4	5	5	6	7
57	7559	7566	7574	7582	7589	7597	7604	7612	7619	7627	1	2	2	3	4	5	5	6	7
58	7634	7642	7649	7657	7664	7672	7679	7686	7694	7701	1	1	2	3	4	4	5	6	7
59	7709	7716	7723	7731	7738	7745	7752	7760	7767	7774	1	1	2	3	4	4	5	6	7
60	7782	7789	7796	7803	7810	7818	7825	7832	7839	7846	1	1	2	3	4	4	5	6	6
61	7853	7860	7868	7875	7882	7889	7896	7903	7910	7917	1	1	2	3	4	4	5	6	6
62	7924	7931	7938	7945	7952	7959	7966	7973	7980	7987	1	1	2	3	3	4	5	6	6
63	7993	8000	8007	8014	8021	8028	8035	8041	8048	8055	1	1	2	3	3	4	5	5	6
64	8062	8069	8075	8082	8089	8096	8102	8109	8116	8122	1	1	2	3	3	4	5	5	6
65	8129	8136	8142	8149	8156	8162	8169	8176	8182	8189	1	1	2	3	3	4	5	5	6
66	8195	8202	8209	8215	8222	8228	8235	8241	8248	8254	1	1	2	3	3	4	5	5	6
67	8261	8267	8274	8280	8287	8293	8299	8306	8312	8319	1	1	2	3	3	4	5	5	6
68	8325	8331	8338	8344	8351	8357	8363	8370	8376	8382	1	1	2	3	3	4	4	5	6
69	8388	8395	8401	8407	8414	8420	8426	8432	8439	8445	1	1	2	2	3	4	4	5	6
70	8451	8457	8463	8470	8476	8482	8488	8494	8500	8506	1	1	2	2	3	4	4	5	6
71	8513	8519	8525	8531	8537	8543	8549	8555	8561	8567	1	1	2	2	3	4	4	5	5
72	8573	8579	8585	8591	8597	8603	8609	8615	8621	8627	1	1	2	2	3	4	4	5	5
73	8633	8639	8645	8651	8657	8663	8669	8675	8681	8686	1	1	2	2	3	4	4	5	5
74	8692	8698	8704	8710	8716	8722	8727	8733	8739	8745	1	1	2	2	3	4	4	5	5
75	8751	8756	8762	8768	8774	8779	8785	8791	8797	8802	1	1	2	2	3	3	4	5	5
76	8808	8814	8820	8825	8831	8837	8842	8848	8854	8859	1	1	2	2	3	3	4	5	5
77	8865	8871	8876	8882	8887	8893	8899	8904	8910	8915	1	1	2	2	3	3	4	4	5
78	8921	8927	8932	8938	8943	8949	8954	8960	8965	8971	1	1	2	2	3	3	4	4	5
79	8976	8982	8987	8993	8998	9004	9009	9015	9020	9025	1	1	2	2	3	3	4	4	5
80	9031	9036	9042	9047	9053	9058	9063	9069	9074	9079	1	1	2	2	3	3	4	4	5
81	9085	9090	9096	9101	9106	9112	9117	9122	9128	9133	1	1	2	2	3	3	4	4	5
82	9138	9143	9149	9154	9159	9165	9170	9175	9180	9186	1	1	2	2	3	3	4	4	5
83	9191	9196	9201	9206	9212	9217	9222	9227	9232	9238	1	1	2	2	3	3	4	4	5
84	9243	9248	9253	9258	9263	9269	9274	9279	9284	9289	1	1	2	2	3	3	4	4	5
85	9294	9299	9304	9309	9315	9320	9325	9330	9335	9340	1	1	2	2	3	3	4	4	5
86	9345	9350	9355	9360	9365	9370	9375	9380	9385	9390	1	1	2	2	3	3	4	4	5
87	9395	9400	9405	9410	9415	9420	9425	9430	9435	9440	0	1	1	2	2	3	3	4	4
88	9445	9450	9455	9460	9465	9469	9474	9479	9484	9489	0	1	1	2	2	3	3	4	4
89	9494	9499	9504	9509	9513	9518	9523	9528	9533	9538	0	1	1	2	2	3	3	4	4
90	9542	9547	9552	9557	9562	9566	9571	9576	9581	9586	0	1	1	2	2	3	3	4	4
91	9590	9595	9600	9605	9609	9614	9619	9624	9628	9633	0	1	1	2	2	3	3	4	4
92	9638	9643	9647	9652	9657	9661	9666	9671	9675	9680	0	1	1	2	2	3	3	4	4
93	9685	9689	9694	9699	9703	9708	9713	9717	9722	9727	0	1	1	2	2	3	3	4	4
94	9731	9736	9741	9745	9750	9754	9759	9763	9768	9773	0	1	1	2	2	3	3	4	4
95	9777	9782	9786	9791	9795	9800	9805	9809	9814	9818	0	1	1	2	2	3	3	4	4
96	9823	0827	9832	0836	9841	9845	9850	9854	9859	9863	0	1	1	2	2	3	3	4	4
97	9868	9872	9877	9881	9886	9890	9894	9899	9903	9908	0	1	1	2	2	3	3	4	4
98	9912	9917	9921	9926	9930	9934	9939	9943	9948	9952	0	1	1	2	2	3	3	4	4
99	9956	9961	9965	9969	9974	9978	9983	9987	9991	9996	0	1	1	2	2	3	3	3	4

FORMULAE

Time Series

Additive Model:

Series = Trend + Seasonal + Random

Multiplicative Model:

Series = Trend * Seasonal * Random

Regression Analysis

The linear regression equation of *Y* on *X* is given by:

$$Y = a + bX \quad \text{or} \quad Y - \overline{Y} = b(X - \overline{X})$$

where

$$b = \frac{Covariance(XY)}{Variance(X)} = \frac{n\sum XY - (\sum X)(\sum Y)}{n\sum X^2 - (\sum X)^2}$$

and

$$a = \overline{Y} - b\overline{X}$$

or solve

$$\sum Y = na + b\sum X$$
$$\sum XY = a\sum X + b\sum X^2$$

Exponential $Y = ab^x$

Geometric $Y = aX^b$

The Examiner for IMPM offers to future candidates and to lecturers using this booklet for study purposes, the following background and guidance on the questions included in this examination paper.

Section A — compulsory

Question One comprises 10 objective test sub-questions, designed to complement the syllabus coverage of the remainder of the paper, and overall this question addresses a number of different learning outcomes.

Section B — compulsory

Question Two is taken from syllabus section (iii) – *Costing Systems and Decision Making* and addresses three learning outcomes:

"Apply and evaluate the use of activity-based, absorption, marginal and process costing and throughput accounting in the content of planning and decision making";

"Explain total quality management" and

"Apply and evaluate relevant costs and actions."

Section C – one question from two

Question Three is taken from syllabus section (i) – *Standard Costing* and addresses the learning outcome *"Prepare and discuss a report which reconciles budget and actual profit using absorption and/or marginal costing principles."*

Question Four is taken from syllabus section (ii) – *Budgeting* and addresses the learning outcomes:

"Calculate future sales and costs using forecasting techniques and evaluate the results" and

"Explain and interpret the effect of amendments to budget/plan assumptions".

Section D – one question from two

Question Five is taken from syllabus section (ii) – *Budgeting* and addresses the learning outcome *"Evaluate the balanced scorecard."*

Question Six is taken from syllabus section (iii) – *Costing Systems and Decision Making* and addresses the learning outcome *"Apply and evaluate the use of activity-based, absorption, marginal and process costing and throughput accounting in the content of planning and decision making."*

CIMA

The Examiner's Answers for Management Accounting – Performance Management

SECTION A

Answers to Question One

1.1	**A**	**(B)**	**C**	**D**
1.2	**A**	**B**	**C**	**(D)**
1.3	**A**	**(B)**	**C**	**D**
1.4	**A**	**B**	**C**	**(D)**
1.5	**A**	**B**	**(C)**	**D**
1.6	**A**	**B**	**(C)**	**D**
1.7	**A**	**(B)**	**C**	**D**
1.8	**A**	**B**	**C**	**(D)**
1.9	**A**	**B**	**C**	**(D)**
1.10	**A**	**B**	**(C)**	**D**

Explanations follow for answers to objective test questions involving calculations

1.1 3,400 kgs x £2·60/kg = £8,840

Therefore the answer is B

1.2

Service	*P1*	*P2*	*P3*
Contribution/service	£220	£230	£200
Processing hours/service	5	4	3
Contribution/processing hour	£44·00	£57·50	£66·67
Rank	3rd	2nd	1st

Therefore the answer is D

1.3 Absorption rate = £100,000/10,000 machine hours
= £10/machine hour

Budgeted hours 10,000
Actual hours 10,300

300 hours x £10 = £3,000 F

Therefore the answer is B

1.4 Absorption rate = £10/hour

Actual units = 4,800

Budgeted hours/unit = 10,000/5,000 units = 2 hours

Actual units should take (4,800 x 2 hours) = 9,600 hours

Actual hours 10,300 hours

700 hours x £10 = £7,000 A

Therefore the answer is D

1.5 Total contribution from one unit of each service = £40 + £70 + £25 = £135

Total contribution required = £140,000/£135 = 1,037 units of each service

Sales value of one unit of each service = £100 + £200 + £100 = £400

Sales value required = £400 x 1,037 = £414,800

Therefore the answer is C

1.6 Use the high/low method to determine the fixed and variable costs:

	Cost	*Kilometres (000)*
High	£148,000	640
Low	£96,000	380
Difference	£52,000	260

Variable cost = £52,000/260,000 kilometres = £0·20/kilometre

		£
Total cost of 640,000 kilometres	=	148,000
Variable cost of 640,000 kilometres = 640 x £200	=	128,000
Fixed cost	=	20,000

		£
Budget cost allowance:		
Variable 490,000 x £0·20	=	98,000
Fixed	=	20,000
		118,000

Therefore the answer is C

1.9

	Actual litres	*Std mix litres*	*Difference litres*	*Std price*	*Variance*
PF4	81,800	74,836	6,964	£8·00	55,712 A
SE5	55,400	62,364	(6,964)	£6·00	41,784 F
	137,200	137,200	Nil		13,928 A

Therefore the answer is D

1.10 Actual input 137,200 litres

Expected output:		
1,000/1,100 x 137,200	=	124,727 litres
Actual output	=	123,500 litres
Yield loss		1,227 litres

Std cost/litre of output:

PF4	600 x £8 =	£4,800
SE5	500 x £6 =	£3,000
		£7,800

£7,800/1,000 litres of output = £7·80/litre

1,227 litres x £7·80 = £9,570·6

Therefore the answer is C

Answer to Question Two

Requirement (a)

Process account

	tonnes	*£*		*tonnes*	*£*
Opening WIP	200	450	Z	4,800	24,000
R1	24,000	60,480	T5	28,800	135,234
R2	24,000	24,000	Closing WIP	200	836
Conversion costs					
- variable		36,125	Normal loss	14,400	
- fixed		39,015			
	48,200	160,070		48,200	160,070

Equivalent units table

	Materials %	*eu*	*Conversion* %	*eu*
Started & finished	100	28,600	100	28,600
Opening WIP	0	0	70	140
Closing WIP	100	200	80	160
		28,800		28,900
		£		£
Period costs		84,480		75,140
By product Z proceeds		(24,000)		
		60,480		75,140
£/equivalent unit		2·10		2·60
Started & finished		60,060		74,360
Opening WIP		0		364
Closing WIP		420		416

Note: The cost of 28,800 tonnes of output of T5 is made up as follows:

	Material	*Conversion costs*	*Total*
	£	£	£
Units started and finished	60,060	74,360	134,420
Opening WIP b/fwd			450
Completing WIP		364	364
			135,234

Requirement (b)

(i) New mix = 32,000 tonnes of R1 and 16,000 tonnes of R2

Extra input cost = 8,000 x [(£60,480/24,000) - (£24,000/24,000)]
= 8,000 x £(2·52 - 1·00)
= £12,160

Extra output = 7,200 tonnes which earn a contribution of £6 per tonne = £43,200

Net benefit (£43,200 - £12,160)	£31,040

(ii) Variable processing cost/tonne
= £36,125/28,900 = £1·25 per tonne

40% of this would be saved in respect of the loss units	£0·50/tonne

Testing costs per tonne tested = £0·20 per tonne
PLUS fixed costs £1,000 per month

Based on input of 48,000 tonnes:

	£
Loss units processing costs saved 14,400 tonnes x £0·50 per tonne	7,200
Testing costs Variable: 48,000 tonnes x £0·20	(9,600)
Fixed	(1,000)
NET LOSS	3,400

The change in mix is worthwhile, but the quality programme is not if the benefits are restricted to those financial benefits identified in the data provided.

Requirement (c)

REPORT

To: Board of Directors

From: Management Accountant

Subject: Quality Control Programme

Date: 24 November 2004

Introduction
Further to our discussions, I set out below the costs and benefits that can be expected following the introduction of a quality control programme.

Costs and Benefits
A number of costs and benefits are likely to arise from the introduction of a quality control programme. Some of these costs and benefits are more easily quantified than others, but difficulties in measuring should not be a reason to ignore them.

Four quality cost classifications are often used:

- Appraisal costs
- Prevention costs
- Internal failure costs
- External failure costs

Appraisal and Prevention costs are sometimes referred to as Costs of Conformance, whereas Internal & External Failure costs are often referred to as Costs of Non-Conformance. There is usually a trade off between these two groups of cost, as the more care that is taken to eliminate poor quality, the less likely failures are to occur.

Appraisal costs are the costs of measuring conformity with the required quality target. This would include the costs of inspecting raw materials, work in progress and finished items.

Prevention costs are those costs incurred in trying to avoid failures occurring. These would include training of employees, routine servicing and preventative maintenance of equipment used in the process and the designing of quality into the product.

Internal failure costs are those costs that are incurred as a result of faulty items being discovered prior to their despatch. This category would include the costs of re-working (if it is possible).

External failure costs are those costs that arise due to the discovery of failures by customers, that is after the items have been despatched. These costs include the costs of replacement including any transportation costs, the costs of handling customer complaints and any compensation payments. In addition, this category includes the cost of the loss of customer goodwill though this may be difficult to quantify.

Apart from the obvious quantifiable benefits of avoiding the costs of non-conformance described above, we can expect a number of benefits from introducing the quality programme.

Such a programme demonstrates that the company is keen to improve the quality of its products and has a responsible attitude to improving the quality of the items it produces. This company attitude should spread to its employees so that they take pride in the work that they do. This in itself should improve the quality of the items produced as employees take responsibility for the quality they achieve.

As the quality of the company's product improves, customers will begin to appreciate its quality and thus will value this and may be prepared to pay a higher price for the quality they are receiving. Furthermore, a satisfied customer will recommend the company to others.

Suppliers will also be encouraged to supply quality materials as they know that the company is inspecting their supplies. This should improve the quality of the items that we receive so that, in time, it may be possible to reduce the amount of inspection that takes place.

Conclusion
I should be pleased to discuss this further at our next meeting.

SECTION C

Answer to Question Three

Requirement (a)

Budgeted contribution:			
S3 (10,000 x $13)			$130,000
S5 (10,000 x $11)			$110,000
			$240,000
Fixed costs:			
Production		$51,000	
Administration		$34,000	$85,000
Budgeted profit			$155,000

Requirement (b)

Actual sales:			
S3 (12,200 x $96)			$1,171,200
S5 (8,350 x $145)			$1,210,750
			$2,381,950
Costs incurred		$2,489,370	
Increase in closing stock:			
S3 (800 x $87)	$69,600		
S5 (1,050 x $124)	$130,200	$199,800	$2,289,570
Actual profit			$92,380

Requirement (c)

	$	$	$
Budgeted profit			155,000
Sales volume variance			
S3 (2,200 x $13)		28,600 F	
S5 (1,650 x $11)		18,150 A	10,450 F
Standard profit on actual sales volume			165,450
Selling price variance			
S3 (12,200 x $4)		48,800 A	
S5 (8,350 x $10)		83,500 F	34,700 F
			200,150

Cost Variances

	Adverse	*Favourable*	
Material X price		23,600	
Material X usage	53,400		
Liquid Z price	88,200		
Liquid Z usage		99,000	
Direct labour rate	69,150		
Direct labour efficiency		20,400	
Variable overhead total	40,600		
Fixed production expenditure		3,450	
Fixed administration expenditure	2,870		
	254,220		107,770 A
Actual profit			92,380

(ii) The main issues include:

- Favourable sales variances, both price and volume significantly increase profit;
- Adverse variable cost variances are, in total, very high, significantly reducing profit;
- There are some quite high individual cost variances, both favourable and adverse. Some of these individual variances are as high as 13% of the actual costs incurred and these will need investigating;
- There are compensating variances on all of the variable costs; for example an adverse usage variance is partially compensated by a favourable price variance. The reasons for some of these compensatory variances may well be linked and an investigation could prove useful;
- The fixed overhead variances are, in absolute terms, quite low and are probably not worth investigating further until the more serious variable cost variances are brought under control and/or the standards investigated.

Answer to Question Four

Requirement (a)

Average quarterly production = 31,115 units

Since production is the same in each quarter and there are no changes in the cost levels the production cost is the same in each quarter.

		£	£
Direct materials	£15 x 31,115 x 95%		443,389
Direct labour	£25 x 30,000	750,000	
	£38 x 1,115	42,370	792,370
Variable overheads	£10 x 31,115		311,150
Fixed overheads	£100,000 x 1·20		120,000
			1,666,909

Average marginal production cost per unit £49·72

Quarter	*Production cost*	*Stock adjustment*	*Cost of sales*
	£	£	£
1	1,666,909	(264,311)	1,402,598
2	1,666,909	(349,880)	1,317,029
3	1,666,909	181,378	1,848,287
4	1,666,909	432,813	2,099,722
Totals	6,667,636		6,667,636

Requirement (b)

Quantity produced = Quantity sold, so Production cost = Production cost of sales

	Q1	*Q2*	*Q3*	*Q4*	*Total*
Units	25,799	24,078	34,763	39,820	124,460
	£	£	£	£	£
Materials	386,985	361,170	495,373	567,435	1,810,963
Labour:					
- basic	644,975	601,950	750,000	750,000	2,746,925
- overtime			180,994	373,160	554,154
Overhead:					
- variable	257,990	240,780	347,630	398,200	1,244,600
- fixed	100,000	100,000	120,000	120,000	440,000
Totals	1,389,950	1,303,900	1,893,997	2,208,795	6,796,642

Requirement (c)

An analysis of each cost element for the year is as follows:

	Current production method	*Just In Time*	*Difference*
	£	£	£
Materials	1,773,556	1,810,963	(37,407)
Labour	3,169,480	3,301,079	(131,599)
Variable overhead	1,244,600	1,244,600	nil
Fixed overhead	480,000	440,000	40,000
Total			**(129,006)**

The main reasons for these higher JIT production costs are:

- Material costs are higher because the 5% quantity discount cannot be obtained on all materials every quarter;
- Labour costs are higher because the uneven pattern of production results in the higher labour charge having to be paid for more units;
- There are savings on fixed overheads however, because the fixed overhead stepped threshold is breached in only two quarters.

Requirement (d)

Any of the four quarterly sales units figures given for 2005 can be used to derive the trend value, for example if quarter 3 is used the solution is found as follows:

2005 quarter 3 = 34,763 units = 110% of trend

2005 quarter 3 trend = 34,763/110% = 31,603 units

	Trend Units		*Forecast Units*
2005 Q4	33,183		
2006 Q1	34,842	x 0·9	31,358
2006 Q2	36,584	x 0·8	29,267
2006 Q3	38,413	x 1·1	42,254
2006 Q4	40,334	x 1·2	48,401

SECTION D

Answer to Question Five

REPORT

To: Board of Directors

From: Management Accountant

Subject: Performance Measures

Date: 24 November 2004

Introduction

Further to your request, I consider in this report our existing performance measures and then set out explanations of the balanced scorecard and benchmarking approaches and how our performance could improve if we introduced these alternative performance measures.

(a) Existing performance measures

Our present performance measures focus attention on our profitability and our level of chargeable hours, the latter of course being a key factor in achieving our profitability targets.

These targets are set in the form of a budget which is based upon increasing our performance by 5% over that previously budgeted. This arbitrary increase does not necessarily reflect the change in the circumstances in which HJL operates. As a result, the budget may become dysfunctional. It also suggests that the organisation's sole performance indicator is one that focuses on financial aspects. There are many other aspects that contribute towards the company's performance which need to be monitored.

(b) The Balanced Scorecard

The balanced scorecard is an approach to the provision of information to management to assist strategic policy formulation and achievement. It emphasises the need to provide the user with a set of information which addresses all relevant areas of performance in an objective and unbiased fashion.

The balanced scorecard comprises four perspectives: Financial perspective, Customer perspective, Internal business perspective, and Innovation & Learning perspective.

The financial perspective considers how we look to our shareholders and thus focuses on measures of short-term and long-term profitability and growth. Our present performance measures of profitability and number of chargeable hours is very much focused on these financial measures, but they should not be the only measures that are used.

The customer perspective considers how our customers see us. This is important because if our customers are pleased with the service they receive then we will continue to be their preferred supplier and hopefully they will recommend us to their business contact group so that we obtain more work. Measures that could be used include the number of customer referrals received, the proportion of quotations accepted by the customer, the extent to which our projects and recommendations are delivered on time to our customers.

The internal business perspective monitors what we must excel at if we are to succeed. This perspective looks at our ability to remain up to date and design new communications systems in an efficient manner. We need to compare our systems with those recommended by our competitors and measure the time taken to introduce new systems that take advantage of technological developments.

The innovation and learning perspective considers whether we can continue to improve and create value by the advice that we give to our customers. Measures that could be used in this area include our position in the industry in relation to introducing new systems compared to our competitors, and the amount of expenditure on training per employee.

The overall concept of the balanced scorecard is that all four types of performance measure are equally important to ensure the continuing success of a company.

(c) Benchmarking

There are two types of benchmarking: intra group and inter-industry.

Intra group benchmarking involves groups of companies in the same industry agreeing to pool data on their processes. Best practices are identified from this pooled data and as a result the performance of all of the group companies can improve.

Inter-industry benchmarking is used by non-competing businesses that have similar processes. HJL could consider using this type of benchmarking by working with other consultancy businesses who provide services other than those connected with communications, such as marketing consultants.

Benchmarking enables a company to improve its performance by learning best practice from other organisations. Benchmarking establishes targets and comparators and through their use relative levels of performance (particularly areas of underperformance) can be identified. By the adoption of identified best practices it is hoped that performance will improve.

Conclusion
I should be pleased to discuss these matters with you at our next meeting.

Answer to Question Six

REPORT

To: Board of Directors

From: Management Accountant

Subject: Activity Based Costing

Date: 24 November 2004

Introduction

I detail below the weaknesses of our present cost attribution method, the principles of Activity Based Costing (ABC), and how we could attribute our costs using ABC.

Details

(a) The present system has identified two groups of indirect costs: warehousing costs and retail outlet costs both of which are attributed to product units using similar bases that are essentially sales values. This is similar to a traditional absorption costing system that was developed by manufacturing organisations, but it has been modified to be appropriate to retail/distribution organisations.

The problem with the current approach to attributing indirect costs to individual product units is that it assumes that there is a single basis of sharing such costs between individual products that provides a fair cost per unit. Where the level of such indirect costs is relatively small, then this simple basis may be sufficiently accurate, but if such costs are significant (as they are in many modern organisations) such a simplification may lead to inappropriate plans and decisions.

This simplified approach does not require managers to have any real understanding of the causes of costs. If costs are to be controlled, this implies that actions will be taken to reduce costs where appropriate. However if the cause of the cost is not known, then there will be significant elements of trial and error that occur as the manager attempts to take action which it is hoped will reduce the cost. Equally, a manager making a decision is often choosing a particular course of action because they believe that such action will have a positive effect on costs and profitability. Without a detailed understanding of the causes of costs, managers will take such actions without any real knowledge of the likelihood that they will have the desired effect.

(b) The main principles of ABC are:

- that costs are caused by activities, rather than the volumes or values of output units;
- that costs should be collected for each activity;
- that the costs of each activity should be attributed to products on the basis of their use of each activity.

(c) Warehousing costs have already been analysed between storage facilities and distribution and the products have been identified as being of different sizes. There are also significant differences between the distances from the warehouse to each retail outlet.

Thus storage costs could be attributed to products based on the amount of storage space that is required for each unit, since storage area is probably the cost driver for a majority of the storage costs. If any items require specialist storage facilities which cause specific costs to be incurred, then these costs should be attributed to those products that require such specific storage facilities.

The distribution costs would be driven by the distances that the items have to be transported from the warehouse to the retail outlet, but this is not the only causal factor. A vehicle has a limited volume of storage per delivery, so the size of the items being transported will also affect the costs per unit. Also some items may require specialist handling equipment or the need to include a driver's mate to assist with the unloading of the items at their destination.

Retail outlet costs also seem to be able to be divided into those related to storage area and those incurred due to the specialist knowledge and time of staff in selling the items. Again different products require different quantities of space and specialist knowledge and time. These should be used as the basis of attributing the retail outlet's indirect costs to individual products.

(d) As a result of implementing an activity based approach, DFR should benefit in a number of ways. In the initial phase of introducing ABC, there will be a large amount of time spent analysing costs and their causes. This will be time well spent because it should greatly improve management's understanding of the causes of costs. Additionally, as costs will have been more accurately attributed to products, the profitability of individual product lines will be better understood. ABC may also provide the basis for more appropriate, and profitable, product pricing.

If the cause is known then in the second phase the planning and control of costs should be much better. In the longer term, the use of ABC will improve budgeting and decision making which will benefit the overall performance of the business.

Conclusion

I would be pleased to discuss this with you further at our next meeting.

CIMA

November 2004 Examinations

Intermediate Level

Management Accounting – Decision Making

(IDEC – Paper 9)

Question Paper	1
Examiner's Brief Guide to the Paper	17
Examiner's Answers	18

The answers published here have been written by the Examiner and should provide a helpful guide for both lecturers and students.

Published separately on the CIMA website (www.cimaglobal.com/students) from the end of March 2005 is a Post Examination Guide for this paper, which provides much valuable and complementary material including indicative mark information.

CIMA

Intermediate Level

Management Accounting – Decision Making

9

IDEC

24 November 2004

Wednesday afternoon

INSTRUCTIONS TO CANDIDATES

Read this page before you look at the questions

You are allowed three hours to answer this question paper.
Answer the ONE question in Section A (this has 7 sub-questions). Answer the ONE question in Section B. Answer ONE question ONLY from Section C. Answer ONE question ONLY from Section D.
Maths tables and formulae are provided.

SECTION A – 20 MARKS

ANSWER *ALL* SEVEN SUB-QUESTIONS

Question One

1.1 The standard output from a joint process was 5,000 litres of Product K, 3,000 litres of Product L and 2,000 litres of Product M. The total cost of the joint process was £156,000. The company is now deciding if it should modify Product K by putting it through an additional process.

In order to help with that decision the best way to apportion the joint costs of £156,000 to the products is

A in the ratio of 5 : 3 : 2.

B in the ratio of the sales value at the split off point.

C in the ratio of the sales value after further processing.

D £52,000 each (that is one third each).

E none of the above methods.

(2 marks)

1.2 The times taken to produce each of the first four batches of a new product were as follows:

Batch number	**Time taken**
1	100 minutes
2	70 minutes
3	59 minutes
4	55 minutes

Based upon the above data, the rate of learning was closest to

A 85·0%

B 84·3%

C 78·6%

D 70·0%

E 69·3%

(4 marks)

---

*The following information relates to questions **1.3** and **1.4***

A company is considering buying a new machine. The machine will cost £200,000 and make annual profits, after depreciation, of £28,000. The machine will be depreciated on a straight-line basis over its four-year life and it will have no residual value.

The company uses three techniques to appraise the proposed investment: net present value (NPV), first year residual income (RI) and cash payback (PB). The company has a 15% cost of capital and requires projects to pay back within three years.

1.3 The recommendations arising from each of the appraisal techniques will be (✓ = accept, X = reject)

	NPV	RI	PB
A	✓	✓	✓
B	✓	X	✓
C	✓	X	X
D	X	✓	X
E	X	X	X

(4 marks)

1.4 The internal rate of return for the machine is closest to

A -£120,060.
B £22,690.
C 10%.
D 15%.
E 20%.

(2 marks)

1.5 The budgeted profit statement for Product X for next year shows that it has a margin of safety equal to 20% of budgeted sales and a unit selling price of £10. Product X has a contribution to sales (c/s) ratio of 60% and budgeted fixed costs of £120,000 for the year.

The percentage increase in the unit variable cost that would result in Product X breaking even is

A 20%.
B 25%.
C 30%.
D 40%.
E 80%.

(3 marks)

*The following information relates to questions **1.6** and **1.7***

Trialpha Ltd produces and sells three products (R, S and T). The company uses a standard costing system. Budgeted and actual data for last year is shown in the table below.

	Selling price (£/unit)		*Sales volume (units)*	
	Budget	*Actual*	*Budget*	*Actual*
R	£3·00	£2·50	10,000	12,000
S	£6·00	£7·00	6,000	7,000
T	£8·00	£10·00	4,000	3,000

1.6 The total sales mix revenue variance for last year was

A £8,700 A.

B £5,800 A.

C £1,280 A.

D £1,000 A.

E £2,080 A.

(3 marks)

1.7 The total sales volume revenue variance for last year was

A £2,000 F.

B £3,500 F.

C £4,000 F.

D £4,200 F.

E £9,800 F.

(2 marks)

(Total = 20 marks)

End of Section A

SECTION B – 30 MARKS

ANSWER THIS QUESTION

Question Two

X manufactures and sells audio-visual products. Over the last two years it has developed a DVD recorder (the DVDR). The company is currently deciding whether it should manufacture the DVDR itself or sell the design to another manufacturer for $3 million net of tax.

Information relating to the in-house manufacture and sale of the DVDR is as follows:

Investment

The equipment needed to manufacture the DVDR would cost $5·12 million and could be sold for $1·12 million at the end of year four. The equipment would be depreciated in equal amounts over four years.

Working capital of $1·2 million will be needed.

Sales

The Managing Director of X thinks that a target costing based approach should be adopted. As a result of a market research survey that has already been conducted at a cost of $750,000, it has been decided that the selling price of the DVDR will be set, and held, at $180 per unit. It is thought that this price will be lower than that charged by competitors.

The annual unit sales forecasts for the DVDR are:

Year	*Unit sales*
1	190,000
2	200,000
3	150,000
4	100,000

It is thought that the DVDR will be obsolete in Year 5 due to further advances in audio-visual technology.

Costs

The Management Accountant expects that the variable costs will reduce as a result of the impact of a learning curve. She has forecast the following relationship between the unit variable cost of a DVDR and the selling price:

Year	*Variable Cost/Selling Price*
1	105%
2	85%
3	60%
4	60%

The annual fixed costs directly attributable to the DVDR project are forecast to be:

Depreciation	$1·00 million
Manufacturing overhead	$0·90 million
Administration overhead	$0·10 million
Marketing and distribution overhead	$0·35 million

Taxation
X pays tax at 30%. This is payable at the end of the year after that in which profits are earned. An annual writing down allowance of 25% on a reducing balance basis will be available on the manufacturing equipment. The company has sufficient profits from other activities to offset any losses that may arise on the DVDR project.

Cost of Capital
X has an after tax cost of capital of 14% per year.

Required:

(a) Prepare calculations that show, from a financial perspective, whether X should manufacture the DVDR. State clearly your recommendation based upon your calculations.

(17 marks)

(b) Discuss any other factors that the management of X should consider before making the decision.

(6 marks)

(c) (i) Briefly explain "target costing".

(2 marks)

(ii) Identify and explain evidence from the scenario that X has adopted "target costing".

(5 marks)

Total for requirement (c) = (7 marks)

(Total = 30 marks)

End of Section B

SECTION C – 25 MARKS

ANSWER ONE QUESTION ONLY

Question Three

C Ltd excavates, mixes, processes and then distributes a variety of materials that are used to surface roads and pedestrian walkways. The business works to capacity every year and usually earns annual profits of £24 million.

Another company, Z Ltd, has developed a new product, "Flexicrete", which can be used to provide a softer and safer surface than traditional coverings. Flexicrete is made by passing traditional coverings through an additional process. Z Ltd has developed this finishing process, but does not have access to the earlier stages of the process or a distribution network. Consequently, Z Ltd has offered to lease the machinery needed for the finishing process to C Ltd.

There are three sizes of machinery that could be leased. However, the machines are not reliable. Their possible annual outputs and associated probabilities are shown in the table below. The annual lease payments are also shown.

	Probability		
Annual output (m^3)	*Machine A*	*Machine B*	*Machine C*
1 million	0·8	0·4	-
5 million	0·2	0·3	0·6
8 million	-	0·3	0·4
Annual lease (£ million)	£20	£30	£40

Operating costs
If C Ltd processed Flexicrete, it would not be able to sell any of its traditional products. Due to the unreliability of the machinery, rectification problems, overtime working and possibly the need to reduce the output of the earlier processing plants, the costs per cubic metre (m^3) will vary with the type of machine and its output. The uncertainty is so great that even for a given output there is a range of possible costs. Z Ltd will dictate the selling price of Flexicrete. The accountant for C Ltd has produced the following forecasts of profit per cubic metre and their probabilities.

	Machine A		*Machine B*		*Machine C*	
Annual output (m^3)	*Profit (£ per m^3)*	*Prob*	*Profit (£ per m^3)*	*Prob*	*Profit (£ per m^3)*	*Prob*
1 million	35	0·7	5	0·4	-	-
1 million	25	0·3	-5	0·6	-	-
5 million	35	0·4	25	0·4	10	0·3
5 million	15	0·3	15	0·3	5	0·5
5 million	5	0·3	5	0·3	-5	0·2
8 million	-	-	25	0·5	25	0·6
8 million	-	-	5	0·5	5	0·4

Note: The profit per cubic metre is after charging all costs except the lease payments.

Required:

(a) Draw a decision tree that shows the situation facing C Ltd.

(7 marks)

(b) Using the decision tree, or any other method, calculate for **each** machine

(i) the expected value of the total profit;

(ii) the probability of at least breaking even.

(9 marks)

(c) As management accountant, write a report to the management of C Ltd that recommends the action it should take. The report must support your recommendation by evaluating the situation and include a discussion of the appropriateness of the methodologies used in part *(b)*.

(9 marks)

(Total = 25 marks)

Question Four

Part (a)

The Premier Cycle Company has two divisions: the Frame Division and the Assembly Division. One type of frame produced by the Frame Division is a high quality carbon frame for racing bicycles. The Frame Division can sell the frames directly to external customers as "frame only" or the frames can be transferred to the Assembly Division where they are assembled into complete racing bicycles.

Company policy
It is current company policy for the managers of each division to seek to maximise their own divisional profits. Consequently, the transfer price of a carbon frame is set by the manager of the Frame Division to be the same as the external selling price.

Frame Division
The relationship between the selling price of carbon frames and the annual quantity demanded by external customers is such that at a price of £4,000 there will be no demand, but demand will increase by 500 frames for every £250 decrease in price. The variable cost of producing a carbon frame is £1,000. The division has a maximum annual output of 10,000 frames and fixed costs of £2 million each year.

Assembly Division
The relationship between selling price and annual demand for a complete bicycle is such that at a price of £7,000 there will be no demand, but demand will increase by 300 bicycles for every £100 decrease in price. The Assembly Division has a maximum annual capacity of 30,000 assemblies and fixed costs of £1·2 million each year. The total variable costs of additional parts and assembling are £1,750 for each bicycle.

Note: If the relationship between Price (P) and quantity demanded (x) is represented by the equation $P = a - bx$ then Marginal Revenue (MR) will be given by $MR = a - 2bx$.

Required:

(i) Calculate the unit selling price of an assembled bicycle and the quantity that would be demanded given the current company policy;

(8 marks)

(ii) Calculate the unit selling price, and quantity demanded, of an assembled bicycle that would maximise the profit of the Premier Cycle Company.

(4 marks)

Total for requirement (a) = (12 marks)

Part (b)

Freezer Foods Ltd is a divisionalised company that specialises in the production of frozen foods. Each division is a profit centre. The Pizza Division produces frozen pizzas. In order to ensure a regular supply of suitable packaging, Freezer Foods Ltd recently acquired a company that produces high quality packaging. This company is now the Box Division.

Bonus scheme
Freezer Foods Ltd will pay a fixed bonus to each Divisional Manager next year if he/she earns a minimum profit equivalent to at least 12% of his/her division's fixed costs.

Pizza Division
The manager of the Pizza Division has just won a fixed price contract to supply 7 million pizzas to a chain of food shops. This contract will fully utilise all of the capacity of the Pizza Division for the next year.

Budget details for the next year are:

Variable cost per pizza	£0·89 (this does ***not*** include the box)
Fixed costs	£4·50 million
Revenue	£11·55 million
Capacity	7 million pizzas

Box Division
Budget details for the Box Division for the next year are:

Variable production cost	£0·025 per box
Fixed costs	£1 million
External market demand	32 million boxes

Required:

(i) Calculate the price per box that the Box Division will want to charge the Pizza Division if this is to equal the budgeted external selling price;

(3 marks)

(ii) Calculate the maximum price per box that the Pizza Division would be willing to pay;

(3 marks)

(iii) Discuss the validity of using relevant costs as a basis to set transfer prices for internal performance measurement. You should use data from Freezer Foods Ltd to illustrate your answer.

(7 marks)

Total for requirement (b) = (13 marks)

(Total = 25 marks)

End of Section C

SECTION D – 25 MARKS

ANSWER ONE QUESTION ONLY

Question Five

B Ltd produces a wide variety of differently flavoured confectionery products (candy bars, chews and other sweets) in batches using various combinations of highly automated processes. These processes include mixing, cooking and packaging. Some, but not all, of the processes are common to all products. Each type of product has its own manager. The performance of each Product Manager is evaluated by the profit that their products earn and the managers' salaries are linked to those profits.

The Managing Director has received complaints from some Product Managers about the amount of costs being charged to their products. He has also heard about the growing rivalry and tension between Product Managers that has been caused by this profit-focused performance appraisal system. The Managing Director thinks that the problems would be solved by using activity based costing (ABC) instead of the traditional absorption costing system currently used. He believes the biggest benefit of introducing ABC will be better product costings and that this will lead to more appropriate selling prices, so that Product Managers will have no grounds for complaint.

Required:

(a) Discuss the applicability of ABC to B Ltd's situation.

(13 marks)

(b) Discuss the intended use of ABC to

(i) set selling prices by B Ltd;

(6 marks)

(ii) support B Ltd's performance appraisal system.

(6 marks)

Total for requirement (b) = (12 marks)

(Total = 25 marks)

Question Six

Traditional cost classifications, terminology and the dominance of periodic financial accounts must be challenged if managers are to be provided with information that is focused on decision-making in a modern manufacturing environment.

Required:

(a) Discuss the above statement.

(7 marks)

(b) Explain how EACH of the following has responded to the challenges:

(i) Activity Based Costing (ABC);

(ii) Throughput accounting;

(iii) Life cycle costing.

Note: Your answers to part *(b)* should focus on how each **one** of the above has challenged traditional cost classifications, terminology and/or periodic accounting; *simply describing* ABC, throughput accounting and life cycle costing will **not** answer the question.

(18 marks)

(Total = 25 marks)

End of paper

Maths Tables and Formulae follow

MATHS TABLES AND FORMULA

TABLES

LOGARITHMS

	0	1	2	3	4	5	6	7	8	9	1	2	3	4	5	6	7	8	9
10	0000	0043	0086	0128	0170						4	9	13	17	21	26	30	34	38
						0212	0253	0294	0334	0374	4	8	12	16	20	24	28	32	37
11	0414	0453	0492	0531	0569						4	8	12	15	19	23	27	31	35
						0607	0645	0682	0719	0755	4	7	11	15	19	22	26	30	33
12	0792	0828	0864	0899	0934	0969					3	7	11	14	18	21	25	28	32
							1004	1038	1072	1106	3	7	10	14	17	20	24	27	31
13	1139	1173	1206	1239	1271						3	7	10	13	16	20	23	26	30
						1303	1335	1367	1399	1430	3	7	10	12	16	19	22	25	29
14	1461	1492	1523	1553							3	6	9	12	15	18	21	24	28
					1584	1614	1644	1673	1703	1732	3	6	9	12	15	17	20	23	26
15	1761	1790	1818	1847	1875	1903					3	6	9	11	14	17	20	23	26
							1931	1959	1987	2014	3	5	8	11	14	16	19	22	25
16	2041	2068	2095	2122	2148						3	5	8	11	14	16	19	22	24
						2175	2201	2227	2253	2279	3	5	8	10	13	15	18	21	23
17	2304	2330	2355	2380	2405	2430					3	5	8	10	13	15	18	20	23
							2455	2480	2504	2529	2	5	7	10	12	15	17	19	22
18	2553	2577	2601	2625	2648						2	5	7	9	12	14	16	19	21
						2672	2695	2718	2742	2765	2	5	7	9	11	14	16	18	21
19	2788	2810	2833	2856	2878						2	4	7	9	11	13	16	18	20
						2900	2923	2945	2967	2989	2	4	6	8	11	13	15	17	19
20	3010	3032	3054	3075	3096	3118	3139	3160	3181	3201	2	4	6	8	11	13	15	17	19
21	3222	3243	3263	3284	3304	3324	3345	3365	3385	3404	2	4	6	8	10	12	14	16	18
22	3424	3444	3464	3483	3502	3522	3541	3560	3579	3598	2	4	6	8	10	12	14	15	17
23	3617	3636	3655	3674	3692	3711	3729	3747	3766	3784	2	4	6	7	9	11	13	15	17
24	3802	3820	3838	3856	3874	3892	3909	3927	3945	3962	2	4	5	7	9	11	12	14	16
25	3979	3997	4014	4031	4048	4065	4082	4099	4116	4133	2	3	5	7	9	10	12	14	15
26	4150	4166	4183	4200	4216	4232	4249	4265	4281	4298	2	3	5	7	8	10	11	13	15
27	4314	4330	4346	4362	4378	4393	4409	4425	4440	4456	2	3	5	6	8	9	11	13	14
28	4472	4487	4502	4518	4533	4548	4564	4579	4594	4609	2	3	5	6	8	9	11	12	14
29	4624	4639	4654	4669	4683	4698	4713	4728	4742	4757	1	3	4	6	7	9	10	12	13
30	4771	4786	4800	4814	4829	4843	4857	4871	4886	4900	1	3	4	6	7	9	10	11	13
31	4914	4928	4942	4955	4969	4983	4997	5011	5024	5038	1	3	4	6	7	8	10	11	12
32	5051	5065	5079	5092	5105	5119	5132	5145	5159	5172	1	3	4	5	7	8	9	11	12
33	5185	5198	5211	5224	5237	5250	5263	5276	5289	5302	1	3	4	5	6	8	9	10	12
34	5315	5328	5340	5353	5366	5378	5391	5403	5416	5428	1	3	4	5	6	8	9	10	11
35	5441	5453	5465	5478	5490	5502	5514	5527	5539	5551	1	2	4	5	6	7	9	10	11
36	5563	5575	5587	5599	5611	5623	5635	5647	5658	5670	1	2	4	5	6	7	8	10	11
37	5682	5694	5705	5717	5729	5740	5752	5763	5775	5786	1	2	3	5	6	7	8	9	10
38	5798	5809	5821	5832	5843	5855	5866	5877	5888	5899	1	2	3	5	6	7	8	9	10
39	5911	5922	5933	5944	5955	5966	5977	5988	5999	6010	1	2	3	4	5	7	8	9	10
40	6021	6031	6042	6053	6064	6075	6085	6096	6107	6117	1	2	3	4	5	6	8	9	10
41	6128	6138	6149	6160	6170	6180	6191	6201	6212	6222	1	2	3	4	5	6	7	8	9
42	6232	6243	6253	6263	6274	6284	6294	6304	6314	6325	1	2	3	4	5	6	7	8	9
43	6335	6345	6355	6365	6375	6385	6395	6405	6415	6425	1	2	3	4	5	6	7	8	9
44	6435	6444	6454	6464	6474	6484	6493	6503	6513	6522	1	2	3	4	5	6	7	8	9
45	6532	6542	6551	6561	6571	6580	6590	6599	6609	6618	1	2	3	4	5	6	7	8	9
46	6628	6637	6646	6656	6665	6675	6684	6693	6702	6712	1	2	3	4	5	6	7	7	8
47	6721	6730	6739	6749	6758	6767	6776	6785	6794	6803	1	2	3	4	5	5	6	7	8
48	6812	6821	6830	6839	6848	6857	6866	6875	6884	6893	1	2	3	4	4	5	6	7	8
49	6902	6911	6920	6928	6937	6946	6955	6964	6972	6981	1	2	3	4	4	5	6	7	8

LOGARITHMS

	0	1	2	3	4	5	6	7	8	9	1	2	3	4	5	6	7	8	9
50	6990	6998	7007	7016	7024	7033	7042	7050	7059	7067	1	2	3	3	4	5	6	7	8
51	7076	7084	7093	7101	7110	7118	7126	7135	7143	7152	1	2	3	3	4	5	6	7	8
52	7160	7168	7177	7185	7193	7202	7210	7218	7226	7235	1	2	2	3	4	5	6	7	7
53	7243	7251	7259	7267	7275	7284	7292	7300	7308	7316	1	2	2	3	4	5	6	6	7
54	7324	7332	7340	7348	7356	7364	7372	7380	7388	7396	1	2	2	3	4	5	6	6	7
55	7404	7412	7419	7427	7435	7443	7451	7459	7466	7474	1	2	2	3	4	5	5	6	7
56	7482	7490	7497	7505	7513	7520	7528	7536	7543	7551	1	2	2	3	4	5	5	6	7
57	7559	7566	7574	7582	7589	7597	7604	7612	7619	7627	1	2	2	3	4	5	5	6	7
58	7634	7642	7649	7657	7664	7672	7679	7686	7694	7701	1	1	2	3	4	4	5	6	7
59	7709	7716	7723	7731	7738	7745	7752	7760	7767	7774	1	1	2	3	4	4	5	6	7
60	7782	7789	7796	7803	7810	7818	7825	7832	7839	7846	1	1	2	3	4	4	5	6	6
61	7853	7860	7868	7875	7882	7889	7896	7903	7910	7917	1	1	2	3	4	4	5	6	6
62	7924	7931	7938	7945	7952	7959	7966	7973	7980	7987	1	1	2	3	3	4	5	6	6
63	7993	8000	8007	8014	8021	8028	8035	8041	8048	8055	1	1	2	3	3	4	5	5	6
64	8062	8069	8075	8082	8089	8096	8102	8109	8116	8122	1	1	2	3	3	4	5	5	6
65	8129	8136	8142	8149	8156	8162	8169	8176	8182	8189	1	1	2	3	3	4	5	5	6
66	8195	8202	8209	8215	8222	8228	8235	8241	8248	8254	1	1	2	3	3	4	5	5	6
67	8261	8267	8274	8280	8287	8293	8299	8306	8312	8319	1	1	2	3	3	4	5	5	6
68	8325	8331	8338	8344	8351	8357	8363	8370	8376	8382	1	1	2	3	3	4	4	5	6
69	8388	8395	8401	8407	8414	8420	8426	8432	8439	8445	1	1	2	2	3	4	4	5	6
70	8451	8457	8463	8470	8476	8482	8488	8494	8500	8506	1	1	2	2	3	4	4	5	6
71	8513	8519	8525	8531	8537	8543	8549	8555	8561	8567	1	1	2	2	3	4	4	5	5
72	8573	8579	8585	8591	8597	8603	8609	8615	8621	8627	1	1	2	2	3	4	4	5	5
73	8633	8639	8645	8651	8657	8663	8669	8675	8681	8686	1	1	2	2	3	4	4	5	5
74	8692	8698	8704	8710	8716	8722	8727	8733	8739	8745	1	1	2	2	3	4	4	5	5
75	8751	8756	8762	8768	8774	8779	8785	8791	8797	8802	1	1	2	2	3	3	4	5	5
76	8808	8814	8820	8825	8831	8837	8842	8848	8854	8859	1	1	2	2	3	3	4	5	5
77	8865	8871	8876	8882	8887	8893	8899	8904	8910	8915	1	1	2	2	3	3	4	4	5
78	8921	8927	8932	8938	8943	8949	8954	8960	8965	8971	1	1	2	2	3	3	4	4	5
79	8976	8982	8987	8993	8998	9004	9009	9015	9020	9025	1	1	2	2	3	3	4	4	5
80	9031	9036	9042	9047	9053	9058	9063	9069	9074	9079	1	1	2	2	3	3	4	4	5
81	9085	9090	9096	9101	9106	9112	9117	9122	9128	9133	1	1	2	2	3	3	4	4	5
82	9138	9143	9149	9154	9159	9165	9170	9175	9180	9186	1	1	2	2	3	3	4	4	5
83	9191	9196	9201	9206	9212	9217	9222	9227	9232	9238	1	1	2	2	3	3	4	4	5
84	9243	9248	9253	9258	9263	9269	9274	9279	9284	9289	1	1	2	2	3	3	4	4	5
85	9294	9299	9304	9309	9315	9320	9325	9330	9335	9340	1	1	2	2	3	3	4	4	5
86	9345	9350	9355	9360	9365	9370	9375	9380	9385	9390	1	1	2	2	3	3	4	4	5
87	9395	9400	9405	9410	9415	9420	9425	9430	9435	9440	0	1	1	2	2	3	3	4	4
88	9445	9450	9455	9460	9465	9469	9474	9479	9484	9489	0	1	1	2	2	3	3	4	4
89	9494	9499	9504	9509	9513	9518	9523	9528	9533	9538	0	1	1	2	2	3	3	4	4
90	9542	9547	9552	9557	9562	9566	9571	9576	9581	9586	0	1	1	2	2	3	3	4	4
91	9590	9595	9600	9605	9609	9614	9619	9624	9628	9633	0	1	1	2	2	3	3	4	4
92	9638	9643	9647	9652	9657	9661	9666	9671	9675	9680	0	1	1	2	2	3	3	4	4
93	9685	9689	9694	9699	9703	9708	9713	9717	9722	9727	0	1	1	2	2	3	3	4	4
94	9731	9736	9741	9745	9750	9754	9759	9763	9768	9773	0	1	1	2	2	3	3	4	4
95	9777	9782	9786	9791	9795	9800	9805	9809	9814	9818	0	1	1	2	2	3	3	4	4
96	9823	0827	9832	0836	9841	9845	9850	9854	9859	9863	0	1	1	2	2	3	3	4	4
97	9868	9872	9877	9881	9886	9890	9894	9899	9903	9908	0	1	1	2	2	3	3	4	4
98	9912	9917	9921	9926	9930	9934	9939	9943	9948	9952	0	1	1	2	2	3	3	4	4
99	9956	9961	9965	9969	9974	9978	9983	9987	9991	9996	0	1	1	2	2	3	3	3	4

PRESENT VALUE TABLE

Present value of £1 ie $(1+r)^{-n}$ where r = interest rate; n = number of periods until payment or receipt.

Periods (n)	Interest rates (r)																			
	1%	2%	3%	4%	5%	6%	7%	8%	9%	10%	11%	12%	13%	14%	15%	16%	17%	18%	19%	20%
1	.990	.980	.971	.962	.952	.943	.935	.926	.917	.909	.901	.893	.885	.877	.870	.862	.855	.847	.840	.833
2	.980	.961	.943	.925	.907	.890	.873	.857	.842	.826	.812	.797	.783	.769	.756	.743	.731	.718	.706	.694
3	.971	.942	.915	.889	.864	.840	.816	.794	.772	.751	.731	.712	.693	.675	.658	.641	.624	.609	.593	.579
4	.961	.924	.888	.855	.823	.792	.763	.735	.708	.683	.659	.636	.613	.592	.572	.552	.534	.516	.499	.482
5	.951	.906	.863	.822	.784	.747	.713	.681	.650	.621	.593	.567	.543	.519	.497	.476	.456	.437	.419	.402
6	.942	.888	.837	.790	.746	.705	.666	.630	.596	.564	.535	.507	.480	.456	.432	.410	.390	.370	.352	.335
7	.933	.871	.813	.760	.711	.665	.623	.583	.547	.513	.482	.452	.425	.400	.376	.354	.333	.314	.296	.279
8	.923	.853	.789	.731	.677	.627	.582	.540	.502	.467	.434	.404	.376	.351	.327	.305	.285	.266	.249	.233
9	.914	.837	.766	.703	.645	.592	.544	.500	.460	.424	.391	.361	.333	.308	.284	.263	.243	.225	.209	.194
10	.905	.820	.744	.676	.614	.558	.508	.463	.422	.386	.352	.322	.295	.270	.247	.227	.208	.191	.176	.162
11	.896	.804	.722	.650	.585	.527	.475	.429	.388	.350	.317	.287	.261	.237	.215	.195	.178	.162	.148	.135
12	.887	.788	.701	.625	.557	.497	.444	.397	.356	.319	.286	.257	.231	.208	.187	.168	.152	.137	.124	.112
13	.879	.773	.681	.601	.530	.469	.415	.368	.326	.290	.258	.229	.204	.182	.163	.145	.130	.116	.104	.093
14	.870	.758	.661	.577	.505	.442	.388	.340	.299	.263	.232	.205	.181	.160	.141	.125	.111	.099	.088	.078
15	.861	.743	.642	.555	.481	.417	.362	.315	.275	.239	.209	.183	.160	.140	.123	.108	.095	.084	.074	.065
16	.853	.728	.623	.534	.458	.394	.339	.292	.252	.218	.188	.163	.141	.123	.107	.093	.081	.071	.062	.054
17	.844	.714	.605	.513	.436	.371	.317	.270	.231	.198	.170	.146	.125	.108	.093	.080	.069	.060	.052	.045
18	.836	.700	.587	.494	.416	.350	.296	.250	.212	.180	.153	.130	.111	.095	.081	.069	.059	.051	.044	.038
19	.828	.686	.570	.475	.396	.331	.277	.232	.194	.164	.138	.116	.098	.083	.070	.060	.051	.043	.037	.031
20	.820	.673	.554	.456	.377	.312	.258	.215	.178	.149	.124	.104	.087	.073	.061	.051	.043	.037	.031	.026

CUMULATIVE PRESENT VALUE OF £1

This table shows the Present Value of £1 per annum, Receivable or Payable at the end of each year for n years $\frac{1-(1+r)^{-n}}{r}$.

Periods (n)	Interest rates (r)																			
	1%	2%	3%	4%	5%	6%	7%	8%	9%	10%	11%	12%	13%	14%	15%	16%	17%	18%	19%	20%
1	.990	.980	.971	.962	.952	.943	.935	.926	.917	.909	.901	.893	.885	.877	.870	.862	.855	.847	.840	.833
2	1.970	1.942	1.913	1.886	1.859	1.833	1.808	1.783	1.759	1.736	1.713	1.690	1.668	1.647	1.626	1.605	1.585	1.566	1.547	1.528
3	2.941	2.884	2.829	2.775	2.723	2.673	2.624	2.577	2.531	2.487	2.444	2.402	2.361	2.322	2.283	2.246	2.210	2.174	2.140	2.106
4	3.902	3.808	3.717	3.630	3.546	3.465	3.387	3.312	3.240	3.170	3.102	3.037	2.974	2.914	2.855	2.798	2.743	2.690	2.639	2.589
5	4.853	4.713	4.580	4.452	4.329	4.212	4.100	3.993	3.890	3.791	3.696	3.605	3.517	3.433	3.352	3.274	3.199	3.127	3.058	2.991
6	5.795	5.601	5.417	5.242	5.076	4.917	4.767	4.623	4.486	4.355	4.231	4.111	3.998	3.889	3.784	3.685	3.589	3.498	3.410	3.326
7	6.728	6.472	6.230	6.002	5.786	5.582	5.389	5.206	5.033	4.868	4.712	4.564	4.423	4.288	4.160	4.039	3.922	3.812	3.706	3.605
8	7.652	7.325	7.020	6.733	6.463	6.210	5.971	5.747	5.535	5.335	5.146	4.968	4.799	4.639	4.487	4.344	4.207	4.078	3.954	3.837
9	8.566	8.162	7.786	7.435	7.108	6.802	6.515	6.247	5.995	5.759	5.537	5.328	5.132	4.946	4.772	4.607	4.451	4.303	4.163	4.031
10	9.471	8.983	8.530	8.111	7.722	7.360	7.024	6.710	6.418	6.145	5.889	5.650	5.426	5.216	5.019	4.833	4.659	4.494	4.339	4.192
11	10.368	9.787	9.253	8.760	8.306	7.887	7.499	7.139	6.805	6.495	6.207	5.938	5.687	5.453	5.234	5.029	4.836	4.656	4.486	4.327
12	11.255	10.575	9.954	9.385	8.863	8.384	7.943	7.536	7.161	6.814	6.492	6.194	5.918	5.660	5.421	5.197	4.988	4.793	4.611	4.439
13	12.134	11.348	10.635	9.986	9.394	8.853	8.358	7.904	7.487	7.103	6.750	6.424	6.122	5.842	5.583	5.342	5.118	4.910	4.715	4.533
14	13.004	12.106	11.296	10.563	9.899	9.295	8.745	8.244	7.786	7.367	6.982	6.628	6.302	6.002	5.724	5.468	5.229	5.008	4.802	4.611
15	13.865	12.849	11.938	11.118	10.380	9.712	9.108	8.559	8.061	7.606	7.191	6.811	6.462	6.142	5.847	5.575	5.324	5.092	4.876	4.675
16	14.718	13.578	12.561	11.652	10.838	10.106	9.447	8.851	8.313	7.824	7.379	6.974	6.604	6.265	5.954	5.668	5.405	5.162	4.938	4.730
17	15.562	14.292	13.166	12.166	11.274	10.477	9.763	9.122	8.544	8.022	7.549	7.120	6.729	6.373	6.047	5.749	5.475	5.222	4.990	4.775
18	16.398	14.992	13.754	12.659	11.690	10.828	10.059	9.372	8.756	8.201	7.702	7.250	6.840	6.467	6.128	5.818	5.534	5.273	5.033	4.812
19	17.226	15.679	14.324	13.134	12.085	11.158	10.336	9.604	8.950	8.365	7.839	7.366	6.938	6.550	6.198	5.877	5.584	5.316	5.070	4.843
20	18.046	16.351	14.878	13.590	12.462	11.470	10.594	9.818	9.129	8.514	7.963	7.469	7.025	6.623	6.259	5.929	5.628	5.353	5.101	4.870

Formula:

Learning and experience curve

$Y = aX^b$

Where:
- Y = the cumulative average time/cost per unit
- a = the time/cost for the first unit
- X = the cumulative number of units
- b = the index of learning

The Examiner for IDEC offers to future candidates and to lecturers using this booklet for study purposes, the following background and guidance on the questions included in this examination paper.

Section A — compulsory

Question One consists of 7 objective test sub-questions, designed to cover a variety of syllabus topics and addressing a selection of learning outcomes in all sections of the syllabus.

Section B — compulsory

Question Two part (a) requires candidates to prepare calculations showing whether from a financial perspective a company should manufacture a product it has developed. Part (b) asks candidates to discuss any other non-financial factors that should be considered prior to making the decision to manufacture the product. Part (c) asks for an explanation of target costing and an identification of evidence that the company concerned has adopted this method. The question addresses the learning outcomes *"Prepare project cashflows that take account of taxation and inflation"* from syllabus section (iii) *Investment Appraisal* and *"Apply and evaluate life cycle costing"* from syllabus section (ii) *Costing and Accounting Systems.*

Section C – one question from two

Question Three part (a) requires candidates to draw a decision tree showing the situation facing the company in the question. Part (b) asks for calculations of expected value of total profit and the probability of breaking even. Part (c) requires candidates to write a report to the management of the company concerned recommending what action to take. The question addresses the learning outcome *"Apply and discuss decision trees"* from syllabus section (i) *Decision Making.*

Question Four part (a) requires candidates to calculate unit selling prices and quantities demanded of a product made by the company concerned given current company policy and also to maximise profit. Part (b) then requires candidates to calculate prices of a product based on what one division will charge another division of the same company, as well as the maximum price that the division would pay for it. Candidates are then required to discuss the validity of using relevant costs as a basis for setting transfer prices for internal performance measurement using data from the question. The question addresses the learning outcome *"Explain and demonstrate transfer pricing"* from syllabus section (i) *Decision Making.*

Section D – one question from two

Question Five part (a) requires candidates to discuss the applicability of using activity based costing in a manufacturing company which currently uses traditional absorption costing. Part (b) asks candidates to discuss the intended uses of ABC if introduced. The question addresses the learning outcome *"Apply and evaluate activity-based costing and activity-based management"* from syllabus section (ii) *Costing and Accounting Systems.*

Question Six part (a) requires candidates to discuss a statement given in the question and then, in part (b), to explain how three methods have responded to the challenges made in the statement. The question addresses the learning outcomes *"Apply and evaluate alternative costing and accounting systems; backflush accounting, just-in-time, standard costing, throughput accounting, overhead allocation (Japanese), absorption costing, marginal costing, activity based costing"* and *"Apply and evaluate life cycle costing"* from syllabus section (ii) *Costing and Accounting Systems.*

CIMA

The Examiner's Answers for Management Accounting – Decision Making

SECTION A

Answers to Question One

1.1	A	B	C	D	(E)
1.2	A	(B)	C	D	E
1.3	A	(B)	C	D	E
1.4	A	B	C	D	(E)
1.5	A	B	(C)	D	E
1.6	A	(B)	C	D	E
1.7	A	B	(C)	D	E

Explanations to the answers to Objective Test Questions

1.1 The decision should look at incremental costs and incremental revenues. The joint costs are irrelevant.

Therefore the answer is E

1.2 (100 + 70 + 59 + 55) = 284. Cumulative average time for 4 units = 284/4 = 71 hours/unit
$0{\cdot}71 = r^2$
$r = 0{\cdot}8426$

Therefore the answer is B

1.3

NPV = -200,000 + (78,000 x 2·855) = £22,690. Therefore accept.
RI = 28,000 - (200,000 x 0·15) = -£2,000. Therefore reject.
Payback = 200,000/78,000 = 2·56 years. Therefore accept.

Therefore the answer is B

1.4 200,000/78,000 = 2·56. This is the annuity factor for the IRR. Searching the annuity tables on the four year line shows that this is close to 20%.

Therefore the answer is E

1.5

Contribution per unit = 10 x 60% = £6
Break-even point = 120,000/6 = 20,000 units
Margin of safety = 20%. Therefore budgeted output = 25,000 units
Profit at 25,000 units = (25,000 x 6) - 120,000 = £30,000
Variable costs at 25,000 units = 25,000 x (10 - 6) = £100,000

Therefore variable costs could rise by £30,000 before the product fails to break even. This gives a sensitivity of 30,000/100,000 = 30%

Therefore the answer is C

1.6 Standardised mix = 11,000R, 6,600S and 4,400T

	£
(12,000 - 11,000) x 3 =	3,000 F
(7,000 - 6,600) x 6 =	2,400 F
(3,000 - 4,400) x 8 =	11,200 A
Total	5,800 A

Therefore the answer is B

1.7 (actual sales - budgeted sales) x standard price

	£
(12,000 - 10,000) x 3 =	6,000 F
(7,000 - 6,000) x 6 =	6,000 F
(3,000 - 4,000) x 8 =	8,000 A
Total	4,000 F

Therefore the answer is C

SECTION B

Answer to Question Two

Requirement (a)

The development costs and the cost of the market research report are sunk costs and are therefore not relevant to the decision. Depreciation is not a cash cost and is also irrelevant. The decision should be taken "looking forwards" to evaluate the difference between the two options.

Calculation of Tax allowances

Year	*1*	*2*	*3*	*4*
	$	*$*	*$*	*$*
Opening value	5,120,000	3,840,000	2,880,000	2,160,000
Allowance	1,280,000	960,000	720,000	540,000
Final WDV				1,620,000
Sale value				1,120,000
Balancing allowance				500,000

Tax calculation

Year	*1*	*2*	*3*	*4*
Selling price$	180	180	180	180
VC/SP %	105	85	60	60
	$	*$*	*$*	*$*
Variable cost	189	153	108	108
Contribution per unit	-9	27	72	72
Unit sales	190,000	200,000	150,000	100,000
Total contribution	-1,710,000	5,400,000	10,800,000	7,200,000
Fixed costs	-1,350,000	-1,350,000	-1,350,000	-1,350,000
WDA	-1,280,000	-960,000	-720,000	-540,000
Balancing allowance				-500,000
Taxable profit	-4,340,000	3,090,000	8,730,000	4,810,000
Tax	-1,302,000	927,000	2,619,000	1,443,000

The tax will be paid one year later.

Cash flows

	0	*1*	*2*	*3*	*4*	*5*
	$	*$*	*$*	*$*	*$*	*$*
Equipment	-5,120,000				1,120,000	
Work Cap	-1,200,000				1,200,000	
Contribution		-1,710,000	5,400,000	10,800,000	7,200,000	
Fixed Costs		-1,350,000	-1,350,000	-1,350,000	-1,350,000	
Tax			1,302,000	-927,000	-2,619,000	-1,443,000
Cash Flow	-6,320,000	-3,060,000	5,352,000	8,523,000	5,551,000	-1,443,000
Disc factor	1	0·877	0·769	0·675	0·592	0·519
Present value	-6,320,000	-2,683,620	4,115,688	5,753,025	3,286,192	-748,917

Net Present Value = $3,402,368

The DVDR design and all rights could be sold for $3 million. Therefore it can be seen, from a financial perspective, that X should manufacture the DVDR.

Requirement (b)

The calculations in requirement *(a)* above reveal that the net benefit of manufacturing and selling the DVDR "in-house" is relatively small ($402,368) when compared with the overall scale of the project. A major problem would be "managing" the project and the many control issues that would be associated with a project on this scale.

Hence, the management of X need to carefully consider the following issues before proceeding with the DVDR project:

- X's ability to survive the negative cashflows in the early years of the project. The initial investment in the project is $6·32 million and in the first year of operation the project has a negative cash flow of just over $3 million. This should be contrasted with the immediate inflow of $3 million if the patent is sold. Management of X must ensure that they have sufficient cash resources to absorb these negative cash flows.

- The accuracy of the sales forecasts. Sales forecasting is notoriously difficult especially when the forecast period extends to four years in such a technologically developing product market. Relatively small errors in the forecasts could have a large impact on the net worth of the project.

- Management's attitude to risk. Management should undertake a sensitivity analysis on the project to test the vulnerability of the decision to changes in the variables. Critical factors (given the projected life span) appear to be the selling price, sales forecasts and the impact of the learning curve.

- The learning curve effect. The management accountant expects to observe a learning curve effect in the production of the DVDR but any miscalculations in this regard could prove very costly in terms of the project's outcome.

- Competitors' reactions. The success or otherwise of the DVDR project appears to hinge, to a large extent, on the assumption that our product will be purchased because it is cheaper than the competitors' offerings and that it will continue to be bought at this price. If this is "new technology" would it be possible to skim the market? Are there any rival products? If so competitors may react by reducing their own selling prices when the DVDR is launched. Does the DVDR have a unique selling point?

> **Examiner's Note:**
> Other sensible points that are related to the scenario are equally acceptable, for example possible loss of "know how", could the funds be used elsewhere (for example development and sale of a more advanced version of the DVDR) and so on.

Requirement (c)

(i) "Target costing" is a customer-orientated approach to product pricing and costing, whereby the seller: (i) sets the product price based on their knowledge of what customers are willing to pay, and (ii) ensures that the product cost is either currently at, or is driven down to, a level which ensures that a pre-determined target margin is earned on each unit sold. In this sense, target costing is the reverse of traditional "cost plus margin" approaches to pricing.

In some settings, the firm's actual cost may be at or below the level required to achieve a target profit. However, for most firms, the task of driving the cost down to the level that ensures that the target margin is achieved creates many challenges. Meeting these challenges typically requires a combined organisational effort involving many different functional areas (for example engineering, design, marketing and accounting).

(ii) X has employed the target costing philosophy in the following ways:

Price setting: X is aiming to undercut competitors and the price of $180 appears to be the most appropriate from the perspective of what customers are willing to pay. Hence, because the price is driven by what customers are willing to pay, the company is adhering to one of the basic principles of target costing.

Avoiding a short-term perspective: in the first year, the price of the DVDR product is even lower than its variable cost. However, the management of X appear to be taking a longer-term perspective and are willing to increase volume as a means of benefiting from the learning effect. In turn, the learning effect will ultimately reduce the cost of manufacture.

The importance of the long-run target margin: management of X appears to be aiming for a target contribution margin (ignoring fixed costs) of 40%. While this will not be achieved in the first two years of production, as demonstrated by the workings in requirement *(a)* above, the contribution generated when this target is achieved is substantial and is the major contributor to the positive NPV reported above.

Examiner's Note:

Other issues raised about the target costing approach (which are relevant to the DVDR project) are equally acceptable.

SECTION C

Answer to Question Three

Requirement (a)

See Decision Tree on page 25.

Requirement (b)

(i) and (ii)

	Machine A			Machine B			Machine C		
Output	*Prof*	*Prob*	*EV*	*Prof*	*Prob*	*EV*	*Prof*	*Prob*	*EV*
1	35	0·56	19·60	5	0·16	0·80			
	25	0·24	6·00	-5	0·24	-1·20			
5	175	0·08	14·00	125	0·12	15·00	50	0·18	9·00
	75	0·06	4·50	75	0·09	6·75	25	0·30	7·50
	25	0·06	1·50	25	0·09	2·25	-25	0·12	-3·00
8				200	0·15	30·00	200	0·24	48·00
				40	0·15	6·00	40	0·16	6·40
		1·00	**45·6**		**1·00**	**59·60**		**1·00**	**67·9**

(the profits in the above table are before charging the lease payments)

Machine A

Probability of breaking even = 100%
EV of profit = 45·60 - 20 = £25·60 million

Machine B

Probability of breaking even = 51%
EV of profit = 59·60 - 30 = £29·60 million

Machine C

Probability of breaking even E = 58%
EV of profit = £67·90 - 40 = £27·90 million

Requirement (c)

REPORT

To: Management of C Ltd

From: Management Accountant

Subject: Recommended action

Date: 24 November 2004

Based on the decision tree, Machine B is the preferred option. But issues to consider:

The expected values of the profits from all three machines are close to the current profit of £24 million. This business is known and offers very little risk. Do the extra profits offer sufficient reward for the risks involved in undertaking the new venture?

B has the highest expected value, but the lowest probability of breaking even. Is this acceptable? It is impossible to say without knowing the management's attitude to risk.

A has the smallest expected value, but based on the outcomes presented it will always return a profit.

C has an expected value close to that of Machine A, but offers the potential for the largest outputs (that is 5 million or 8 million). However C also presents the possibility of the largest loss.

The choice between the machines is very sensitive to the forecasts of outputs and costs and their associated probabilities. For example if, for Machine C, the profit per cubic metre for the production of 8 million cubic metres was certain to be £25, then the expected value would rise to £53·50 million. This is far higher than the other machines and much higher than the profit currently being earned.

Expected value is an averaging technique based on probability estimates and therefore its use for a "one-off" decision is questionable. The use of a small number of point probabilities also weakens the technique.

Expected value gives no measure of the spread of results that could occur. A simulation (modelling) technique may be a better methodology to appraise such projects.

Answer to Question Three *Requirement (a)* **Decision Tree**

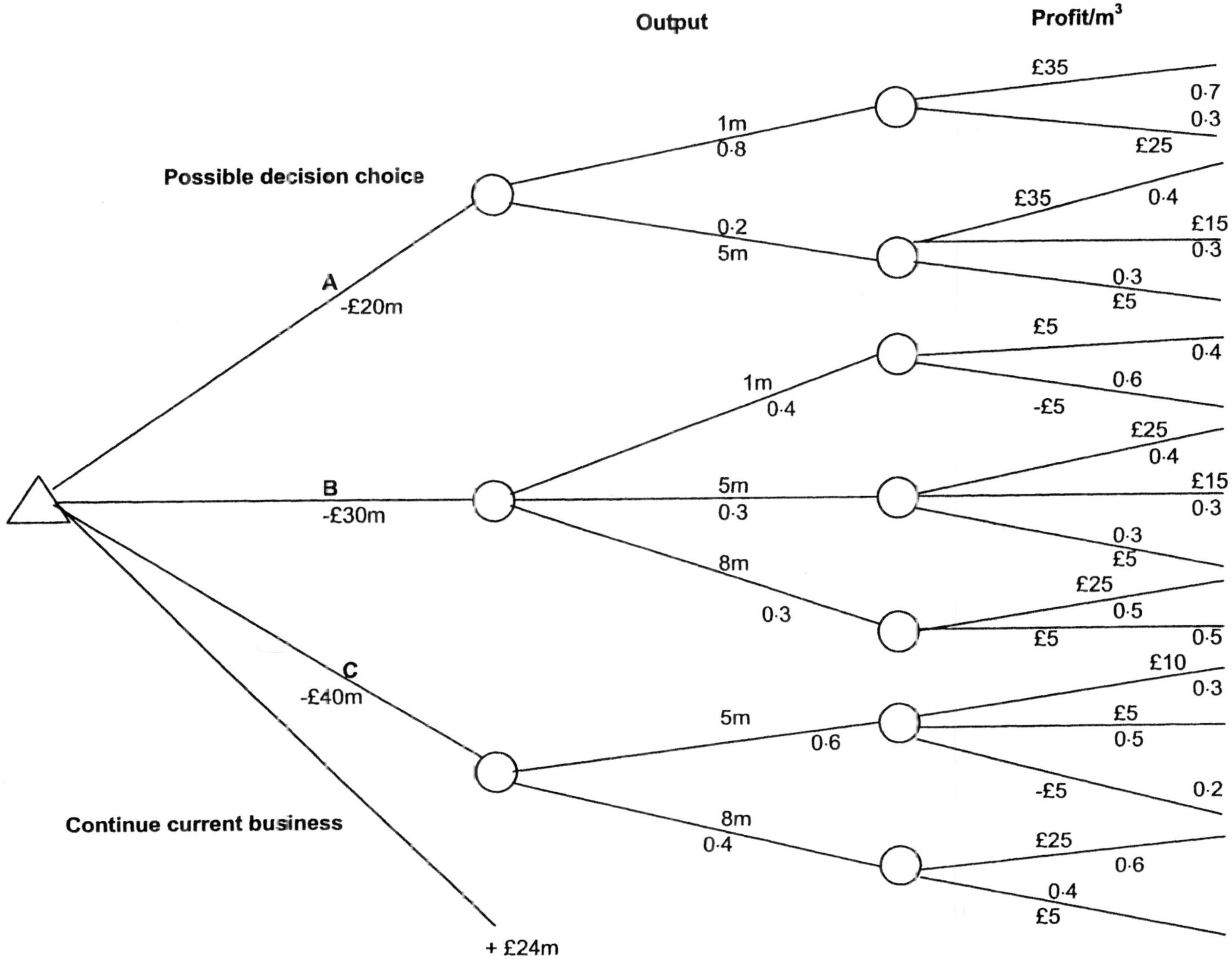

Answer to Question Four

Requirement (a)

(i) *Frame Division*

P = 4,000 - 0.5x
MR = 4,000 - x
MC = £1,000
Max profit when MC = MR
1,000 = 4,000 - x
x = 3,000
Substitute in price equation to give P = 2,500

Assembly Division

P = 7,000 – x/3
MR = 7,000 – 2x/3
MC = 2,500 + 1,750 = 4,250 (transfer price plus the assembly division's own variable cost)
Max profit when MC = MR
4,250 = 7,000 - 2x/3
x = 4,125 bicycles
Substitute in price equation to give price = £5,625 per assembled bicycle

(ii) The marginal cost of an assembled bicycle for the company as a whole is £2,750.

MC = 1,000 + 1,750 = 2750
Max profit when MC = MR
2,750 = 7,000 - 2x/3
x = 6,375 bicycles
P = £4,875

Requirement (b)

(i) Fixed Cost = £1 million. Therefore Profit required = £0·12 million
Therefore total contribution required = £1·12million
32 * x = 1·12 (x = contribution per box)
x = 0·035
Therefore transfer price = 0·035 + 0·025 = £0·06 per box

(ii) Fixed Cost = £4·5 million. Therefore Profit required = £0·54 million
Therefore total contribution required = £5·04 million
(1·65 – x) x 7 = 5·04 (note 1·65 = 11·55 million/7 million)
x = 0·93

The current variable costs are £0·89 therefore the maximum price that would be paid per box is £0·04.

(iii) A relevant cost equals the sum of the cash and opportunity costs.

There are a number of roles of a transfer price. These include:

- Promotion of goal congruence;
- To encourage autonomy;
- To encourage optimal allocation of resources;
- To facilitate performance appraisal;
- To motivate managers and employees.

There are a number of extreme values of transfer price that could be used in Freezer Foods Ltd.

Marginal cost: no "reward" is given to the supplying division. May be acceptable if there is spare capacity. (Marginal cost per box = £0·025)

Market price: this should be used if there is a perfectly competitive market. The selling division will, if operating efficiently, be expected to earn a profit and the buying division should be happy to buy at this price as the only alternative is the open market. The price should be reduced for any "internal" savings (for example packaging).

Using relevant costing as a basis would enable the above extremes to be recognised. If the Box Division can sell all of its output externally, then the opportunity cost would be the selling price. Consequently, it should not be penalised by having to accept a lower price from the Pizza Division. If there is spare capacity, then the Pizza Division should be allowed to benefit and could then be charged just the marginal cost.

However, there could be complications caused by the performance appraisal system and the effects of this on the willingness of the managers to "trade" must be considered. One solution to this could be to use "dual pricing".

SECTION D

Answer to Question Five

Requirement (a)

It is claimed that ABC is particularly useful in companies when:

- Overheads are a large percentage of total cost;
- Volume does not drive costs;
- Diverse product range;
- Varying demands on resources.

These factors will apply to B Ltd. The production process is highly automated and a wide variety of products are produced. The products are likely to consume/cause different costs in their manufacture and it highly unlikely that volume drives many of the costs. For example, the question states that the products pass through a combination of common processes: one such process could be a mixing machine. The machine can continue working for as long as the current flavour that is being mixed is needed but when a new flavour is needed the machine has to be stopped and cleaned out. This causes costs. Therefore, it can be seen that the driver of this cost is "flavour change", not volume.

If B Ltd allocates the costs of the mixing machine based on volume, the products that have very few flavours will be bearing too much cost. Consequently, their Product Managers will be unhappy.

Other implications include the fact that production runs for the mixer should be determined by flavour not final product.

However, B Ltd will need to think very carefully about the nature of the costs. The scenario says that there are "common processes". How can these be costed? It is very doubtful that ABC can offer much help here. ABC will help with the activities that surround the processes for example set-ups, sluicing and so on rather than the process itself.

Does B Ltd have knowledge of the production flow? Does the current cost allocation system follow that flow? This might seem as if it should be taken for granted but in many companies the accounting has, over the years, become detached from the reality of the "shop floor". Is that the case in B Ltd? The manager will need to investigate this.

The manager must undertake a cost benefit analysis. Perhaps the biggest benefit that could arise would be an awareness of what drives cost and therefore activity based management.

Requirement (b)

(i) The question implies that B Ltd uses, or intends to use, cost-plus pricing. Is this possible given:

The confectionery market. Can selling prices be based on cost-plus given the nature of the competition, incidental purchases/consumer habits and so on. Most products will be in a mature market and competitors will try to hold market share through the differentiation caused by their product's flavour/ingredients, brand name and so on. It is highly unlikely that they will spark a price war.

The processes involved. Full cost plus could be problematic given the common processes – how can they be shared out? Marginal cost plus: again problems may arise in identifying the true nature of the costs.

From a cost perspective, it can be seen that "accurate" costs will be very hard to ascertain. The market will judge the "accuracy" of the selling prices – and this will be done regardless of B Ltd's costs.

(ii) Why is the performance of the Product Managers based on profit?

The current costing system is obviously causing problems. This is due to the perceived arbitrary way that costs are allocated to the products. Given the common processes, there will always be problems with this. ABC could lead to greater awareness of some drivers of costs and therefore this will lead to a more robust and defendable base for those costs. This will, in turn, make the managers responsible for their actions, for example requesting flavour changes and the scheduling of production runs.

Introducing ABC will not solve the issues discussed. The Managing Director should be aware of this fact. There is possibly a sign of weak management here – he appears to want to hide behind the perceived accuracy and robustness of ABC. ABC will enable a better view of cost drivers to be formed and should therefore lead to better activity management but it will not cure the problems of an inappropriate performance appraisal system.

Answer to Question Six

Requirement (a)

Traditional cost classifications, terminology and periodic financial accounts focus on the need to determine the total costs and revenues that have occurred. This approach matches the need to measure profit and to value stocks and work in progress in accordance with external account reporting requirements. These approaches therefore focus on the past which may not be appropriate for decision making.

Decision making should be based on relevant costs; that is costs that are affected by the decision that is taken. Thus relevant costs are those that are:

- Future;
- Differential; and
- Involve cash.

Thus it can be seen that there is a very significant difference between the traditional approaches that are based upon the past, and the information needs of managers for decision making which are focussed on the future.

The modern manufacturing environment emphasises changes in production flows to meet the demands of customers and the holding of little or no stocks. This means that the company must be very flexible in order to meet the demands of its customers. In addition, there must be a very strong focus on quality and quality related practices as there is no buffer stock to resolve any quality failures which occur. Thus, there is potential stoppage of production resulting in a possible loss of customers.

Information for decision making in this environment must therefore be based on the principles of relevant costs outlined above, but determined in the context of the modern manufacturing environment.

Requirement (b)

(i) **Activity Based Costing (ABC)**

ABC is a system that is based on the principle that it is activities that cause costs to be incurred rather than the number of units of product/service that are produced.

Traditional cost accounting analyses overhead costs according to how they change in relation to changes in the volume of output and thus classifies costs as being either fixed (because they are unaffected by volume changes) or variable (because they change in proportion to volume changes). This simplistic approach assumes that costs are only affected by volume and not by other factors and thus perhaps provides a misleading analysis of fixed and variable overhead costs.

The modern environment is much more mechanised than traditional manufacturing and, consequently, the proportion of overhead costs to total costs is much greater than it was when the traditional costing systems were devised. It is these changes that have resulted in the need for a more appropriate method of recognising the causes of costs. As a consequence, costs that were previously thought of as being fixed and indirect can now often be recognised to be variable costs that can be clearly identified with a particular activity and the number of times that the activity is performed.

If a manager knows what drives the cost then the driver can be thought of as being incremental and, therefore, decision specific.

ABC will accumulate costs at various levels, for example batch, product and organisational levels. As such it can be thought of as being similar to marginal costing and thereby, if used correctly, an appropriate aid to decision making.

(ii) **Throughput Accounting (TA)**

TA evolved from the "Theory of Constraints" that Goldratt and Cox developed to improve profitability.

TA is concerned with the rate at which a business can generate profit. It is a short run optimisation technique that seeks to obtain the maximum benefit from the throughput. Consequently, it focuses on the bottleneck in the production process. Therefore, it can be seen to be very similar to the marginal cost/decision-making technique needed when there is a scarce resource, that is to maximise contribution per unit of scarce resource.

However, TA redefines marginal cost and hence contribution. Only direct material is viewed as being a variable cost; all other costs are assumed to be fixed. Products are ranked according to their contribution per unit of time on the key resource. This is identical to the concept of allocating a scare resource under short run decision making except for the definition of contribution.

It can be seen that TA has responded to the needs of decision making in the new manufacturing environment by challenging the classification of certain costs.

(iii) **Life cycle costing (LCC)**

With LCC the objective is to maximise the profit over the product's (or customer's) life, that is it views the project from "cradle to grave".

Factors to consider include:

- Designing quality/value added;
- Engineering costs;
- Minimising time to market;
- Managing cash flows;
- Managing the length of the life cycle.

Viewing cash flows and profits over the entire life runs contrary to the need for periodic financial reporting. It should be expected that "poor" performance in one period might be necessary to promote strong returns in another. Increased investment in design and engineering (an increased cash outflow before production starts) can give rise to greater demand and large cost savings later.

It could be argued that investment appraisal techniques also cut across the periodic view but very often the appraisal concentrates on a predetermined time scale.

CIMA

November 2004 Examinations

Intermediate Level

Systems and Project Management

(ISPM – Paper 10)

Question Paper	1
Examiner's Brief Guide to the Paper	9
Examiner's Answers	10

The answers published here have been written by the Examiner and should provide a helpful guide for both lecturers and students.

Published separately on the CIMA website (www.cimaglobal.com/students) from the end of March 2005 is a Post Examination Guide for this paper, which provides much valuable and complementary material including indicative mark information.

CIMA

Intermediate Level

Systems and Project Management

10 ISPM

25 November 2004

Thursday morning

INSTRUCTIONS TO CANDIDATES

Read this page before you look at the questions

You are allowed three hours to answer this question paper.
ALL questions are based on the scenario. Answer the THREE questions in Section A. Answer ONE question ONLY from Section B.

SCENARIO

READ THIS SCENARIO FIRST.

ALL QUESTIONS ARE BASED UPON THIS SCENARIO.

THE QUESTIONS ARE IN TWO SECTIONS AND ARE ON PAGES 7 – 9.

ANSWER ALL THREE QUESTIONS IN SECTION A AND ONE ONLY FROM SECTION B.

This scenario is structured in two sections. Section 1 introduces CFO, the organisation under review, and Section 2 introduces the systems implementation project being undertaken by CFO.

SECTION 1

Background
CFO Ltd is an organisation based in the United Kingdom. It offers a range of financial services, including home, life and car insurance products, personal and business loans and home loans (known as "mortgages").

The structure of CFO is shown below:

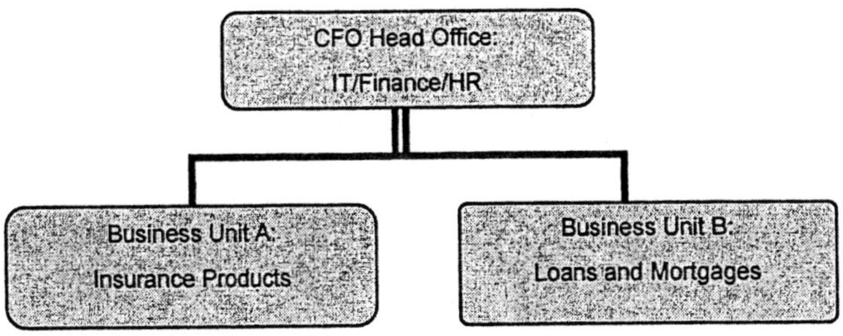

Business Unit A
Business Unit A operates five call centres located throughout the country, selling home, life and car insurance products. As the larger of the two business units, the management team of Business Unit A has frequently over-used the resources of the whole organisation to meet their aggressive and often over-ambitious deadlines and targets. In recent years, Business Unit A has lost market share to rivals, largely due to its slowness in introducing information technology to deliver its products to customers.

Business Unit B
Business Unit B is smaller and less technologically innovative, operating from two call centres. CFO loan and mortgage customers are less likely to require on-line website facilities than insurance product customers, instead being more interested in high quality customer care and on-going customer service.

Head Office IT department
The IT staff consists of 6 technicians/analysts, 2 designers (one of whom is an expert in core CFO systems and one who is a web designer), and 2 help-desk advisers (both of whom have experience of training in previous jobs). In the past, the IT team has only been involved in core technical work and not involved in training or customer support of new systems. The IT manager believes that only IT staff have the necessary skills to be involved in IT projects.

Market environment
The financial services industry has become increasingly regulated in recent years, and a number of job losses have occurred in CFO as a result of increased competition and falling profits. This has resulted in low morale. For the last two years, CFO has been a member of a benchmarking group called "The Forum for Quality in Lending", the aim of which is to improve the quality of customer service and standards of excellence in the mortgage industry.

SECTION 2

IT infrastructure upgrade : Project scope
At the start of May, the CFO board of directors committed to a new operating system and the re-design of the organisation's website and intranet. The official project start date, as set by the IT department manager, was 1 June 2004. (However, the systems analysis phase of the re-designed website had already been completed in May.) The operating system must be fully installed by mid-September, and the website must be up and running by the first week of November. CFO has already announced to the public that the re-designed website would be available at the beginning of November. As a result of problems which had occurred during previous systems projects, at the beginning of July the board of directors of CFO brought in a team of management consultants, EZ, to oversee the project.

You are a senior management consultant working for EZ.

Findings by EZ of initial review of CFO organisation
On review of the organisation, the management consultants have discovered the following issues:

- After carrying out a detailed systems analysis in May, Business Unit A announced to the public the new website (to be linked to the internal intranet) to improve customer interface and management;
- Business Unit B staff are more interested in a stable desktop environment and user friendly operating system, than a state-of-the-art intranet and website;
- The IT department has a history of forcing ill-suited and poorly tested technology on the staff, with IT technicians of CFO controlling entire projects and dismissing user suggestions;
- There is an apparent inability for both business units to work together with the IT department.

By the end of July, the management consultants had also uncovered the following issues relating to the project activities up to that date.

1: Project team work
The IT department was responsible for organisation of the project team. True to its past history, the IT department had put together a project team with no members from the business units. When the IT team went into each individual call centre, users were not asked for input into the overall plan.

2 : Agreement of project objectives
The IT department manager set the objectives and timescales for the roll out of the new operating system and updated website and produced a project plan for the IT team only (see Figure 1), with no input from the staff of the two business units.

PRIVATE AND CONFIDENTIAL

TO: IT DEPARTMENT STAFF
FROM: HEAD OF IT

TWO PHASE INFRASTRUCTURE UPGRADE

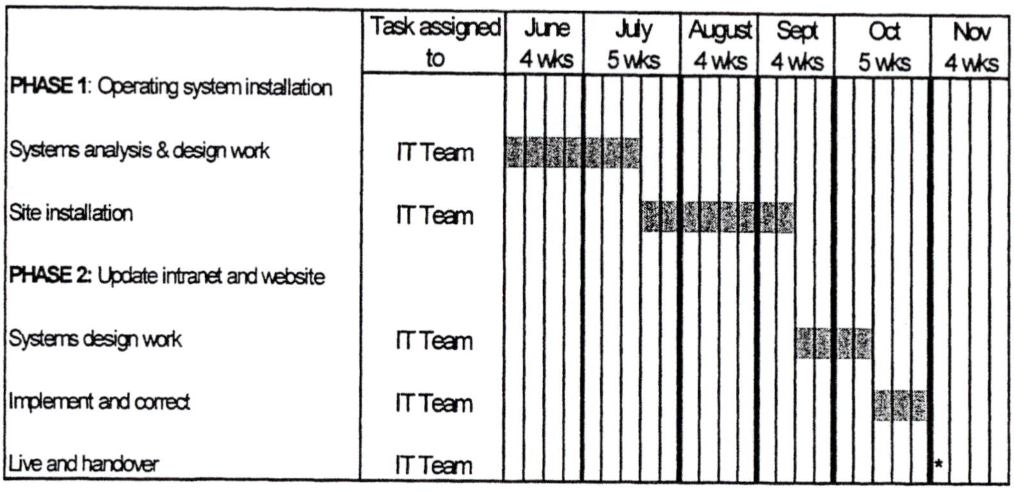

Figure 1

The IT manager planned to complete the roll out of the new operating system by the middle of September. There is to be one roll out completed each week. That is, it will take eight weeks to install the operating system in all of the call centres and at Head Office.

3: User focused implementation
All six IT technicians/analysts travel to the installation site for the week, three to carry out the main installation work and the other three to act as back up, providing any extra assistance required. They do this during normal working hours, displacing individuals from their desks and completing the installation at each site to a rigidly defined timetable.

The plan shown in Figure 1 has no defined pilots, training or contingencies and has no agreed method for handling the calls that would normally be received during the planned installation time. During the two installations which took place during July, the management consultants estimated that several hundred telephone calls (approximately 20% of the total number of calls expected during this period) from existing and potential customers were missed due to the displacement of call centre staff.

4: Support infrastructure
The IT department has a poor track record of supporting the technology they deliver and has no resources planned to train staff. In the past this has resulted in frustration for IT staff and users. There have also been complaints from customers in the past as a result of slow service and errors made by call centre operators. Many staff have an incomplete understanding of some of the basic functions of the current systems as they have never been properly trained.

5: Ownership
As the IT department has taken full responsibility for running and implementing the project, users have shown little enthusiasm for, or interest in, the system. Support in design or attempts to generate ideas or innovation are non-existent, as most users do not feel that the operating system is anything to do with them.

6: Updated website and intranet
The updated website will allow customers to review all products on offer, to obtain quotes, to compare quotes with rival companies, to send email queries and to instantly sign up for insurance products and make payments electronically.

A basic website is already in existence (showing all current products on offer, the ability to make comparisons with rivals, and the ability to get on-line quotes), but, as at the end of July, the enhanced features had not been designed, as both designers have been working full time on the new operating system.

In early July, the web designer informed the IT manager that he believed his time would be better spent on the re-design of the new website, and suggested that developing a prototype web page in order to test customer acceptance would help to improve design and customer acceptance. The web designer estimated this would only take 4 weeks. However, development of the prototype would need to begin at the end of July if the web site is to be in operation by early November. The IT manager dismissed this suggestion, stating that time would be better spent working on operating system problems.

Part of the systems analysis work on the website was carried out on the arrangements for credit facilities and discounts that are to be automatically applied to each on-line sale (under the current system these were done over the phone). Under the planned system, if the on-line enquiry is for car insurance, then no credit terms will be offered to the customer. If the enquiry is for home or life insurance, then credit is automatically offered. Customers with existing insurance policies with CFO are offered credit at 6% interest, whereas new customers to CFO are offered credit facilities at 8% interest. In addition, existing customers get a 5% discount on all new sales, but new customers get no discount on the first sale.

Following these investigations, the board of directors has appointed **you as the project manager until the end of the project**. You called a meeting with the project team and other relevant members of CFO which took place on 2 August.

The meeting of 2 August
Present at the meeting were the IT department manager, who was previously the leader of the project, and the IT staff who had been assigned to work on the project. In addition, the general manager of each business unit was also present. The main issues raised by the participants were as follows:

The general manager of Business Unit A was worried about the security of the new website, particularly as it was planned to introduce electronic payments by customers. He was concerned that insufficient time had been allowed in the project to test security of the website.

The general manager of Business Unit B was concerned that the introduction of the new operating system was being done too quickly, with little regard for the needs of the staff, and with no training or after support being provided. He reminded the IT department manager that, as a member of the Forum for Quality in Lending, CFO had a duty to customers to maintain a high standard of performance, which was being threatened by this project.

The IT department manager was most concerned with achieving the project deadline within the allocated budget. One of the IT department staff raised concerns that no training had been built into the plan and that resulting increased workload would put pressure on the IT staff after the system was up and running. She was most concerned that the high workload of the very limited and over stretched IT department would reduce morale, which was already very low in the department.

Today's date is 3 August. You have been asked by the board of directors to prepare a number of documents relating to the above information.

SECTION A – 80 MARKS

Read the scenario before you attempt the questions

ANSWER ALL THREE QUESTIONS

Question One

Required:

The board of directors of CFO has asked you, as the Project Manager, to prepare an internal memo to the IT department manager which will

(a) identify and explain the problems with the plan prepared by the IT department manager, as shown in Figure 1 on page 4.

(10 marks)

(b) recommend **four** main improvements that should have been made to the plan, as prepared by the IT department manager, at the start of the project. You should clearly explain how these would have overcome the problems identified in part *(a)* of your answer.

(12 marks)

(Total = 22 marks)

Question Two

Required:

Prepare a second internal memo for the staff of both business units of CFO which will

(a) *(i)* explain the term "operating system", and describe **four** main features of commonly used operating systems such as *Microsoft Windows,* and

(ii) identify the benefits of these features to CFO.

(15 marks)

(b) *(i)* explain the importance to CFO of an updated website; and

(6 marks)

(ii) produce a decision table for the on-line credit and discount facilities.

(12 marks)

(Total = 33 marks)

Question Three

Required:

The board of directors of CFO is particularly concerned about the management of the IT department and the inability of the IT department staff to work effectively with the other departments. It is also concerned that poor management may lead to poor control.

The board has asked you to prepare a report for them which will

(a) propose a plan for an audit of the management activities of the IT department manager in respect of this project. Clearly explain the aim of each stage of the audit.

(15 marks)

(b) explain the importance to CFO of ensuring adequate security controls to be included in the new website, and the importance of testing these security controls during and after the project.

(10 marks)

(Total = 25 marks)

End of Section A

SECTION B – 20 MARKS

Read the scenario before you attempt a question

ANSWER ONE QUESTION ONLY

Question Four

YOU ARE TO ASSUME THAT YOU ARE THE PROJECT MANAGER FOR QUESTION FOUR ONLY

On 1 August, you were preparing for the meeting which was to take place on 2 August.

Required:

(a) Discuss the challenges faced by you, as the new project manager of the project, when you conduct the project meeting which is to take place on 2 August.

(12 marks)

(b) Explain the skills required of a project manager when trying to improve staff morale in relation to the project.

(8 marks)

(Total = 20 marks)

Question Five

The Forum for Quality in Lending is a benchmarking group specifically set up to improve standards of excellence and quality of customer service for organisations working in the mortgage industry.

Required:

(a) Identify **four** advantages for organisations of benchmarking, explaining the advantages to organisations like CFO of being a member of a benchmarking group.

(12 marks)

(b) Identify and explain **four** reasons why improvements in staff training in CFO (both in the use of the technology and in the products sold), could improve quality of customer service.

(8 marks)

(Total = 20 marks)

End of paper

The Examiner for ISPM offers to future candidates and to lecturers using this booklet for study purposes, the following background and guidance on the questions included in this examination paper.

This scenario is based upon a financial services organisation, CFO, which is currently undertaking a project to upgrade its existing operating system and website.

The main issues covered by the scenario are:

- Project leadership, communication and management skills;
- Project planning;
- Information technology features and controls;
- The management of quality through benchmarking.

Section A – compulsory

Question One examines part (i) of the syllabus – *Project Management.* Requirement (a) relates to the learning outcome *"Evaluate the project management process"* and examines candidates' ability to identify the problems with the current situation of the project plan. Requirement (b) relates to the learning outcome *"Produce a management plan for a simple project"* and tests candidates' ability to produce an improved plan for the scenario project based upon the weakness identified in requirement (a).

Question Two examines part (ii) of the syllabus – *Information Technology and Systems.* Requirements (a) and (b)(i) relate to the learning outcome *"Explain the features and operation of commonly used Information Technology hardware and software".* These questions are designed to test both the candidates' knowledge of operating systems and their ability to identify how they can be utilised by the organisation in the scenario. Requirement (b) (ii) relates to the learning outcome of *"Apply the main tools and techniques used in gathering and analysing information relating to an information system."* This question primarily tests candidates' ability to use and apply a decision table tool.

Question Three examines part (iv) of the syllabus – *Audit of Activities and Systems*, and part (iii) – *Control of Activities and Resources.* Requirement (a) relates to an audit issue and specifically relates to the learning outcome *"Produce a plan for the audit of various organisational activities including management, accounting and information systems".* The question tests candidates' ability to produce an outline management audit plan for the managers mentioned in the scenario. Requirement (b) relates to control, and specifically the learning outcome *"Evaluate and recommend improvements to the control of Information Systems including those using Information Technology"* and tests candidates' understanding of security controls and testing.

Section B – one question from two

Question Four examines part (i) of the syllabus – *Project Management.* Requirement (a) relates to the learning outcome *"Identify the main problems associated with meetings and recommend how these problems might be avoided or solved".* It is designed to test the candidates' ability to identify the problems faced in a difficult meeting situation. Requirement (b) relates to the learning outcome *"Explain the skills required of a project manager"* and tests the candidates' knowledge of key project management skill areas in difficult projects.

Question Five examines part (v) of the syllabus – *Management of quality* and part (ii) – *Information Technology and Systems.* Requirement (a) relates to the learning outcome *"Evaluate the features, benefits and drawbacks of contemporary approaches to the management of quality"*, and tests candidates' understanding of benchmarking. Requirement (b) relates to the learning outcome *"Explain the processes of systems design and development and analyse the issues arising at those stages."* This question tests candidates' understanding of the importance of training as part of the systems development process.

CIMA

The Examiner's Answers for Systems and Project Management

SECTION A

Answer to Question One

Requirement (a)

INTERNAL MEMORANDUM

From:	Project Manager, EZ
To:	IT Department Manager
Date:	3 August 2004

Issues relating to the current project plan

The Board of Directors of CFO has asked me to review and appraise the current project plan, and in the light of these findings to propose a number of recommendations for improvement to this plan.

Problems with the current project plan

Lack of user input

The first problem is procedural rather than technical. No information was initially gathered from the users and staff of CFO, relating to how the project should be appropriately planned in terms of timescales or resources.

Without this key user input, key issues within the planning process could be missed or underestimated. For example, there is no extra time indicated in the plan to deal with the calls that will need to be taken during the time when the implementation is taking place in each centre. As a result it is evident that business is potentially being lost due to the high number of missed calls. Had the users been involved in planning, the issue would probably have been raised as an important planning consideration. This lack of user involvement in planning is likely to reduce user co-operation and commitment to the system.

No visible allocation of responsibility for planning tasks

The current plan only indicates that the IT team is responsible for all of the stages within the project. There is no indication of individual areas of responsibility or reporting.

Without this information, it will be very difficult to identify whether individual workloads of the IT staff are realistic. It will also lead to ambiguity and lack of direction for the IT team as it will not be clearly directed. Again, this may lead to lack of commitment to individual tasks within the project and may lead to reduced motivation of the IT team.

Key project phases omitted

Some key stages of the project are not highlighted on the plan. This may be because they are not in fact part of the plan itself, but nevertheless, they are key omissions. For example, there is no time allowed in the plan for testing or training of staff. It may be that these are included somewhere else in the plan (for example, within "Site installation" in Phase 1, or in "Implement and correct" in Phase 2). However, it would be much clearer to the project team and the users if these were separated out on the plan.

Without this clarification, these key aspects of the project may be omitted or overlooked, or sufficient time may not be allowed for them. If it is the case that these elements of the project are not in fact to take place, then these are serious omissions. It is vital to ensure thorough testing before allowing the users to use the system. If testing is not done, then errors will almost certainly occur and may result in lengthy and time consuming re-design of the system while it is meant to be up and running. It will also lead to much user dissatisfaction and probably more significantly for CFO, customer dissatisfaction.

Lack of training is also likely to have a similar negative effect on the project. Poor training will lead to misuse, resulting in a high error rate, and both user and customer dissatisfaction. In a highly competitive market place, CFO cannot afford to have a system that customers do not use or feel that the operators cannot use efficiently to process their requests. As raised by one of the IT staff, lack of training will also result in additional pressure on the IT staff, causing even lower morale in the IT department.

No contingency

This again may be built into individual stages within each phase, but it is not highlighted separately on the plan.

Having contingency built into the plan is critical, as it is most unlikely that every stage will go according to plan. As the IT department of CFO is so busy and low morale is a potential problem, then it would be wise to include contingency to cover staff absence. It may be that there is no contingency in the current plan because the IT manager does not believe there to be any spare time within the project.

However, with improved testing, allocation of responsibilities and greater user involvement, time can be used more efficiently on the project and contingency could be built in.

No milestone reviews

Without this, project time slippage can occur for too long before any remedial action is taken. Similarly, without milestone reviews, a holistic view of project progress will be lost whilst addressing individual stages. With this particular project, given the fact that in the plan all stages follow directly after each other, opportunities for synergy and reduction in time are being missed because too much emphasis is being placed on each individual stage.

Requirement (b)

Changes to original plan (any 4 of the following)

1. An initial stage to collect data from staff of their requirements should be carried out. The first two or three weeks of the project should be allowed for meeting staff in order to consult, explain and collect requirements. If this is done, then time is likely to be saved in later stages due to better understanding of systems requirements.

2. The plan should be distributed to all project team members, both within the IT department and any other staff used by the team in other parts of the organisation. The plan should not be private and confidential to the IT department. All CFO staff are affected by the project so should have access to the plan.

3. Tasks assigned should be more clearly defined. Although it may not be possible to be absolutely specific, a revised plan should indicate more clearly which person/group of people should carry out a task. In particular, in Phase 1 three systems analysts could be assigned to each roll out, rather than all six analysts at each roll out. This should save time and allow for more roll outs to be carried out in a shorter period of time.

4. Phase 1 and 2 both should include a stage for testing. This could occur after the design work has been done, but before any implementation gets underway.

5. Phase 1 and 2 both should include a stage for training. The IT department has 2 help desk advisers who are both skilled trainers. They should be used to assist in training whilst the analysts are on each site. While roll out is occurring, training can be taking place and the trainers could stay on each site for 3 or 4 days after the implementation to assist with any post implementation issues.

6. Milestone reviews. It is important that the project manager should review project progress periodically. In both phases of the project this could occur directly after design and testing to ensure that all issues or problems are addressed before implementation begins.

7. Contingency should be included in both phases. Hopefully, with improved analysis, testing and training, contingency time will be limited, but it should nevertheless be included on the plan.

8. Phase 2 should start earlier, at the start of September to allow a little more time for testing of the system and to build in some contingency. By allowing the web designer to work exclusively on web design rather than on the operating system is a more efficient use of resources.

9. In Phase 2, a prototype should be built into the project. It is evident that the expert web designer believes this to be an important phase of the project. The web designer should not be spending all of his time working on the operating system when his time could be better spent on the design of the new website.

10. More overlap of resources. In the original plan, each stage followed directly on from the previous stage, due to the fact that all of the IT department were allocated to work on each aspect of the project. However, the revised plan could allow for some overlap, in order to overcome the over allocation of resources to some stages and the mis-match of skills to others. For example, the web designer should not be working on the operating system design. Also, the help desk advisers could utilise their skills more effectively in training than in basic help desk or IT assistance.

Answer to Question Two

Requirement (a)

INTERNAL MEMORANDUM

From:	Project Manager, EZ
To:	Staff of Business Units A and B
Date:	3 August 2004

The importance of the new operating system and upgraded website to CFO

The Board of Directors of CFO has asked me to explain the importance of the current information systems project to all staff within CFO. The following memo will highlight the benefits to CFO of the new operating system and the upgraded website, and will also explain the tool which is used by the system to decide on-line credit and discount facilities.

An operating system

The operating system is the system software that manages the control activities of the computer. It can be seen as the chief manager of the computer system, determining which resources the computer system will use, scheduling the use of those resources and monitoring their activities. The operating system controls the links between other hardware devices, such as keyboards, printers or faxes, and makes sure they are ready to use. It is also responsible for the efficient storage of your data, files and directories, and it monitors storage space within a computer and how best this should be used. The operating system schedules all of the thousands of tasks your computer does and it co-ordinates different parts of the computer so that many tasks can be done simultaneously, thus improving efficiency.

Four main features of an operating system and their benefits to CFO

Multi-programming

The operating system allows multiple computer programs to use the computer's resources at the same time. For example, a user can be inputting new or updated data relating to a customer on the customer database, whilst at the same time the user can be printing off a separate report on weekly activities. This allows the user to be more productive and therefore will hopefully improve both internal and external customer satisfaction. Customers of CFO require up to date, efficient information, thus the operating system facilitates this requirement.

Multi-tasking

Multi-tasking allows the user to run two or more programs concurrently on a single computer. For example, a user in Business Unit B may wish to use the mortgage customer database to refer to customer information, whilst also preparing a spreadsheet report on overdue mortgage accounts. Multi-tasking will allow the user to display both programs on screen at the same time and work on them both simultaneously, without having to close one program down to work with the other. This obviously is a great advantage to users in Business Unit B, as it again will improve productivity through time saving and it will improve accuracy, as the user always knows that they are using the most recent database information and not a copy printed off earlier.

Graphical User Interface

Users interact with the operating system through the user interface of that particular operating system. Modern operating systems, such as *Windows*, *Windows NT*, *OS2*, *UNIX* and *Systems 7*, all use a graphical user interface (GUI) to represent common commands and computer operations. GUI's use a range of icons, buttons, symbols, pull down menus and bars to represent programs and files, which can be activated using a mouse or cursor. For the users of

CFO, GUI's can assist new users to master the system more quickly and without extensive training. The commands in GUI's tend to be the same in all programs used by the operating system, which again reduces systems complexity and makes it easier for the user to operate without additional training or reference manuals.

CFO is likely to have a number of separate programs including a mortgage customer database, the intranet, separate files and programs relating to all of the insurance products and the intranet. If all of these use the same GUI, then users will be able to navigate their way around all parts of the system without too much difficulty or need to re-learn, which again will improve productivity and efficiency. It should also improve confidence in the system and the users will also feel greater confidence as users.

Security and password controls

Operating systems will have strict password control systems to prevent unauthorised access to data and files. The operating system can be programmed to ensure that users can only access recognised areas of the system. It can also monitor who has logged on and off a system, unauthorised attempts at systems access and it notifies users of password changes and errors. The operating system will also be responsible for validation checks on data entry to ensure that any data entered fits within a recognised criterion within each part of the system.

For CFO, security of data is paramount, as a great deal of data relating to customers will be held on various parts of the system and customers will want to be assured that their data is not at risk. If customers feel assured that appropriate security controls exist then they are more likely to do business with CFO.

Validation checks are an important part of the system for CFO. A wide variety of different data is likely to be held within different files and it is important that this is not duplicated or input incorrectly within each part of the system. Validation checks will ensure that only the correct data is stored within each file and directory, thus improving the efficiency of the system and it also helps the users to ensure accuracy.

Requirement (b)

Importance of an updated website

It is clear that Business Unit A customers expect up to date technology, as it has lost customers in recent years by being slow to introduce technological delivery of its products. Therefore, if Business Unit A is to maintain and regain its customer base it must respond to its customers expectations. Customer satisfaction will be key in maintaining its position in the market and this could be achieved partly by improved customer service through on-line delivery of Business Unit A products. The additional features proposed for the website are designed to enhance customer satisfaction and improve customer interaction with the company. Business Unit A has already announced to the public that the new website will be available in November. Therefore, achievement of the date for phase 2 is critical to its credibility.

Part of the new website functions will be the ability to produce on-line decisions for credit and discount facilities. This should improve speed of response for the customer, thus increasing productivity in decision making, as the system, rather than the operator, can now make a decision.

The updated website will allow cross selling of products between the five call centres as customers will be able to see all products on-line. This is likely to be key to future growth for CFO.

Decision table for on-line credit and discounts

The Conditions:

1. If the enquiry is for car insurance then no credit.
2. If the enquiry is for home or life insurance then credit is offered. Existing customers are offered credit at 6% interest and new customers at 8% interest.
3. Existing customers with other insurance policies with CFO get a 5% discount. New customers get no discount on the first policy.

Condition Entry = $2^2 = 4$

CONDITIONS	**CONDITION ENTRY**			
Car Insurance	Y	Y	N	N
Existing Customer	Y	N	Y	N
ACTIONS	**ACTION ENTRY**			
No Credit given	X	X		
Credit given at 6% interest			X	
Credit given at 8% interest				X
Discount of 5% given	X		X	

Answer to Question Three

Requirement (a)

REPORT

To:	Directors of CFO
From:	Project Manager, EZ Consultants (working for CFO systems implementation project)
Date:	August 2004

An analysis of the management and control activities within the CFO systems implementation project

Introduction

It is evident from research and observation undertaken by the consultants of EZ that there are some managerial and organisational problems within CFO. These have led to problems of mistrust and lack of communication between departments and low morale. The following report will produce a plan for a management audit of the IT manager within CFO, in order to identify and evaluate any management weaknesses which could be causing the aforementioned problems. In addition, the report will consider the importance to CFO of adequate control and security measures in both the planning of the systems project and in its subsequent day to day operations.

A management audit plan for CFO

The official CIMA terminology defines a management audit as:

"An objective and independent appraisal of the effectiveness of managers and the corporate structure in the achievement of entity objectives and policies. It aims to identify existing and potential management weaknesses and to recommend ways to rectify them."

It is important that the audit is done as objectively as possible and that, for this particular management audit, the scope will be limited to the objectives of the systems project being undertaken.

The management audit plan, the activities within each stage of the plan and the aim of each stage is provided on the next page.

Management audit plan: Stage	Actions at each stage	Aim of each stage
1. Plan the audit	• Determine the approach of the audit with consultation and agreement of approach with the IT manager. • Identify the aim, scope and methods to be used and the protocol for fact finding and investigation.	To accomplish the audit in an effective and orderly manner and to ensure that all parties are fully aware of the process of the audit.
2. Identify management activities during the stages of the project	**Planning:** • Identify whether the manager sufficiently planned the resources. • Identify whether customer requirements were included in the project plan, that is examine whether customers were involved in the systems analysis stage. • Examine whether all staff are aware of project responsibilities and whether all members of the IT department fully understood their role in the project plan.	To determine whether sufficient management time has been allocated to this critical project phase by the IT department manager. A good plan should form a sound foundation for a successful project, but if there are weaknesses in the planning then it is likely to lead to problems as the project progresses.
	Motivating: • Conduct confidential interviews with IT staff to survey staff attitude to project and IT management. Do staff feel ownership of their tasks on this project? • Identify targets set by the IT manager for staff and whether these are appropriate and motivate achievement of overall project objective. • Interview IT staff and IT manager to identify their attitudes towards quality and customer service. • Identify how much delegation of tasks occurs and how much responsibility is passed down to lower levels for decision making.	An important part of the IT manager's role is to motivate the staff to achieve their objectives. Therefore the management audit must review both the manager's attitude to motivation, and the IT staff opinion on motivation and targets of the project. Motivation can not be achieved if the IT staff do not feel ownership of the project nor if they are not givon cufficient levels of authority.
3. Evaluate management activities	• Identify those areas of the IT manager's activities which are successful in achieving the project objectives, and those which are not successful.	It is important to identify both effective and ineffective management activities so that the weaknesses can be addressed and improved and the strengths can be reinforced and built upon.

4. Review findings	• Present initial findings to the IT manager	Allow the IT manager to respond to some of the key points and make explanations for some/all of his activities
5. Report findings and make recommendations	• Present report to the Board of Directors with recommendations to improve key areas in planning, staff management, control activities and motivation techniques	Allow senior managers to decide appropriate actions for the future management of IT and role of the IT manager

Requirement (b)

The importance of security controls in the new CFO website

Security controls in the new website are likely to include firewalls, data validation and encryption controls, data back up procedures and virus protection software.

Having a website means that the organisation is open to the risk of malicious external interference, such as hackers or those spreading deliberate viruses. Hackers could cause fraudulent insurance claims or corruption of key customer information. This could lead to loss of customers and reputation in the industry. Firewalls are a common method of protecting against unwanted external interference.

During the project, the testing of how effectively the firewall system deals with external interference will be critical in stopping any long term damage to the organisation's business and reputation.

Data validation controls are important to ensure that information relating to credit card and personal customer information remains confidential both on the system and during transmission. Encryption technology, such as using an SSL protocol, could be used to transmit personal information to CFO and thus reduce the chances of errors or fraud in transmission.

Again, during the project the IT team should identify which information needs to be transmitted using SSL and should adequately test the encryption process to ensure that all confidential customer information is protected.

Regular data and systems back up is also important to protect the system and its information. If the system failed, then there must be back up data to use immediately in order to ensure that the organisation and the system can continue to operate. Back up is likely to be done on at least a daily basis, probably twice daily in order to ensure adequate accuracy of information in a dynamic financial industry such as this. If back up is not done sufficiently, this could lead to bad publicity and low customer satisfaction which again could be damaging to business. Testing of back up procedures during the project should ensure that CFO is aware of exactly what back up procedures are required and at what frequency. Therefore, back up resources can be minimised but focused upon the key information areas.

A further security control to consider is virus protection. This appears to be a common and recurring problem for many organisations using the internet and e-mail technology. As CFO will be regularly communicating electronically with thousands of external customers, then it is at risk of virus attack. Viruses can cause severe damage to an organisation's system and to its ability to function as a business. Just one day's loss of business activity due to a virus attack could have a severe financial affect upon CFO and could also lead to loss of business and reputation.

Therefore, adequate virus software protection must be put in place to prevent this risk. Again, testing of possible weaknesses in the system to virus attack, that is e-mail systems should be undertaken and periodic review of this must be done at very regular intervals. The nature of viruses is changing every day and testing of virus protection control should not be limited to the duration of the project. Awareness of security risks from virus attack should be an on-going process for the IT team, both during the project and after it is implemented.

Conclusion

A management audit of the activities of the IT manager could highlight some key managerial problems which have occurred in the project, which may indicate wider issues in the management of the IT department. It is important that the audit is carried out openly and objectively, and that the IT manager is made fully aware of the methods and objectives of the audit. Adequate controls and security are a critical aspect of the system under development and it is important that the managers in the organisation do not underestimate the importance of this aspect of the project. The security and control measures mentioned in the report are critical features which must be built into the system in order to protect it from unauthorised or malicious use.

SECTION B

Answer to Question Four

Requirement (a)

All of the participants in the meeting have different goals and objectives for the project. In fact, some of the participants see no relevance to certain aspects of the project. Managing these conflicting objectives during the meeting will be difficult. The IT manager is likely to have the objective of completing the project scope on time, which may be to the detriment of quality. Business Unit A manager will have the objective of satisfying customer demand and improving Business Unit A sales and market share. Business Unit B manager wants the system to maintain stability and customer satisfaction. At the moment these goals seem to be at odds with each other, and therefore it is the role of the project manager to ensure that all of the goals can be achieved without sacrificing the overall outcome of the project's successful implementation. This has to be a primary outcome of the meeting; an understanding by all parties of the differing objectives of each other. Therefore, managing the mutual understanding of these different objectives and communicating and encouraging alignment of goals will be a major task.

A further problem will be taking over the role of project manager from the current IT manager. He is likely to resent my appointment and may attempt to be disruptive or unsupportive in the future stages of the project. In particular, the first meeting will be difficult as I may have to defer to him on aspects of the project that have already occurred and this may lead to confusion during this first meeting. However, he will have much of the key knowledge and understanding of the new system and therefore it is important to retain him on the team and to try to encourage his commitment.

Taking over the project at this late stage, with only three months to go before the website is due to be up and running, means that it is going to be difficult to achieve the technical objectives and to encourage the necessary high levels of team commitment and enthusiasm. As an outsider, it will take time to build up a relationship with the team and therefore motivation to achieve the tight deadline may be difficult. This first team meeting is an opportunity for me as the project manager to meet the team members, to understand their own perspectives of the project and their role within it and their levels of enthusiasm. Again, as the IT manager will be present, it may be difficult to get the IT staff to open up and be honest about their opinions and levels of motivation.

As I do not fully understand the complexities of the insurance and loans business, this may cause a very steep learning curve at the beginning of my project management process. I therefore very quickly need to appreciate as much as possible about the business, its environment and the new system. It would be useful for me to have had some information relating to the business operations prior to the first project meeting.

This lack of understanding may result in pressure from divisional managers or other staff. I must be aware of any internal politics and personal agendas that may be taking place in the meeting and must make sure that the focus of the meeting is upon project success and completion, not political in fighting.

I may also appear to have a lack of authority in the early stages of the project as an external consultant. This needs to be overcome by clear communication of my role and my level of authority from the Board of Directors.

Requirement (b)

Involvement and communication

It is important to make all staff feel involved in the project, not just the project team members but all of the staff affected by the new system. If staff is to feel ownership and commitment to the new system, then they must be involved in the system. Therefore, from this point onwards, all staff will receive updated information relating to the project progress and will be informed on a regular basis on how development will affect them. Staff will be asked their opinions as to the development of the system and should be allowed to put forward suggestions if they wish. Team members should also be in regular contact and communication, with weekly project meetings and reports on progress. Communication with all stakeholders is also critical, from senior managers who will want to be kept updated on project progress, to external customers who may need to be involved in discussion on the development of a prototype.

Leadership

Leadership is a critical skill in any project environment. In order to get staff motivated and working hard on the project to ensure its successful implementation, the project manager should lead by example. Leadership will involve clear direction, and strength in dealing with the current problems with lack of goal congruence. The leader must set the direction of the project clearly and should ensure that everyone is aware and working towards the same project outcome.

Technical skills

As this is a systems project, ideally the project manager will have a level of technical understanding of the hardware and software implications of the project. Detailed systems analysis or design knowledge may not be necessary, but a competence in systems would be useful in order to understand the system objectives and to lead the team and assign responsibilities.

Delegation skills

Delegation is critical when working with staff who are highly skilled and who require delegation to ensure continued motivation and support. The project manager cannot undertake every aspect of the project and should allow responsibility to those who have knowledge of specialist areas. For example, delegating responsibility for the design of the website prototype to the website designer would improve his motivation and the chances of the website being correct.

Analytical and problem solving skills

This project, like any other technical project will require analytical and problem solving skills. This may involve analysing the allocation of scarce resources to maximise their use, or complex technical problems relating to the design of the system. The project manager must be able to create realistic plans and to make sensible and realistic decisions based upon the available resources, knowledge and timescales.

Business and commercial skills

A strong business acumen will also be necessary, as this is a critical business system and the project manager must understand the impact this system will have on business operations. Understanding the nature of the customer, the business environment and the decision making process of the organisation is critical in the delivery of a successful business system such as the Business Unit website.

Answer to Question Five

Requirement (a)

Four advantages of benchmarking (Candidates may discuss any four of the following)

Focus upon competitive advantage

Benchmarking provides organisations with the opportunity to benchmark themselves against other organisations which are considered to be the best at what they do. This could mean comparing themselves against the best mortgage lender (competitor benchmarking) or it could mean comparing a particular process being carried out by the organisation against another organisation who does a similar process. For example, sales order processing or customer complaints procedures (process benchmarking). In this case, CFO is part of the Forum for Quality in Lending so it is able to compare itself against other mortgage providers. This way it can identify the attributes of other mortgage providers that customers most value and it can also identify where it needs to improve to stay competitive. This will give it a competitive advantage over those mortgage providers who are not part of the benchmarking group.

Reduces complacency within organisations

By using a type of league table measure of performance based upon key indices, it challenges an organisation to improve its performance in order to remain competitive and to maintain its position in the rankings. As some of the ratings are based upon customer measures, then this forces CFO and other lenders to be outward looking and focus upon customer satisfaction. It means that CFO will have to continually keep up to date with new ideas and approaches to lending and in particular, in customer service.

Focuses upon improvement

Organisations who undertake benchmarking tend to be more dynamic and forward thinking. They are more open to change and to improvement in delivery of service. Traditionally, Business Unit B has been less dynamic and innovative, but it may have to be more innovative and responsive to customers now that it is part of the Forum for Quality in Lending. An advantage to CFO is that this focus on continual improvement should improve customer relations.

Allows organisations to focus on areas in need of improvement

Benchmarking allows organisations to allocate scarce resources to those areas most in need of improvement. CFO could use the indices provided by the benchmarking forum to identify its main areas of weakness and could ensure that those processes were the first to be allocated resources such as money, staff time and expertise. For example, if the indices provided by the benchmarking group identified response rates to customer queries as a key index of poor performance, then CFO management could allocate managerial and staff time to identifying and implementing new and improved systems to rectify this.

Provides a good marketing tool

Being part of an industry-wide and recognised quality body will be a key marketing tool for CFO and should help to retain existing customers and attract new customers. It is also a valuable tool to attract and retain high quality staff. Being part of a recognised quality body builds confidence and is a recognition of standards in performance. This is likely to be important to mortgage customers spending high value amounts.

Requirement (b)

Improvements in staff training

Speed of response

Improved training should result in an increase in the speed at which staff is able to deal with queries and provide customer advice. Effective training can give staff the tools and techniques, both in the technology used and in the products offered, to analyse administrative processes in order to operate at maximum efficiency. For example, training may allow the staff member to immediately recognise the optimum mortgage product for the customer. This will mean that they can focus upon this option without time consuming discussion of other products which are not suitable.

Understanding and Empathy

Staff training can help staff to relate better to the customers and provide a higher level of personal service and attention. Customers clearly expect good customer service and this will include interacting with staff who understand their financial and personal situations. Training in telephone manner, communication skills and detailed knowledge of the products themselves, should assist in improving staff understanding of the customers.

Reliability and accuracy

The mortgage and insurance industries are both complex financial areas and it is important that staff understand these areas in order to provide the optimum advice. It is critical that any advice given to customers is technically correct and accurate. Most of the products offered by CFO, in particular the mortgages offered, will require a detailed technical knowledge if effective customer support is to be offered. Errors or mis-selling of products will have a negative impact on the business and may result in expulsion from the Forum for Quality in Lending. Therefore, training in the mortgages and insurance products offered, training in the effective manipulation of the computer system and product databases will all help to ensure reliability and accuracy of service to customers.

Dolivery of tangibles

Quality of customer service can be affected by poor paperwork or inaccurate or unclear documentation. Poor layout of forms or key documents can cause confusion and lead to customer dissatisfaction. Training in the use of IT tools, such as spreadsheets and letter or report formats, could assist staff in presenting and designing more helpful and user friendly documentation.

CIMA

November 2004 Examinations

Intermediate Level

Organisational Management

(IORG – Paper 11)

Question Paper	1
Examiner's Brief Guide to the Paper	10
Examiner's Answers	11

The answers published here have been written by the Examiner and should provide a helpful guide for both lecturers and students.

Published separately on the CIMA website (www.cimaglobal.com/students) from the end of March 2005 is a Post Examination Guide for this paper, which provides much valuable and complementary material including indicative mark information.

CIMA

Intermediate Level

Organisational Management

11

IORG

25 November 2004

Thursday afternoon

INSTRUCTIONS TO CANDIDATES

Read this page before you look at the questions

You are allowed three hours to answer this question paper.
Answer the ONE question in Section A (this has 10 sub-questions). Answer the TWO questions in Section B. Answer TWO questions ONLY from Section C.

SECTION A — 20 MARKS

ANSWER *ALL* TEN SUB-QUESTIONS – 2 MARKS EACH

Question One

1.1 Which of Porter's competitive strategies is based on providing products/services that command a superior price?

A Cost leadership

B Diversification

C Concentration

D Differentiation

1.2 When behaviour in an organisation is influenced by a set of moral principles and values it is called

A a mission environment.

B the rule of law.

C a corporate code of ethics.

D corporate culture.

1.3 The operations function in most organisations produces a mixture of both products and services.

Which ONE of the following businesses is closest to producing a pure service?

A A consultancy company

B A restaurant

C A bank

D A steel company

1.4 Those who are praising the merits of standardisation are probably describing the

A simple structure.

B team structure.

C matrix structure.

D bureaucracy.

1.5 Which ONE of the following statements most closely reflects recommended best practice for staff appraisal?

A The appraisal system should focus on the faults of those being appraised.

B Appraisal reports should always be "closed" so that managers are able to give a frank and honest appraisal.

C One appraisal per year is sufficient for any employee within any organisation.

D Staff should be able to view their appraisal report to ensure the consistency of the report with verbal feedback from their manager.

1.6 A selection test that fails to produce similar results over time when taken by the same person would be considered

A unstable.

B contradictory.

C unreliable.

D non-specific.

1.7 At which stage in the process of group development do members begin to set agreed standards and allocate roles?

A Performing

B Storming

C Norming

D Forming

1.8 A manager who allows his/her subordinates to make the majority of the decisions is demonstrating which of the following leadership styles?

A Autocratic

B Participative

C Democratic

D Laissez-faire

1.9 An organisational development tool used for assessing the discrepancy of perceptions among organisational members and so helping to solve any differences that arise is known as

A sensitivity training.

B survey feedback.

C process consultation.

D inter-group development.

1.10 Divestment as a strategic option may be considered where

A an organisation is unable to secure sufficient resources or competences.

B a change occurs in the expectations of a stakeholder with low power and low interest.

C an organisation is unable to change its competences.

D the intrinsic value of a company's products or assets does not change over time.

(Total = 20 marks)

End of Section A

SECTION B – 40 MARKS

ANSWER BOTH QUESTIONS

Question Two

K Company, a manufacturer of small appliances is facing very difficult times. Many years of steady growth have recently ended with a sharp decline in its sales and a consequent fall in its profits and share price. The CEO has decided in consultation with the Finance Director that urgent action is required and has proposed a plan to turnaround K Company from its current decline.

This plan involves reducing the workforce by 50% to 3,000 and closing six domestic assembly plants, four of which are in the same town. Most of the production is to be moved to other parts of the world where labour costs are lower. K Company's loyal workforce is shocked by the proposals and the trade unions are determined to fight the proposed job cuts with all the means at their disposal.

The plan also involves the sourcing of many components from overseas, a proposal which has shocked its long established domestic suppliers.

Finally, the board of directors is not entirely united behind the plan and there are rumours that the Production and Marketing directors are considering resignation.

Required:

(a) Identify the internal and external stakeholders that are likely to be affected if the proposed plan is implemented. Describe the impact of the proposed changes on each stakeholder group.

(10 marks)

(b) Describe the sources of power available to each stakeholder group. Explain how each group might try to influence the outcome of the proposed plan.

(10 marks)

(Total = 20 marks)

Question Three

On appointment to her new post as Head of Finance in the Z Company, H discovers that the training and development of the finance staff has been badly neglected. This lack is all the more surprising to H when she reflects on the many changes that have affected the work of accounting and finance professionals in the last decade.

The Company does not have a specialist human resource management function so departmental heads have to organise training and development for the staff within their departments.

Required:

(a) Describe the potential problems associated with the neglect of staff training and development in a time of rapid change for:

(i) Z Company's finance staff

(ii) The Z Company

(8 marks)

(b) Discuss the activities that must be undertaken in order to provide a set of effective training and development programmes for Z Company's finance staff.

(12 marks)

(Total = 20 marks)

End of Section B

SECTION C – 40 MARKS

ANSWER TWO QUESTIONS ONLY

Question Four

Until recently, C Company could have been described as a single product, medium sized company structured along functional lines with the clearly defined polices and procedures typical of a classical bureaucracy. But things are changing rapidly; a new CEO has been appointed who is committed to growing the Company by diversification into new products and new markets.

Such a strategy entails coping with new competitors in a dynamic and unstable international environment, the use of new technology for the production and distribution of its new products and the employment of local managers and production-line workers in overseas subsidiaries.

Required:

(a) Compare and contrast the contingency approach to organisational design with that of the classical management approach.

(10 marks)

(b) Using the contingency approach, explain how the changes described in the above scenario are likely to affect the future organisational structure and design of C Company.

(10 marks)

(Total = 20 marks)

Question Five

Despite the diverse composition of its workforce, the higher grades of management in X Company are dominated by middle-aged males from one ethnic group.

Required:

(a) Discuss the implications for the performance of X Company of promoting only the members of a particular gender/ethnic group.

(8 marks)

(b) Discuss the various ways in which

(i) X Company can ensure fair treatment of all its employees.

(ii) Governments can assist in the prevention of discrimination in the workplace.

(12 marks)

(Total = 20 marks)

Question Six

T Company was, until recently, a national telephone company that enjoyed monopoly status, but a decision to deregulate by the government means that it is now exposed to aggressive competition from new entrants. T Company's competitive position has also been undermined by developments in wireless technology. As customers increasingly choose to use mobile phones, T Company's vast investment in fixed line technology is becoming increasingly uneconomic. This change in technology and the associated shift in consumer tastes have left T Company with no option but to invest in mobile technology itself.

T Company also suffers from its history as a monopoly provider; its bureaucratic culture and structure means that it tends to be slower to respond to market changes than the new entrants. The high proportion of telephone engineers who belong to the telecoms trade union does not help this situation. When earlier this year, T Company announced job cuts, the trade union members voted for industrial action that lasted for several weeks and cost the Company millions in lost revenue.

The development of broadband digital technology, however, allows high speed access to the Internet. This has meant a new lease of life for fixed line operators like T Company because existing fixed line systems can be adapted for broadband use. This opportunity has been seized by T Company's senior management. The Company has been successful in attracting 50,000 subscribers to the new broadband service in its first year of operation. The Company has also introduced a service that allows people on the move to access the Internet at selected public venues using a wireless enabled laptop.

This installation of broadband does, however, require training in new skills and the engineers required to undertake this training have threatened strike action in support of a large pay increase to compensate them for using the new skills required for the job.

Required:

(a) Identify the internal and external triggers for change in the strategy and operations of T Company. Discuss the difficulties that the Company is likely to experience in introducing the change programme.

(10 marks)

(b) Evaluate the success of T Company in managing the change process to date. By application of any model of change management, explain how T Company might go about managing change in the future.

(10 marks)

(Total = 20 marks)

Question Seven

Company A has acquired Company B. As part of a wide ranging effort to integrate Company B into its operations, systems and procedures, the management of Company A has decided to combine the two existing finance departments. A new finance department will be formed in the headquarters building of Company A. The move by Company B Finance staff to Company A headquarters will mean, for most, a daily road journey of some 20 miles each way.

Required:

(a) Discuss the concerns that Company B finance staff will have as they consider their move to Company A headquarters. Explain why an induction programme is necessary for Company B staff.

(10 marks)

(b) Produce an induction programme that will help support Company B finance staff in their move to Company A, and which will enable them to contribute productively to the enlarged Company.

(10 marks)

(Total = 20 marks)

End of paper

The Examiner for IORG offers to future candidates and to lecturers using this booklet for study purposes, the following background and guidance on the questions included in this examination paper.

Section A – compulsory

Question One presents 10 multiple-choice sub-questions designed to cover the whole of the IORG syllabus and to test candidates' knowledge, understanding and application.

Section B – compulsory

Question Two concerns a manufacturing company in decline and attempts, led by the CEO of the company, to turn it around. It is taken from syllabus section (i) *Organisational Management* and addresses the learning outcome *"Identify the stakeholders of an organisation and explain their influence on its management and structure."*

Question Three concerns the problems facing a company without a specialist human resource management function and the attempt by a new Head of Finance to introduce effective staff training and development programmes. It is taken from syllabus section (iii) *Human Resource Management* and addresses the learning outcome *"Produce a training and development plan for the staff of a finance department and analyse the major problems associated with the design and implementation of such a plan."*

Section C – two questions from four

Question Four (a) concerns the implementation of new strategy, changing a company from one with a classical management approach to one with a contingency approach. It is taken from syllabus section (i) *Organisational Management* and addresses the learning outcome *"Explain the usefulness of both classical and contemporary theories of management in practical situations."* Requirement (b) is taken from syllabus section (ii) *The Functional Areas of Organisations* and addresses the learning outcome *"Recommend and evaluate changes in the structure of organisations."*

Question Five concerns discrimination in the workplace. It is taken from syllabus section (iv) *Management of Relationships* and addresses the learning outcome *"Explain the various ways in which fair treatment of employees can be achieved, and the role of government in ensuring this."*

Question Six concerns the management of change in a company that once had monopoly status in it particular business. Requirement (a) is taken from syllabus section (v) *Management of Change* and addresses the learning outcome *"Evaluate the determinants of change in organisations and different levels at which change must be managed."* Requirement (b) is taken from the same syllabus section and addresses the learning outcome *"Recommend ways in which planned change can be implemented at the organisational and departmental levels."*

Question Seven concerns the production and application of an induction programme for staff whose company has been acquired by another. It is taken from syllabus section (iii) *Human Resource Management* and addresses the learning outcome *"Produce a plan for the induction of new staff into the finance department of an organisation."*

CIMA

The Examiner's Answers for Organisational Management

SECTION A

Answers to Question One

1.1	A	B	C	(D)
1.2	A	B	(C)	D
1.3	(A)	B	C	D
1.4	A	B	C	(D)
1.5	A	B	C	(D)
1.6	A	B	(C)	D
1.7	A	B	(C)	D
1.8	A	B	C	(D)
1.9	A	(B)	C	D
1.10	(A)	B	C	D

SECTION B

Answer to Question Two

Requirement (a)

Stakeholders are those individuals or groups that have an interest or "stake" in the organisation. The turnaround plan will affect a range of stakeholders both internal to the organisation and external to it. Beginning with internal stakeholders, these include those directly employed by the Company such as existing directors, senior and junior managers, assembly line workers and other employees and new employees in the countries to which production is being moved.

The most dramatic impact will be on the assembly line and other production workers who will lose their jobs in the plants that are to be closed. Some managers and supervisors will also lose their jobs. For the remaining managers and employees in the home country the future prospects for promotion will be much reduced as the number of senior posts will be reduced.

On the other hand, individuals in the countries to which the assembly/production plants are being moved will benefit from employment and prospects in the Company.

External stakeholders will also be affected by the proposed turnaround plan. These include a wide range of groups such as suppliers, customers, trades unions, local communities, local and national governments and shareholders. Those holding shares may well include many of the internal stakeholders noted above as well as stakeholders external to the business.

Communities in both the home country and the countries to which production is moving will be affected. The effects will impact not only the families of the redundant employees but on local shops and services in the locality of the plants closing or where the new plants are opening. The families of new employees taken on in the new production plants will be fortunate and the local economy in those towns to which production has been moved will benefit from the extra income that the new jobs will bring

Existing domestic suppliers and new overseas suppliers will be affected but in different ways. Existing suppliers will lose contracts, new suppliers will gain contracts

The domestic suppliers will be devastated with the loss of business and new overseas suppliers delighted with the new business that the shift in K Company brings about. The trades unions representing the workforce will be affected in the sense that they will have to muster their resources to attempt to save the jobs or obtain the best severance package for the employees they represent.

Other external stakeholders include local government, in both the home country and the overseas countries to which the plant is moving. Local governments normally have economic development plans that operate to attract new business and jobs into an area and to prevent possible loss of jobs.

Shareholders will necessarily be affected by the outcome of the turnaround plan. If it is successful they will benefit from an increase in dividends and capital growth, if it fails they will receive lower dividends and a reduction in the value of their shareholding.

Requirement (b)

The power of any stakeholder group turns on how dependent the organisation is upon it. The amount of dependency is a function of:

- the degree of uncertainty the stakeholder can create for, or manages on behalf of, the organisation;
- the extent to which the organisation is able to replace the relationship or avoid it;
- the extent to which decisions or actions of the stakeholder could directly disrupt the operations or plans of the organisation.

In the case of K Company, the power of internal stakeholders, like existing employees and lower level managers, derives from their skills and expertise. Their power will, however, be limited in the situation described by the scenario. K Company has every right to move its operations overseas if it wishes to do so and, as the Company can obtain a workforce in the other countries at lower cost, it is not dependent on its existing workforce.

In the case of the production director and the marketing director, they possess not only skills and experience but a vote on the board as to what the future policy of the Company should be. Given that the Board of Directors as a whole has agreed the policy to move production abroad, the production and marketing directors have limited power to change things. The Company is going through a difficult time and they would have to produce an alternative plan to turn the business around to convince their fellow directors. If they do resign, it will be a loss of experience and skill from the K Company but it should be possible to recruit people with similar experience in the field, so again the Company is not dependent on them.

The trades unions have the power to bring production at existing plants to a halt, but if the Company is determined to shut down the production plants in the home country, the influence they can bring to bear is limited.

The power of existing suppliers is also limited in this situation. Their power derives from an ability to disrupt supplies to the Company and the legal power to enforce any contracts they already have with K Company. They may be able to hold K Company to these contracts until the contracts run out but after this they can only protest on moral grounds.

The local government authority and parliamentary representative for the town/area in which K is currently located have the power to influence the Company by moral persuasion but, with the increasing globalisation of markets, politicians recognise their limitations to interfere in the international operation of companies.

The action of shareholders can be crucial for the Company. The shareholders have the power to remove the directors of the board and so change the policy of K Company if they so decide.

The action taken by stakeholder groups to influence the outcome of the proposed plan will range from verbal persuasion to threats of industrial action. Internal stakeholders threatened with loss of jobs will use whatever legal means are at their disposal. In addition to tradess union action, they will use the local media of newspapers, radio and television and participate in marches, demonstrations and industrial action.

The CEO and directors supporting the plan will use their company resources to put the plan into action and they will try to counter the negative publicity in the media by explaining the economic necessity for the plans.

Domestic suppliers about to lose business if the plan is put into operation will try to hold the Company to existing contracts and possibly use the media to seek to bring pressure to bear on the K Company to honour its moral commitments to them as long standing suppliers.

Politicians representing communities from which jobs will be lost may seek to bring pressure to bear on the company and even engage representatives of the State or National government to support the case for keeping jobs in K Company's home country.

By contrast State and local government officials in the countries in which K intends to locate its new plant will welcome the Company's plans and may even offer some form of tax concessions to make the move even more attractive to the Company.

Shareholders could vote to support the plan or not at the Company's Annual General Meeting, or at a special meeting of the shareholders. If they did not support the plan, they could use their voting power to remove the CEO and replace him or her with someone who would pursue an alternative policy.

Answer to Question Three

Requirement (a)

The neglect of training and development during a period of rapid change means that the finance staff in Z Company will learn less efficiently and effectively than if they had had the opportunity for a planned and carefully structured programme of training and development.

Compared with finance staff in other organisations, this will mean that Z's finance staff will pick up new developments in software, accounting techniques, legislative changes and other changes in related fields of management more slowly.

Looked at from an HRM perspective, Z finance staff will be at a disadvantage to competitors' employees in acquiring the knowledge, skills and competences that are increasingly deemed to be the basis of a firm's competitive advantage.

Another downside of neglecting training and development is the effect it has on the motivation of finance staff. Research and experience demonstrate that company training and development programmes are welcomed by employees as they provide tangible evidence that the company values them and has a vested interest both in developing their present skills and in the acquisition of new ones.

This is particularly important for professional staff as many are ambitious to progress in the profession to higher levels of competence and to secure senior posts in either their present company or elsewhere.

The problems for the Z Company are intimately related to the problems that lack of training and development can have for the finance staff.

First, the overall efficiency and effectiveness of Z Company will suffer because Z finance staff will be less able to provide senior management with the financial information that allows them to plan, co-ordinate and control the Company's operations.

Secondly, the fall in motivation and morale of Z finance employees that can arise from the restricted opportunities for training and development will influence staff turnover. The more ambitious staff will leave and the overall quality of finance staff will decline.

Thirdly, the neglect of training and development also means that a key link in the HRM cycle of selection, training and development, appraisal and rewards that leads to good performance will be severely impaired.

Requirement (b)

It is useful to distinguish training from development because the activities necessary for development are somewhat different from those of training.

Training is a learning process whereby individuals acquire knowledge and/or skills to aid in the achievement of specified objectives such as the ability to use a word processing package or the ability to speak a new language.

Development on the other hand can be seen as a longer-term continuing process of learning more often associated with movement of jobs (whether sideways as in a developmental assignment or upwards as a promotion). This is managed internally by organisations or externally by the individual undertaking self development activities and/or applying for more demanding jobs.

Whatever form of training or development is used it ought to be part of a systematic overall training and development system involving the following activities:

First it is necessary to consider the strategy of the Z Company and the finance department's role in helping to implement this strategy. Whatever the strategy happens to be, it will shape the objectives of departments and those of the finance department in particular.

Once these objectives and the means of attaining them have been decided upon, H will be in a position to consider the particular mix of knowledge and skills she requires of her staff.

As H is relatively new to the department and also because staff training has been neglected, it will be necessary for H to conduct a careful analysis of the training needs of her staff. This will entail an audit of existing staff skills and competences and a comparison of these with the skills necessary to fulfil the finance department's obligations.

In considering the skills and competences required, H will need to take account of potential staff retirements and of possible other leavers so that she has a succession plan in place for the department. It follows that during her audit of skills, it would also be useful to find out what the career plans of staff members are.

If performance appraisals have been conducted properly, the information from these should be a useful source of information on career aspirations and training needs but, given the circumstances of neglect in this case, it may be that little useful information is available and that H will have to start from scratch.

Careful observation and monitoring of staff in their current jobs is a useful source of information about their attitudes to work and of the particular skills that they possess.

Once training and development needs for individuals have been ascertained then the next step will be to set training and development objectives for each member of the finance staff.

A clear learning objective describes what it is that the training and development will achieve. This should include not only the aims in broad terms such as "At the end of training, the trainee will be able to use the latest form of spreadsheet" but also try to give a measurable objective expressed as what the employee will be able to do after the training/development, such as lay out a set of accounts on the spreadsheet within a certain time limit.

Objectives stated clearly like this are vital for purposes of evaluating whether the training/development has been effective or not and they form the basis of the detailed training and development programme.

Because most people learn best when they genuinely want to and are motivated to, any training is most likely to be effective if the person to receive training is involved in agreeing his or her training and development plan and in choosing the method or means by which the training/development is to be provided.

Having set the objectives, it then remains to organise a set of training courses and developmental activities to meet the objectives.

This in turn will require consideration of when, and over what period the training/development can take place, the method of training/development, who can offer the most relevant course content and therefore provide the training and where it is best undertaken.

H will also need to be aware of the range of possible training/development methods, possible providers inside or outside the organisation, likely costs and their record of success.

After the training has taken place it will be necessary to conduct an evaluation of the training programmes and the development activities to ensure that the training objectives have been achieved.

SECTION C

Answer to Question Four

Requirement (a)

The classical approach focused attention on the formal structure, technical requirements of the organisation and general sets of principles. Writers who developed this approach assumed rational and logical behaviour on the part of managers and workers. The identification of general objectives and the identification of purposes and responsibilities at all levels of the organisation would, in their view, lead to the most effective structure.

The work of Henri Fayol and Max Weber can be taken as representative of this approach. Fayol developed fourteen basic principles of management, which every organisation needed to address.

Not all of these were concerned with the structure of the organisation but the principles to do with division of work, authority, unity of command, unity of direction, centralisation and the chain of authority most certainly were.

In fact, they are similar in many ways to the features of bureaucracy that Max Weber argued were necessary for the efficient working of an organisation. The features set out by Weber in his "ideal type" of bureaucracy include specialisation, hierarchy, authority, a system of rules and impersonality.

These early approaches to organisation and management believed in one best form of structure and tended to concentrate on limited aspects of an organisation. They also often studied the organisation in isolation from its environment.

These principles and considerations suggest a prescriptive stance towards structure based on the belief that there is one best way of structuring any organisation.

But as customers and shareholders have become more proactive, market-driven strategies and flexible organisations have emerged. The rapidly changing nature of the work environment and consequent demands for flexibility have drawn attention to the need for a contingency approach to organisational design.

The contingency approach can be seen as a development of the systems approach but goes a stage further in relating the environment and other variables to specific structures of an organisation. The contingency approach takes the view that there is no one best universal structure. But there are a large number of variables, or situational factors, which influence organisational design and performance.

The most appropriate structure is dependent, therefore, upon the contingencies of the situation for each individual organisation. These situational factors account for variations in the structure of different organisations.

Expressed rather differently, the contingency approach can be seen as a form of "if-then" matrix relationship. If certain situational factors exist, then certain variables in organisation structure and systems of management are most appropriate.

Requirement (b)

The research into organisational design and resulting structures has found that organisation structure is contingent on a number of key factors. These include size, technology, people, motivation, past experience, pattern of ownership, strategic choice and the environment.

Applying these findings to C Company, we can obtain a fair idea of how the structure of C Company will have to change if it is to compete successfully in future.

Taking the variables in the sequence in which they are described in the scenario, we commence with the appointment of the CEO and his/her ambitions for the Company. Given his/her objectives to grow the organisation through diversification into new products and new markets, it appears likely that C Company will need to adopt some form of divisional structure so that particular divisions can specialise in the production and development of new products and new markets.

The research of Chandler into the relationship between strategy and structure would support this. The reference to the recruitment of employees in countries other than C's own also suggests the possibility of an overseas division as part of the new structure.

The second key change is in the environment of C Company. According to the scenario, this involves a change from a relatively stable environment to a more dynamic unstable environment characterised by new competitors, the use of new technology and the recruitment of employees with different cultural characteristics than those currently employed by the Company.

This change in the environment is likely to push C Company from its current rather mechanistic structure as described by Burns and Stalker to a more organic structure. According to their research findings, this will be necessary because bureaucratic structures are too rigid to cope with rapid change. A more organic task-orientated form of organisation will be required in which employees will be expected to use their own initiative rather than to rely upon detailed rules and procedures.

If C Company should grow as the CEO intends it to, then the structure of the organisation may come under pressure to adopt a more formal structure and emphasise the standardisation of rules and procedures. More control systems may also need to be put in place.

Such changes will inevitably affect the ability of C Company to be flexible and responsive to changes in the market which of course can be detrimental to C Company's operations. In such a case, it is a matter of striking a balance between an organisation structure and procedures that ensures efficient production, on time delivery of quality products and yet is flexible and responsive when required.

The adoption of new technology may also influence how the organisation will be structured. Studies by Woodward, the Aston University team and others have shown that the adoption of a particular production technology such as mass production requires an organisation structure tailored to that kind of technology if it is to operate at maximum efficiency.

Answer to Question Five

Requirement (a)

The effect on the performance of an organisation like X that uses a promotion system that discriminates in favour of any one particular gender/ethnic group is likely to be as follows:

- It is likely to impair the efficiency and effectiveness of the organisation because such a system fails to tap all the potential talents, knowledge and skills of the rest of the workforce. Experience has taught us that talent is not confined to any particular grouping in society. Able and competent individuals exist in all the diverse groupings of society whether we are considering groups characterised by gender, race, ethnicity, physical ability, or sexual orientation.
- Such a system promotes division between groupings and prevents the kind of social integration for good team working that has been increasingly recognised as necessary in organisations where a multiplicity of skills are required to complete a particular task.
- Related to the foregoing, is the de-motivational effect that such an unfair promotion system has on the talented individuals who are outside the exclusive club of middle aged males.
- Related to the above point, there may be more labour turnover and absenteeism amongst staff. These in turn will increase the costs of the Company.
- In a period when other companies are increasingly adopting equality of opportunity programmes, the reputation of the Company can be damaged in the eyes of both potential employees and customers with a consequent loss of both good applicants for jobs and possible loss of Company sales.
- Any form of discrimination may result in costly litigation.

Requirement (b)

(i) The problems of ensuring fair treatment of all employees in Company X can be enormous and success will depend to a considerable extent on the countries in which X is operating. In some countries in the world legislation is in place which makes discrimination in employment illegal whereas in others this is still not yet the case.

Even where legislation exists that outlaws discrimination, women and minority groups continue to be treated in an unequal manner in a covert way that is very difficult to overcome.

Nevertheless, efforts are continuing to try to remove prejudices and discrimination and to create societies and organisations where all individuals are treated equally.

There is no magic formula that will enable Company X to eliminate prejudice and resulting discrimination but the following measures can help:

- The setting of equal opportunities policies that ensure fair treatment in selection, training and development and reward systems including equal access based on merit to senior positions in the Company.
- Awareness needs to be raised via a process of encouraging people to question their attitudes and preconceptions. A variety of workshops, conferences and training programmes can be used for this purpose.
- Positive action programmes for women and minority groups that focus on selection, appraisal, development and coaching that help not only to provide individuals in such groups with necessary skills and competences but encourage them to apply for senior positions in Company X.

- Managing diversity programme to sustain momentum. This can involve the use of a champion, not necessarily from the HRM department, but someone who continues in his or her previous organisation role in addition.
- The continued involvement of senior managers is important, together with trades unions to help harness initiatives from departments. The development of support networks for disadvantaged groups is also useful.
- Also recommended is the measurement of achievements in terms of business benefit, better relationships with customers, improvements in productivity and profitability, all of which need to be communicated to employees.

(ii) Governments can play a role in ensuring fair treatment of employees by introducing legislation that promotes equality of treatment of individuals in the work place. In some countries such as the USA and the European Union countries this legislation is already in place or in the process of being implemented.

In the European Union (EU) for example, a concerted effort is being made to stamp out discrimination and to make the basic principle of respect for fundamental human rights a reality. New laws will soon come into force in all EU countries to protect the right of everyone in the EU to be treated equally and fairly, no matter where they are from or where they live and work.

European laws, called directives, banning discrimination on grounds of racial or ethnic origin, religion or belief, disability, age and sexual orientation were agreed in 2000.

Governments in every country have had to modify their own national laws to bring them into line with these directives. Each country decides how best to do this according to their national traditions and legal systems.

One of the two directives concerned is about achieving racial equality. It prohibits discrimination against anyone because of their racial or ethnic origin and covers most areas of everyday life in which unfair treatment might occur.

These areas include access to jobs, conditions at work, rates of pay and the rights and benefits linked to a job. They also include access to education and training, social security benefits and healthcare and equal rights to buy or rent goods and services, including housing.

The second directive is about establishing equal rights and equal opportunity for people in employment and training, which is key to what people achieve in life and how well they live. The directive, therefore, outlaws discrimination on grounds of a person's ethnicity, gender and religion.

Establishing an effective set of laws against discrimination is an essential part of stamping out unfair treatment. It not only gives protection to those discriminated against, but it creates a climate in which people are discouraged from treating minority groups unfairly. But laws by themselves are not enough. If discrimination is to be eliminated, attitudes and behaviour have to change.

An action programme aimed at helping to bring about these kinds of change needs to be undertaken. This might include measures to support activities to raise the awareness of people, to inform them of their new rights and obligations under the law and to challenge discriminatory attitudes and behaviour wherever they occur.

Answer to Question Six

Requirement (a)

Change may be necessary because of external developments and/or internal organisational factors. Both sources of change can be influenced by organisational decisions, but obviously external developments are less susceptible to control than internal ones.

In the case of T Company the *external triggers* for change include:

- The decision of the government to deregulate the telecommunications industry.
- Developments in wireless technology in the form of mobile phones.
- Development of broadband Internet technology.
- Shift in consumer tastes away from fixed line telephones to mobile phones.
- Action by the trades union to support the workforce of T Company.

Internal triggers

- Decisions by senior management in T Company first to enter the market for mobile telephone services and later to diversify into the market for the delivery of broadband Internet services.
- Decision by managers to downsize the organisation by sacking workers.
- Decision by engineering workers in T Company to take industrial action to try to defend jobs.

The difficulties that the T Company is likely to face in making all the necessary changes are rooted in the history of the Company and in the fears of existing employees. The inherited bureaucratic structure and culture of the organisation with its hierarchical levels and rules and procedures is likely to act as a barrier to change. If the T Company is to change its working practices it is first necessary to change the rules and procedures under which the members of the organisation formerly operated, and this can take time.

Resistance to change by individuals is often based on fear of the unknown. Some employees will fear that they are unable to cope with the jobs created by new technology. Others may be reluctant to cast aside their old skills and ways of doing things and make the necessary effort to learn new skills and new ways of doing things. All workers, noting the loss of jobs at the last shakeout, will be wary of the new technology being introduced and fearful that it may lead to another round of job cuts. In these circumstances, it is perhaps understandable that they will turn to the trades unions for support.

The threat of action by the trades union can only make things more difficult for T Company management as they go about the task of trying to introduce new working practices. It is not just operational level employees who may create difficulties for senior management in introducing necessary changes. Individuals in departments, divisions and even whole organisations may combine to resist the changes proposed by senior management if they see their interests threatened. The political tactics used by groups to further their own interests can apply to middle level mangers just as much as to rank and file employees.

Requirement (b)

The Company to date has a mixed record of success in the management of change.

It has managed, despite its legacy as a monopoly provider and the overhang of a bureaucratic culture and structure, to change from being a provider of only fixed line telephone services to one that now also provides mobile and broadband Internet services.

They have not done this without some costs however, as the management of the last round of job cuts makes clear. Its attempt to slim down the workforce resulted in industrial action that cost T Company many millions. Its current implementation of broadband services is also meeting with resistance from the engineers who have threatened industrial action in support of a large pay increase.

There are no simple prescriptions for the successful management of change. Each case requires careful analysis and implementation. Sometimes it may be appropriate to force changes through regardless of the reasons for resistance, but the inherent danger of this approach is that people will return to the old ways of working once the pressure for change is relaxed.

A useful model for assisting in the design of the change process is that developed by Kurt Lewin.

Lewin recognised that some forces, particularly external forces, may well be outside management's control and so the concentration of management effort should be on internal forces for change and those factors or agents resisting them. Lewin's simple formula for tackling change consisted of a three-step process as follows:

- "Unfreezing" which involves reducing forces that maintain current behaviours and provide people with an understanding of why change needs to occur so that they can more easily accept it.
- Changing behaviour patterns in such a way that the new attitudes, values and behaviour become internalised as part of employees' new ways of thinking.
- "Refreezing" whereby supporting mechanisms are introduced to ensure the new behaviour pattern is maintained such as reward systems and structures.

Applying this model to the situation faced by the T Company, we have to recognise that many of the forces acting upon the company are outside the control of the senior management. There is little that can be done to manage these forces, except to accept the realities of the changes in the market place and to adopt strategies that take account of the threats and opportunities as they emerge.

In order to make changes that will increase its efficiency and effectiveness, the senior management of T Company can use the threat of competition to persuade employees, the trades union and long serving managers that, unless changes are made, the very survival of the company and, therefore, the jobs of employees, are at risk.

The next step of changing behaviour patterns, attitudes and beliefs is more difficult and will require a range of methods to persuade both managers and employees that change is necessary. Such methods will include ensuring that what needs to be changed, (in this case the working practices of T Company's engineers among others) and why, is effectively communicated.

It is also necessary that all employees are involved in the change process through regular meetings and discussions, and that appropriate incentives and penalties are available to drive the changes.

Ideally, change is best achieved through willing participation of all concerned, but experience has taught us that resistance to change is common when the interests of individuals and groups are threatened. It will probably be necessary, therefore, for the senior management team to negotiate changes with the trades union. The threats to the company are so great however, that the management can probably gain the trades unions' acceptance of the need for more efficient working practices.

Once these new working practices are in place, it is necessary according to Lewin's model that the new levels of efficiency are sustained and that management maintains a pressure for constant improvement to raise levels of productivity, so as to ensure continued survival of the business through rewarding desired behaviours.

Answer to Question Seven

Requirement (a)

The concerns of Company B finance personnel will vary depending on such things as age, position in their career and personality characteristics.

For instance, those who have attained senior positions will be concerned with whether or not they will enjoy a similar status in the new organisation.

Those in mid career and hoping to progress in Company B will be concerned about opportunities for progression in the company.

Most members of the B finance staff moving to the A headquarters will be also be concerned about the different policies, practices and procedures of Company A. In particular they will be concerned about the overall benefits package in the new organisation. For instance, there may be concern about pensions, holidays, time off for study and so on. In some countries, state legislation will ensure that the new employment conditions of Company B staff are no worse than they enjoyed in Company B before it was taken over but in other countries this kind of legal protection may not apply.

Most staff will have concerns about the quantity and quality of the work they will be required to do and with technology and systems they will be required to work with.

Related to this they will be concerned about whether they will fit into Company A, given potential differences in organisational culture and management style.

They will also be concerned with whether or not they will be able to work with the new team in Company A.

Finally they will be concerned about more routine matters such as the best way to travel to the new work place and whether there will be room to park their car.

The necessity for an induction programme for Company B staff is evident to some extent from what has been said above about the concerns of the staff as they consider their move to A Company HQ. Any well structured induction programme should address the concerns expressed and so help settle Company B staff into their new organisation.

Without some kind of systematic introduction to their new company, B finance staff may well feel isolated and confused, unaware of company rules and procedures; they may struggle to learn A Company systems because they have received only limited assistance at the outset.

They may unintentionally break safety or disciplinary rules. Furthermore, they may come to question the depth of employers' commitments to people as their most important resource and leave to take up a position elsewhere.

These problems represent a cost to the employer, either in direct financial terms (poor-quality work, time spent on disciplinary issues, re-advertising jobs) or in public relations terms, as potential recruits and customers choose to go elsewhere. It should also be recognised that induction can be a powerful device for integrating new employees into organisations, gaining their commitment, and inculcating them with a sense of belonging and identity which forms a basis for effective performance.

A good induction programme can engender a feeling of belonging to the company, which develops a commitment to organisational goals. The employer then maximises the contribution of the workforce and gets a faster return on investment.

Requirement (b)

An induction programme to assist finance staff from Company B to become quickly effective in Company A will need to meet most of the concerns of B staff as set out in part *(a)*.

Until the incoming finance staff to Company A headquarters are familiar with their new workplace surroundings and the work systems employed in the finance department of Company A, they will not be able to perform to their maximum potential.

Similarly, if the ex B Company employees are worried or otherwise unsettled about their relationships with new colleagues, superiors and subordinates, they will not perform at their best.

An Induction programme for the finance staff of B Company moving to the new location at the headquarters of Company A might take the following form:

Timing	Activity	Induction to be undertaken by
Before the move	Information about the company and the industry, such as a mission statement, history, product markets, organisation structure. Terms of employment and contract of employment covering conditions of service or pay, pension arrangements, employee development opportunities, holiday/sickness arrangements, hours of work, profit sharing and so on, history and rules of organisation, start date, time, location, who to report to, parking facilities.	Human Resource Manager
First Day	Introductions to immediate work colleagues and mentor. Local rules relating to, for example, lunch/tea coffee break arrangements, personal telephone calls, personal emails and use of Internet, location of facilities such as canteen/coffee machines, toilets. Job description, role and performance appraisal details and so on.	Departmental Manager
First week	Legal duties, for example health and safety regulations including fire training, discipline and grievance procedures, trades unions/staff associations.	Human Resource Manager
First Month	Employee involvement and communication, training and development opportunities, orientation to mission goals/ objectives and culture.	Human Resource Manager
First six months	Managerial attention to setting up meetings to check on progress. Use of mentor as point of contact.	Mentor

Order Form

For CIMA Official Study Materials for 2005 Exams

Qty	Title	Authors	ISBN	Price	Total
	CIMA Official *Study Systems*		**Available Now**		
	Performance Evaluation	Scarlett	0750664088	£33.00	
	Decision Management	Wilks	0750664096	£33.00	
	Risk and Control Strategy	Collier / Agyei-Ampomah	075066410X	£33.00	
	Financial Accounting and Tax Principles	Rolfe	0750664118	£33.00	
	Financial Analysis	Gowthorpe	0750664126	£33.00	
	Financial Strategy	Ogilvie	0750664134	£33.00	
	Organisational Management and Information Strategy	Perry	0750664142	£33.00	
	Integrated Management	Harris / Sims	0750664150	£33.00	
	Business Strategy	Botten / Sims	0750664169	£33.00	
	TOPCIMA	Sims / Barnwell	0750664177	£33.00	
	CIMA Official *Revision Cards*				
	Performance Evaluation	Scarlett	0750664819	£6.95	
	Decision Management	Avis	0750664827	£6.95	
	Risk and Control Strategy	Harris	0750664835	£6.95	
	Financial Accounting and Tax Principles	Rolfe	0750664878	£6.95	
	Financial Analysis	Gowthorpe	0750664886	£6.95	
	Financial Strategy	Ogilvie	0750664894	£6.95	
	Organisational Management and Information Systems	Perry	0750664843	£6.95	
	Integrated Management	Harris	0750664851	£6.95	
	Business Strategy	Botten	075066486X	£6.95	
	CIMA Official *Exam Practice Kits*				
	Performance Evaluation	Barnett / Dawkins	0750665882	£14.95	
	Decision Management	Barnett / Dawkins	0750665890	£14.95	
	Risk and Control Strategy	Robertson	0750665920	£14.95	
	Financial Accounting and Tax Principles	Patel / Channer	0750665904	£14.95	
	Financial Analysis	Rodgers	0750665912	£14.95	
	Financial Strategy	Graham	0750665939	£14.95	
	Organisational Management and Information Systems	Robertson	0750665874	£14.95	
	Integrated Management	Best / Dalton	0750665815	£14.95	
	Business Strategy	Graham	0750665823	£14.95	
	TOPCIMA	Little	0750666277	£14.95	
	CIMA CPD *Introduction to Business Tax*	Jones	0750666390	£44.99	
		Postage and packing		£2.95	
		TOTAL			

Elsevier retains certain personal information about you in hard copy form and on computer. It will be used to inform you about goods and services from Elsevier and its associated companies in which you may be interested. ☐ Please tick this box if you do not want to receive this information.

ELSEVIER

CIMA PUBLISHING

Post this form to:

CIMA Publishing Customer Services
Elsevier
FREEPOST (OF 1639)
Linacre House, Jordan Hill
OXFORD, OX2 8DP, UK

Or **FAX** +44 (0)1865 474 010
Or **PHONE** +44 (0)1865 474 014
Email: cimaorders@elsevier.com
www.cimapublishing.com

Name: ________

Organisation: ________

Invoice Address: ________

Postcode: ________

Phone number: ________

Email: ________

Delivery Address if different:

FAO ________

Address ________

Postcode ________

Please note that all deliveries must be signed for

1. Cheques payable to Elsevier.

2. Please charge my:

☐ Visa/Barclaycard ☐ Access/Mastercard
☐ American Express ☐ Diners Card
☐ Switch Issue No.______

Card No. ________

Expiry Date ________

Cardholder Name: ________

Signature: ________

Date: ________

CIMA Publishing is an imprint of Elsevier
Registered Office:
The Boulevard, Langford Lane, Kidlington, Oxford OX5 1GB, UK
Registered in England: 3099304, VAT 494 627212